Where in the Word?

Extraordinary Stories Behind
801 Ordinary Words

David Muschell

Prima
P.O. Box 1260WW
Rocklin, CA 95677
(916) 624-5718

Copy Editing by Brent Goff
Production by Rosaleen Bertolino, Bookman Productions
Typography by Janet Hansen, Alphatype
Interior design by Sandra Popovich
Illustrated by Hatley Mason
Cover design by Kirshner-Caroff

Prima Publishing
Rocklin, CA

Library of Congress Cataloging-in-Publication Data

Muschell, David.
   Where in the word? : extraordinary stories behind
801 ordinary words / by David Muschell.
     p.   cm.
   Includes index.
   ISBN 1-55958-084-4
   1. English language—Etymology.   I. Title.
PE1574.M8   1991
422—dc20   90-49112
                                                          CIP

90 91 92 93 RRD 10 9 8 7 6 5 4 3 2 1

Printed in the United States of America

How to Order:

Quantity discounts are available from the publisher, Prima Publishing, P.O. Box 1260WW, Rocklin, CA 95677; telephone (916) 624-5718. On your letterhead include information concerning the intended use of the books and the number of books you wish to purchase.

U.S. Bookstores and Libraries: Please submit all orders to St. Martin's Press, 175 Fifth Avenue, New York, NY 10010; telephone (212) 674-5151.

For my mother and father
and
Andrew and Judy Boswell,
who made this book possible.

FOREWORD

I've been fascinated by words ever since childhood, when I first began learning the letters on my parents' old Westinghouse refrigerator. That these odd squiggly marks you're reading now can reach into your mind and *mean* something is amazing. In fact, these strange arrangements of symbols can have tremendous power: In a textbook they can reveal the scope of history; in a tragic novel they can bring tears to our eyes; in a love letter they can make our hearts pound faster.

This book looks at the origins and evolution of some of the most common, everyday words. One of the most intriguing things to me is how language gets passed on from generation to generation, from country to country, and how it changes in the passing. The spelling of a word may get altered, the meaning may get changed or expanded, the interpretation may get totally botched ... and yet the word, in some form, hangs around to be used by a new crowd. The word *bozo,* for example, once referred to a young man just starting to shave. But after a TV clown took the word as his name, the meaning was changed forever.

The English language has been tinkered with enormously over the ages. In part this is because it developed on an island that suffered numerous invasions during its early history. Every time some group came in, it left some of its words to be passed about and adapted by the natives. When the Romans came over before the birth of Christ, Latin got added to the mix of Gaelic and Old English. When Latin-speaking priests returned to convert the island's rough tribesmen to Christianity in the fourth and fifth centuries, more Latin got added. In 1066 invaders from Normandy, a powerful state at the time, arrived and imposed their version of the French language and French laws on the stubborn Anglo-Saxons. Eventually it was the English themselves who became the conquerors and picked up words from the people they colonized or conquered. When Europe began sending its explorers, settlers, and traders to the New World, the Americas became a melting pot for words from many languages.

In the early 1980s, as the director of a radio program, I began sharing my fascination for words with my audience, giving them a "word for the day" every day for years. I looked for common words that had unusual origins or amusing histories and tried to entertain my listeners with those stories. I've collected many of those stories in this book. This is not a formal dictionary of extensive listings (though I owe a great deal to the many fine dictionaries and encyclopedias I've used in my research), but more of a conversation with you about something that I've found interesting. I hope it'll be fun for you, too.

Acknowledgments

I would like to thank Joyce Wade, who helped me so much with her suggestions and encouragement. Thanks also go to the very copacetic Laura Glassover and all the people at Prima Publishing who have put this book in your hands.

I've got to give credit to the many fine dictionaries out there whose huge amounts of information I tapped into for this book. You may not want to scour these reference books word by word, as I did over an eight-year period, but even for casual use you'll find a lot more in them than just spelling, pronunciation, and definitions. I found Houghton Mifflin's *The American Heritage Dictionary* a great resource, as was Simon and Schuster's *Merriam-Webster*

Dictionary. I found inspiration in many other works on etymology, and even in the Reader's Digest *Family Word Finder,* which is supposed to be just a thesaurus. Of course, I crosschecked through many books and found one of the most thorough works on word origins to be the *Barnhart Dictionary of Etymology,* published by H. W. Wilson Co. If you enjoyed *Where in the Word?* and want to pursue your own special words, I wish you happy hunting.

David Muschell

aardvark   Origins of the names of Earth's creatures are as varied as the people who name them. This particular anteater gets its name from the old Afrikaners. These Dutch settlers, whose ancestors live in South Africa today, called the beast an "earth pig," probably because when first observed it seemed to be rooting in the dirt with its snout, much like a pig might root in the garden for tasty vegetables. Of course, the aardvark was looking for ants and termites, but the name stuck. Although the Middle Dutch Afrikaans language is now obsolete, the "earth pig" is still raiding the anthills of the world.

abacus   How did this word that we today associate with the oriental counting device actually originate among the Jews? Well, the word derives from a Hebrew word meaning "dust" and was applied to a mathematical counting board covered in dust. Usually, a slab of rock at the marketplace was sprinkled with a coating of sand so that calculations could be made by writing on it with a finger. This device was much cheaper than paper and could be erased easily with a new dose of dust. Later, the Greeks used a similar slab as part of their column construction, keeping the name *abacus*.

abandon   The old French had a term, *metreabandon,* which meant "to put under someone else's power." The verb part of the word, *metre,* got left out along the way as the Norman French conquered the English in 1066 A.D. and imposed their laws and language on the tough tribes of Angles and Saxons. A lot of property and goods were "abandoned" to the French rulers, and the word stuck around; *it* wasn't abandoned. . . . By the way, the *ban* part of the word, which meant "power," is not related to the *ban* meaning "prohibit." The latter word goes all the way back to the Old Norse language and meant "to curse." If something was cursed, it was likely you wouldn't want to use it. It's uncertain if there's any relationship between the French *ban* and the same word in Serbo-Croatian, meaning "warlord." That *ban* came from a Turkish word meaning "rich." It's possible this translated into "power" for the French.

abominable   Here there is disagreement as to origin, though the word clearly goes back to Roman times. It most likely came into our language with Julius Caesar's conquest of England or with the arrival of the first Roman Catholic priests, who used Latin so intensively. Some say the nastiness of *abominable* comes from *ab hominus,* meaning "away from man." Others describe its  origin more magically: that the Latin word *omin,* meaning "omen," is involved, the notion being that you'd stay away from anything that was an omen. The early priests put down all of the magical, pagan religions as "abominations," things for the pious to avoid.

The word seems to have gotten attached to the strange "yeti" snowman because of a terrible smell sometimes claimed to be part of his presence.

abracadabra   Today this harmless, nonsensical magic word is used alongside *hocus pocus* and *mumbo jumbo,* but in ancient times the word had religious power. Some of the earliest Christians divided themselves into sects quite a bit more diverse than our Baptists and Catholics are today. One of these groups, the Gnostics, had an almost voodoo-like notion of Christianity, mixing magic words and spells with what we might consider more normal Christian views. *Abracadabra* derives from the Gnostic term *Abraxas,* a Greek word meaning "almighty God," which the Gnostics used to call up power. The Gnostics scared more traditional early Christians with their secret knowledge and, at times, obnoxious righteousness and they lost a lot of potential converts. The last Gnostics can be found in Iran and Iraq. Those skeptical of all religious beliefs still call themselves *agnostics.*

accent   In today's world an accent can be a coveted thing. You'll hear someone say, "I just love an English accent." Then again, it can be a thing of derision, as many southerners feel when they hear their accents mocked. The word goes back to Roman times, translated from a Greek word. When these empires conquered the surrounding world we began to see the beginnings of class systems based on place of birth and facility with language. Though conquered people might learn the language of the conqueror, they would always show their foreign birth in the way they pronounced it. Actually though, the meaning of the word, "singing speech" seems complimentary.

accident   "Accidents" in ancient times usually came from above: perhaps a volcanic eruption, a landslide or avalanche, or a tree limb falling on one's head. . . . That's why the word, in its original Roman sense, meant "to fall upon." Then too, the gods, the stars, and the heavens were above, but we'll save that for another word.

ace   The playing card reflects the meaning of the word well. Again, we travel to ancient Rome for the word's origin. A certain coin, generally made from copper, was called an *as* and simply meant "one" or "a unit." It was also a name for a Roman unit of weight and, though the coin did not weigh a pound, it could almost certainly buy a pound of something, I know not what. Money has  always been our agreed-upon symbolic measure for "things," as the British pound was equal in value to a pound of silver. And our American paper money was also meant to be the equivalent of gold or silver in its beginnings. *Ace* is also used in dominoes or in tennis when one wins a point in one service stroke. Its use as "topnotch" comes more from the value of the card as the highest in the deck. A pilot or other expert is called an "ace" more for this reason than for any relationship to money. The expressions "to ace a test" or "to ace someone out" also rely on poker or other card games. It is always wise to keep an "ace in the hole."

achieve   The old French knew that the real achievement in life was to finish something. The word literally meant "to bring to a head" in its original form, though it's doubtful that this had any relation to brewery work; we all know that's what happens when the yeast has done its work on the sugar in a brew.

acute   When we think of this word we either think of pain—and the acute kind is very painful indeed—or we think of geometry and those tiny little angles. Both fit the word's origin in that it comes from the Latin for "needle." That sharp pain is like being stuck, and the thin angles taper down to a needle's point.

addict   Roman law would sometimes award conquered people as slaves to those who had been part of the conquering troop or were otherwise deserving. That is where the word *addict* comes from: "to award (as a slave)." That seems appropriate, since when you are addicted to something you are its slave. Though nicotine, cocaine, or heroin may seem odd and varied masters, they certainly have made those enchained to them do strange things to themselves and others in their "masters'" names.

administer   Administrators seem very powerful in today's connotation of the word, running hospitals and businesses, taking care of the distribution of wealth from wills, trust funds, and estates, or making the rules for schools and other bureaucracies . . . but the original meaning of the word again goes back to Rome and was "to be a servant to." Tell that to the boss.

adore   Adoration has always carried with it a sense of worshipfulness, and that reflects the origin of the word.

In Roman times it meant "to pray to a god." Ritualistic speech has always been a part of prayer: special ways of speaking to deities. The root word in *adore* is also part of *oracle,* which was the name for the shrine of god, the priest who prophesied for that god, and the prophesy itself. *Oration* also derives from this root word. After the fall of the Roman Empire, the Latin word was applied to Christ, and that usage is still echoed in the Christmas carol verse "Oh, come let us adore Him." Though the word is still strong in religious and romantic use, by now it has lost much of its power. For example, you'll hear at a party, "I simply *adore* that color of carpet!"

advertise   This is the age of advertising and the American economy runs on it. The competition is fierce to make us notice a product, brand name, or place of business. The original Latin meaning, "to turn toward," is fitting, since an ad certainly wants us to do this.

aggravate   If something aggravates, it can become an irritating millstone around your neck, constantly occupying your thoughts. The Latin root meant "to make heavier," and from that root we also got words like *gravity* and *grief.* Grief can certainly weigh down one's heart as much as an annoyance or a grave situation can burden one's mind. On the other hand, the burial *grave* comes from an Old English word meaning "to dig or scratch," from which we also get *engrave* and *grub.*

agony   "The thrill of victory; the agony of defeat." The idea of pain is today the central meaning of the word *agony,* but to the early Greeks the word meant "contest." When their naked Olympians contested in a sport, they gave their all and could be heroes for life.

But the wrestling, running, and throwing could easily bring on a lot of pain, and that sense has stayed with the word. The idea of a contest is better seen in the two words, *prot*agon*ist* (literally: "one who contests for") and *ant*agon*ist* ("one who contests against").

Alamo Many places are named for landmarks, like rivers or mountains, and sometimes for the plants or animals that abound there. When the Spanish Franciscan monks built their mission in South Texas, they named it for the many cottonwood trees that grew in the area. *Alamo* is the Spanish term for the cottonwood and other poplar trees. Of course, today when students learn the phrase "Remember the Alamo," they're not meant to reminisce about trees, but to recall the 1836 battle at the mission that gave the name entirely new significance in American history.

album The Latin for "white" gives us a word that today has many uses. Originally, an album was a blank tablet, a clean white page ready to be filled. The notion of storing information was carried most strongly as the word progressed through time. Though today's photo and stamp albums start out empty and blank, the object is to fill them. The term *record album* was originally applied to a group of jackets bound together, used to store the platters. It was later applied to the vinyl object itself, which is now fast disappearing. In the 1800s the word was used to describe popular books of illustrations mixed with brief sentimental stories. The idea of "white" can be seen in other words with the same root, like *albino* and *albumen* ("egg white").

alcohol How booze and make-up share origins is a strange tale. You've seen the hieroglyphics of the Egyptian men and women with the darkly colorful

painted eyes? This eye make-up was popular throughout the ancient Middle East and came from a processing
of antimony, a fine metallic, crystalline substance. The
Arabic word for this was *al-kohl*. Somehow or other, it
was the *process* of turning the raw antimony into the
cosmetic that stuck with the word as the Romans got it
from the Carthaginians. The original Arabic word took
on the sense of obtaining the "spirit" of a substance by
distilling it, thus "alcohol." The eye shadow, brought
from Egypt, also kept its name for a while, but soon lost
out in use to the other, drinkable products.

alert   The warning signal of the alert can still be heard
today during tornadoes and safety drills. The word's
origins are linked to Roman times and originally
applied to a high tower. In an age of possible attacks
from marauding opponents, most towns relied on the
eyes of guards in watchtowers to bring the earliest
news of approaching danger. Later, fortress and castle
towns always included a watchtower; the "alert" would
be the shout of the guard on duty. The "tower" sense of
the word never played much of a role in its evolution
from the early Latin to the French to the English. As
faster means of communication replaced the eyes and
the shout, the alert came to signify the warning more
than the watch for danger. By the way, *alarm* comes
from the Old Italian "call to arms," and came from those
who were alert to attack.

algebra   At its height, the Islamic world was widely
known for its medical and mathematical knowledge.
One Arabic word that figured in both those fields is
today part of our vocabulary, and a source of headaches
for many high school math students. *Algebra* comes
from a word meaning "the science of joining broken
parts." In Arabic medicine the word was applied to the

setting of broken bones, while in mathematics it referred to sets of numbers and their many operations as related to other sets. Never mind, I've been trying to avoid all that since tenth grade.

alibi   This word has a logical Latin meaning: "elsewhere." When you use an alibi you are trying to prove you were somewhere else when an event in question occurred. Similarly, the Latin meaning of *alias* is "otherwise." Thus if you're using an alias, you are "otherwise named," as in: David, alias "The Word Nut."

alone   When you are alone, "you" is all you have. The word's formation in England in the 1300s or thereabouts came from "the all is one." Of course, you can be alone and not be lonely, but our word *lone* came later when writers had forgotten the original combining and took the *a* to be an indefinite article (a lone). The word *lone* was usually applied to the widow or the unmarried, and to be lonely was a sad thing indeed.

alphabet   Being able to recite the alphabet is a source of great pride among our littlest learners. But when we say the word *alphabet* we are actually beginning to list the letters of another language, Greek. The first two letters of that tongue are *alpha* and *beta*. The notion of learning your letters goes back farther than that, though. The Greeks took their alphabet from the widely traveling Phoenicians, who probably got their *alpha* from the Hebrew *aleph* (meaning "ox"). The Greeks changed it around both in appearance and pronunciation and headed it toward our modern-day *a*.

amateur   The earliest definition of this word still fits many of our non-professional enthusiasts. The original Latin meant "a lover," and whether you are an amateur baseball player, fisherman, or painter, you must truly love what you're doing to spend so many hours at it. The word can be less than complimentary, however, as when someone says, "He's just an amateur," meaning he's very new at something, or "What an amateur job," meaning that something is sloppy or poorly done. Furthermore, some of today's amateur athletes in football or basketball may not be involved as much for the love of the sport as for the love of the future monetary gains they might receive.

amethyst   You might not realize that this form of purplish quartz or corundum actually was used as a medicine by the ancient Greeks. More accurately, it was believed to be a good hangover treatment and was a mineral that could help sober a person up. The literal translation of *amethyst* is "not to be drunk." This may explain why the gemstone is associated with the month of February, which takes its name from the ancient Roman festival of purification that took place every February 15th. It was probably a good idea to try to seek purification at this time after a long Italian winter cramped up in smoky quarters.

angler   If you think *fisherman* is a sexist term, you can use *angler*, but you aren't referring to anything of 45 or 90 degrees. The word goes back a thousand years to Old English and refers to a fishhook. It doesn't seem to have any relation to the Latin word *angle,* which meant "corner." The name of our language, however, did more than likely derive

from a Roman version of the name of an ancient tribe of fishermen in England, the "Angles." The Romans called them the "Angli," which eventually became the "English." If you get out on the lake or stream by devious means, like calling the boss to say you're sick, we say that you have angled your way out of work. That, too, comes from the Old English for "fishhook," from the notion that good anglers know many tricks to bait their prey to that hook.

Apache   Many Indian tribes were named by other Indians. The Apaches got their name from the pueblo-dwelling Zuñi Indians, and the Spanish added that word, which meant "enemy," to their vocabulary and later to ours. The Ute Indians named the Comanches. "Stranger" was the translation. The Cheyennes were named by the Dakota tribe. *Cheyenne* meant "to speak unintelligibly," which, of course, was just how Cheyenne speech sounded to the Dakotas. The French took the Algonquian Indians' word that their enemies were real snakes, which is what *Iroquois* meant to them.

appendix   This Latin word has a meaning that fits its several uses. Literally, "the part that hangs" makes sense for the leftover organ in the digestive tract and the supplementary material that is "hung" on the end of a book. Things that are *pending* do have the quality of hanging over us, leaving us in *suspense* and even trembling in our *appendages*. Many words come from that first Latin root for "hang." Many a man has kept his pants hanging with good old *suspenders*.

arena   Today, the word *arena* applies to everything from boxing to politics to theater-in-the-round (called arena theater). We took the word from the center area of the Roman amphitheater, where special contests and spectacles had their setting, but the original Latin meaning is more humble. *Arena* meant "sand" to those old Italians because the floor of that part of the amphitheater was covered in sand, not only for traction and making a fall softer, but perhaps, too, for better absorption of blood. Enough said.

arrange   We have been arranging things ever since man decided where he'd put his fur bedding in the cave. Weddings and other appointments are arranged, as are furniture, schedules, and musical scores. The French gave us the word, which meant "to put in a row." Some think it went even farther back, to a word that meant "to put in a circle," as around a hearth or fire. The implied sense of equality changed when chairs were arranged around tables and the most important would be closest to the source of warmth, at the head of the table.

assassin   Arab terrorists have a long tradition going back to the days of the Crusades, when a Moslem sect went about killing and attempting to instill fear, not only in Christian soldiers but in some of their own people as well. The word comes from the Arabic for "hashish addicts," since members of this sect were said to take the drug in great quantities to bring about a crazed, conscienceless state in which they might carry out terrible, bloody acts without remorse. Actually, most of the stories of their drug use are myth. Marco Polo told some of the tales of this group, which were not necessarily based in fact. Though the sect may have started this way, it later turned into a more sophisticated terrorist organization that was finally crushed by the invading Mongols.

athlete   When we call someone an athlete today we usually imply physical prowess, agility, or strength. The Greeks knew well that if you're going to put out all the energy it takes to be good at a sport or game, you'll usually want some reward, whether it's a medal, a ribbon, or a laurel wreath. Their word *athlete* meant "to contest for an award or prize."

atlas   Most of us use this word when referring to a book of maps, but many also know that this was the name given to the poor Titan of Greek mythology who lost out in the war of the gods because his brother, Prometheus, turned against him. Old Atlas was con- demned to hold the pillar separating the heavens and the earth. In drawings he was often depicted carrying the world on his shoul-  ders. Mapmakers in the sixteenth century, an age of exploration that stretched the world's boundaries, made it a tradition to put an illustration of Atlas carrying his burden at the front of the book of maps. The books took the old god's name and that name has continued, though the Titan's role is lost. The Atlantic Ocean took its name from the Greek "sea of Atlas," and later a group of mountains in northwestern Africa also got his name, since part of the story dealt with how Perseus turned Atlas to stone with the Gorgon's head. Even the legendary continent of Atlantis was named after that old Greek immortal.

auction Bridge players will understand the original Latin meaning of this word: "increase." The term is applied to sales done through bidding because that is the goal of the auctioneer: to make a sale after an increase of bids. In auction bridge, the card players also use the increasing of bids as part of the game.

au gratin Today, tasty dishes served with a special cheese sauce might not sound so fancy or delicious if we used the literal translation from the French: "with scrapings." "I'll have the potatoes with scrapings." Yuck! Originally, these French dishes involved scraping dried or toasted bread and mixing it with grated cheese.

autopsy Most of us wouldn't want to look over the coroner's shoulder and watch his sometimes grisly work of discovering the cause of death of the body under his scalpel. The latter half of this word contains the Greek word for seeing, *opsy,* which we find in *optical* and *ophthalmology.* The first half, *auto,* conveys the "self-done" meaning we see in *automatic* and *automobile.* So the word actually translates as "to see for oneself" or "with one's own eyes." In other words, we're not going to accept at face value the notion that a person found washed up on shore died by drowning, or that a pajama-clad person died in bed while sleeping; we're going to see for ourselves. Sometimes, seeing with one's own eyes can lead to surprisingly different conclusions as to the cause of death.

avocado Don't stop eating this tasty tropical fruit just because you've learned it is a South American Indian word for "testicle." Apparently, these Indians expressed either a great deal of humor or pride in giving this tree-grown goodie its name. Even the

Spanish might not have been all too sure of its original meaning when they incorporated the word into their language. Then, too, wild avocados were much smaller than today's cultivated fruit. If the name now makes you uneasy, you can still use the nickname: alligator pear.

awkward Those awkward years: when our bodies have grown big, but our coordination of the parts hasn't quite caught up. The Norse people were right on target when they used this word, meaning "turned backward." In everything from a first kiss to that all-important meeting, we've all worried that things were going to turn out "backward" from our intent.

azalea This beautiful flowering shrub, related to the rhododendron, looks anything but dry when covered in its springtime cloud of blossoms, but that is what its name means in the Greek. It was so named for its tendency to grow well in dry soil.

babble There are actually two words pronounced "babble," and although each is spelled differently and has a different origin, both mean "a confusion of sounds." One has a single *b* in the middle—*babel*—and goes back to the Hebrew and to the Bible story of the "one-tongued" people attempting to build a tower to heaven. They were suddenly struck with a variety of tongues and no United Nations translator. It is an interesting story to both explain different languages and show how prideful Man is punished for thinking he can be on a par with God. The word literally translates as "gate of God" and could apply to the tower and, ironically, to our mouths. The city where this tower was built might have been Babylon, always a pretty wild place. The other word, with double *b,* comes from an entirely different place. The same root that gives us *baby, baboon,* and *barbarian* is at the heart of *babble,* which basically means "to speak incomprehensibly." The French word *baboon* describes the face of the monkey and means both "big-lipped" and "making a face." And the Greek word *barbarian* meant "from a foreign place," and thus, to the civilized Greeks at least, "rude."

baccalaureate   If you've sat through the farewell sermons of a high school graduation ceremony or other speeches given at colleges and universities across the nation, you've actually participated in a tradition that goes back to the days of the knights. In feudal times, if a young and intelligent farmer's son ever wanted to get off the farm and gain higher position without having been born into it, he would have to find a knight of the realm who would let him learn through service and apprenticeship. This might take years of armor-polishing, horse-grooming, and mock fighting, but if the boy proved worthy as he reached manhood he was made a knight in a very special ceremony. Some say the laurel-berry wreath might have been associated with this. Another related word, *bachelor,* also applied to this young man. He was sometimes called a bachelor-at-arms—a young knight who still served an older knight. When the training of these well-born or promising young men came under the wing of universities after the Magna Carta, the ceremonies at the end of a period of study conferred a Bachelor of Arts or Sciences, but the farewell ceremony was still called the baccalaureate.

bald   The bald eagle is definitely not bald as we think of the word, but the Old English term certainly was appropriate, since it meant "having a white head." The root of this word can be found in the Russian *beluga whale,* which described the animal's white color. "To shine brightly" also has a part in the meaning of this word and goes back to a prehistoric spring festival of dancing and  singing around a fire. And it is true that many a bald man has suffered from the teasing of his friends concerning the shine reflected off the bare spot on top.

ballot   In olden days, when paper was expensive (but each vote was still considered important), the Italians used small balls or pebbles to "cast" their votes, throwing them into either one box or another. The problem of stuffing the ballot box is evident with this early method of voting. Although we've made our system fairer, we've kept the term *ballot:* "small ball or pebble."

bandana   If the old westerners who pulled up their bandanas in the face of a sandstorm or to rob a stagecoach knew they were using a Hindu word, they might have taken off their ten-gallon hats and scratched their heads. In Hindi the original word meant "tie-dyed." The first of these colorful scarves and neckerchieves were brought from India by Portuguese traders, who passed the word on.

bank In its original Italian sense this word referred to a moneychanger's table. During the Middle Ages every town or city-state in Italy might have its own form of currency. Thus a traveler from Milan found money-changers important when arriving in Florence or Pisa. Moneychangers and their tables have been a part of our culture since man began trading in symbolic currency. Later developments—having someone hold large sums for you while you were in town, lending money to you for various projects, or even investing your excess capital—were the logical outgrowth of economic progress. *Bankrupt,* another word of Italian origin, meant "broken bench," which was a likely outcome if one of these money dealers had the misfortune to lose his customer's fortune.

banzai For most Americans this Japanese word brings to mind the fierce battle cry of the attacking Nipponese soldier or the kamikaze pilot in a World War II movie. The term was actually both a greeting and a patriotic phrase, as well as a warrior's shout. It meant "May you live ten thousand years," not a likely wish for a kamikaze pilot. Incidentally, *kamikaze* meant "wind of God."

barbecue This popular backyard pastime came from Haiti, where the Creole term referred to a framework of sticks constructed like a spit or grill, depending on what was being cooked. Sometimes a permanent pit was built for this kind of cuisine. Although the word *Creole* came from the Portuguese and was a name for "a

Negro born in his master's house," the term has many meanings today: from a European descendant born in the West Indies, to a person in Louisiana descended from the original French settlers, to mixed black and European descendants, to a special cooking sauce that mixes tomatoes, onions, and peppers (and is spelled *creole* with a small *c*).

bazooka Believe it or not, this important weapon of World War II actually got its name from a comedy act. The American comedian Bob Burns put together a bunch of pipes and tubes and made a crazy-looking wind instrument that he would play in his comedy routines across the country. He called it the "bazooka," probably poking fun at little Dutch horns called *bazoos*. The comedy act became so widely known that when the military introduced the armor-piercing rocket launcher, soldiers thought it resembled Burns's bazooka and called it that in jest. The name stuck.

bead Beads today have much less significance than their ancestors except in the one form that still reflects what the earliest Old English word meant. Rosary beads are still used by Catholics in their prayers, and the *beyed* of over a thousand years ago evokes that in its meaning: "prayer."

bingo Originally, winners in this game had to run to ring a bell, but that rule was changed either because of the game's popularity with older patrons or because the rule might put those seated farther from the bell at a disadvantage when two or more players won at the same time. With the rule change, players were allowed to make the sound of the ringing bell as soon as they had filled the appropriate spots on their cards.

blunder   Today we use this word not only for moving awkwardly but also for social errors or foolish actions of all kinds. There is the political blunder and the blundered construction job. In its first uses the Old Norse word had a simpler sense of *blunder,* which meant "to shut the eyes." This would definitely lead to bumping into things and generally making a variety of mistakes. *Blunderbuss,* the word for the wide-muzzled gun that Pilgrims sometimes carried, had a different origin. It was Dutch for "thunder tube."

bogey   No golfer is pleased with making a bogey unless it prevents a double bogey, but at one time a bogey was considered a fine score. The Scottish and Welsh gave us our "boogie-man," the mischievous evil spirit who causes little children to scurry to their beds in fright, but that word for a hobgoblin was also used on the golf course. When you were doing exceptionally well it 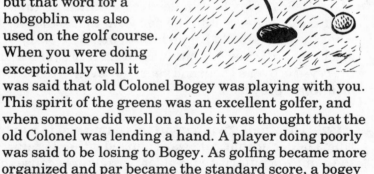 was said that old Colonel Bogey was playing with you. This spirit of the greens was an excellent golfer, and when someone did well on a hole it was thought that the old Colonel was lending a hand. A player doing poorly was said to be losing to Bogey. As golfing became more organized and par became the standard score, a bogey was not the duffer's aim.

bogus   Sometimes a word comes to us out of the blue. When a group of Ohio counterfeiters was caught in 1827, the press questioned folks about the raid. One witness was telling about the items confiscated, including a stamping device used to make coins. He couldn't think of its name and called it a *bogus*. The word made the newspapers and became a slang word for any counterfeiter's press. When the old reporter Mark Twain used it in his fiction the word got stuck in our language for good, meaning anything fake.

bonanza Some might believe this word was the name of the Cartwright ranch and that's that, since the sixties western brought the old gold miner's word into TV-land. It actually came to us from the Spanish and meant "fair weather." They got it from a Latin word meaning "a calm sea." California gold miners applied it to a rich vein of ore, since finding that certainly meant fair financial weather for them. *Bonus* and *boon* also come to us from the American Spanish, used for any good luck.

boondocks When you live "way out in the boon-docks," people understand they're not going to find much in the way of shopping centers or movie theaters nearby. The word, meaning "mountain," comes to us from the native people of the Philippines. On the islands the mountains are probably the least inhabited place, since most food comes from the ocean and the coastline.

boondoggle Today this word refers to a scheme in which taxpayer dollars are wasted on some pork-barrel government project. The Boy Scouts actually gave us the word when, in 1925, a scoutmaster named R.H. Link called a plaited leather cord worn around a Scout's neck a *boondoggle*. The cord had little use and took a long time to make. It thus became associated with time-wasting handicrafts.

boudoir   This Old French word carries a sense of femininity and romance in our language. Entering a woman's boudoir is to discover her very private bedroom. In fact, the word, which refers to a woman's sitting room, dressing room, or bedroom, seems to have a less than complimentary meaning: "a place for sulking or pouting."

boy   Many a young man, no matter what his race, has said, "Don't call me boy!" The sense of insult is never there when the elementary school teacher begins, "Now, boys and girls . . ." Is it just the sense of age that gives *boy* its derogatory quality when applied to new-whiskered fellows? If you look at the earliest use of the word, maybe not. In Greek times, and even through Roman days, a "boy" was one who wore shackles of oxhide or a collar and was a slave. The word stayed with us through the Middle Ages for a manservant or knave. After the French put it into our language it was gradually softened and became our more age-related word of the present day. "He's just a boy" lost its nastier side when it was used for a child.

bozo   Call someone a "bozo" today and you generally are being insulting. Originally, the term was merely slang for a fellow or guy and came from a Spanish word that meant "down on the cheeks of a youth," the peach fuzz of a near-man. So "bozos" were rather naive or inexperienced youngsters, but not necessarily the fool of today's word. The extra weight came from the renown of the clown Bozo. Because of his popularity, the original, harmless slang word has a much more derogatory connotation.

bracket   Brackets are useful devices: They might hold a shelf on the wall, close off words in a sentence, or label taxpayers' liability. Initially, however, a bracket held something much more personal. It got its start from an Old French word meaning "codpiece," that early supporting device for men.

brat Of Gaelic origins, this Scotch-Irish word for a nasty child originally had a much milder meaning. It referred to a coarse cloth usually worn as a bib by a young child to preserve any better garments from a spray of porridge at mealtime. So, very early on, *brat* also came to mean any very young offspring. Over time the word took on harsher connotations, maybe from that child who messed

up his "brat" the most. The word *bib* came from the Middle English and was associated with drinking wine or beer. Since drinking could be a sloppy business, many a gentleman wore a cloth to keep from dripping spirits upon himself. *Bib* came from the word *imbibe*.

bribe Bribery has a very criminal feel to it in our time, but the word started with much less of a wicked taint. In its Old French origins, a bribe was a piece of bread given to beggars. People might carry these little "bribes" to avoid having to give anything of greater value to a persistent beggar. It was probably the French Revolution that brought a more resentful, anti-aristocratic tone to the word.

bridal Many wedding receptions find guests getting just a bit blotto from the champagne or punch in celebration of the happy occasion. Even Jesus kept wedding guests in Canaan happy, changing water into wine. The tradition fits the word, which goes back to an Old English term for the special brew served at the wedding feast: "bride's ale."

buccaneer   Food plays a role in this name for the pirates of the West Indies. The word comes from the French and was used to describe a way of curing meat by cooking it on a barbecue frame. Most of the time, these freebooters had no real base and had to hop from island to island for supplies, cooking on the run. The term *buccaneer* has much better connotations for us than *pirate,* mainly because buccaneers preyed primarily on ships of the Spanish Armada and were thus more acceptable to the English and French. As a side note, *freebooter* didn't refer to any charitable donation of shoes, but came from the Dutch for "free booty."

buck   I can't buck the fact that this word has a bucket full of meanings. When the raw recruit is called a *buck private,* a reference is being made to the Old English word for a stag or a he-goat. This is also where we get our slang for the dollar bill. In pre-colonial days the unit of trade with the American Indian was the buckskin. A "buck" might buy a sack of grain; three "bucks" might purchase a knife. When paper money was introduced, the custom of calling the main unit a "buck" stuck. The deer also played a role in our expression "pass the buck." In early poker games the practice was to use a knife with a buckhorn handle to mark the dealer's place. When the deal changed, the knife was passed. The idea of passing responsibility went with the buck, the nickname for the knife. The tradition fell by the wayside, but passing the buck didn't. Why a ten-dollar bill is called a *sawbuck* goes to a Dutch word for a sawhorse that was translated almost literally into

English: *zaagbok*. Because of the "X" shape of a sawhorse's legs, the name got associated with the early ten-dollar bill, on which a Roman numeral *X* appeared. A buckboard wagon has no relation to deer or Dutch but comes from an Old English word for *belly,* since the center of the carriage reminded the user of the trunk of a body. Now, all you *buckaroos* get your name from a Spanish word for "one who tends cows." For *buckeye* and *buckshot* we go back to the deer. The buckeye nut resembles a deer's eye, while *buckshot* derives from the distance at which a buck could be shot. But *buckle* comes from a Latin word for "cheek," which is where the first ones were found: on straps holding helmets on heads, buckled at the cheek. *Buckwheat* is from the Dutch word for "beachwheat." And if I'm "bucking the system" or need to "buck up," I'm going back to the deer, which tends to leap forward. Whew! Oh, yes, our *buck-toothed* comes from the deer's prominent choppers, and *bucket* goes back to the *belly* origin.

budget If you're living on a budget, you pay close attention to what's coming in or going out of your wallet, and this also takes us to the original meaning of the word. In the beginning, budgets were leather pouches used for carrying money and valuables. Later, with the advent of paper money, *budget* was the initial name for the wallet (which, at first, was a name used for a pilgrim's knapsack). Speaking of money carriers, the purse was carried by both men and women in its first stages of use, but gradually it became associated almost entirely with women. *Purse* comes from a Greek word for "leather." The shipboard accountant still keeps the name in his title: Purser. And the old tradition of keeping prize money in a leather bag is still heard when the boxer wins the "purse."

buff   If you are reading this in the buff, you might be in a hot tub of water or you could just be a bit kinky in your literary habits. No matter which, we all understand that you are naked. Why "in the buff"? The word gets its start from a Greek name for the African antelope—the word from which we get *buffalo*. The skin of this animal got the shortened name *buff,* and the color of that undyed leather also got the same name. If you used that soft hide to polish something, you were *buffing* it. And if you were down to your own skin, you were "in the buff." Why, then, is an expert called a "buff"? That started with the early New York City firemen who were so enthusiastic and dedicated to their jobs that they earned the city's respect. Because of their thick, sturdy leather uniforms, their nickname became "buffs." Later, to be an enthusiast about anything was to be a "buff." The notion of *buffering* something comes from a different source: the French word for a blow, from which we get *"buffeting* winds." To *buffer* was to lessen the shock of the blow (or the jolt of the aspirin). The original game of blind man's buff came from this French word, since the blindfolded participant struck about, trying to find the other players.

bulimia   This word has gotten a lot of attention recently as a dietary dysfunction. It comes from the Greek and means "the hunger of an ox." Those who suffer from this illness tend to eat as much as an ox might, but then regurgitate the excess.

bully How this term for a meanie came from a Dutch word for "sweetheart" is still a bit of a mystery. Originally, a bully was a lover or a fine fellow, and to shout "Bully!" was to say "Way to go!" Along the way the word somehow got applied to pimps, perhaps as the false lover used his "sweetheart" for gain. The use of superior strength over the smaller and weaker began to be the predominant meaning for the word, and even hired thugs were called bullies for their tendency to pick on the helpless.

butter *Butter* has ancient origins. It was the Greek language that gave us the root, meaning "cow cheese." The Romans took the word from the Greeks, as they did so many others, and passed it on to the tribesmen they conquered. The *butterfly* got its name from an old English belief that those insects stole milk and butter when they visited the barn. *Butternuts* were called this because of the oily quality of the nut, but a Confederate soldier or sympathizer was called a "Butternut" because of the bark of that tree. The boiled extract of that bark was used as a dye during the hard economic times of the Civil War South, and this gave the grey uniforms their distinctive color. The extract also made a good laxative.

buxom Though a buxom woman may avoid bending over for many reasons, the original meaning goes back well over a thousand years and meant "easy to bend." It was used for the obedient servants on a lord's lands. As time and women changed, the word was applied to the more lively milkmaids and cheeky cooks and dishwashers. Eventually, it was the vivacious woman with the ample figure who caught most of the attention and, with our tendency to fixate on the bosom, the word began to refer to the larger examples of that portion of the anatomy.

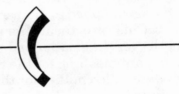

cab Calling out for a cab is a familiar activity in large cities and at airports. If you knew you were actually calling out a shortened version of an old Italian name for "goat," you might smile at the image. The earliest carriages for public hire were apparently so bouncy that they reminded passengers of the bounding goat, dancing about the hillside. The comparison to riding a capering goat stayed with the word. . . . And by the way, the *taxi* part of *taxicab* comes from the fact that you are taxed to ride in one . . . sometimes quite a bit. The word *cab,* referring to that part of a tractor or heavy truck or locomotive, comes from a shortened version of *cabin,* which is an Old French word for "hut."

cabinet This common furnishing has a more secret and seamy beginning than might occur to you when you are taking a glass off the shelf of the kitchen cabinet. The word is an Old French one that originated from a term for a gambling house. The tradition of the small, smoky back room used for the private amusement of gentlemen making wagers goes back many, many years. When craftsmen began making more intricate furniture that had many small compartments for storing or displaying things, they gave it the name *cabinet,* which translated into "little gambling house." The notion of small rooms inspired the name. By the early 1600s groups meeting in private for purposes other than gambling began to be called cabinets, and the term is still used, especially in government circles, where gambling with tax dollars is the pastime.

cadet With the tradition of the oldest son inheriting the lands and title of his father, what were the younger sons to do? In France, where this word got the use we think of today, these boys trained for the military, an honorable occupation that might bring them fame, lands, and titles of their own. In its early form the word *cadet* was applied to the younger son or brother. Later, as warfare became more organized, it was applied to any of the boys attending a school for military training. The Scottish people got hold of the word from the Norman French and used it for a young boy who did odd jobs around the castle or village. One of his primary jobs seemed to be carrying around the lord's golf clubs, thus giving birth to the word *caddie.* When some ungentlemanly fellow is called a *cad,* it reflects back on the original caddies, the young boys who were the "gophers" of Scotland. A tea *caddy* comes from a Malay word for a unit of weight, because of the amount of tea contained in the "caddy."

calendar Economics probably played a major role in the origin of the calendar hanging on your wall. Moneylending led to the need for proper calculation of interest. The Romans used the moon. The "calends" was the day before the new moon and the day when monthly interest was due. The moneylender's account book was called by the Roman name *calendar.* The *ides* was the day of the full moon. The 15th day of March (the one Caesar had to beware of), May, July, or October and the 13th day of other months were the ides in the old Roman measurement of the year. I'll tell more time later on.

caliber   Today, *caliber* is used almost exclusively in talking about the size of bullets and the barrels they travel through, but we get the word from shoemakers. Sandals were easy to fit to feet, but when better coverings were demanded the shoemakers of the Arabic lands took a measure of a person's foot, then matched that size with a series of wooden "feet" in the shop in order to build

the shoe to that particular size. They probably got the idea from the Greeks, but the Arab shoemakers popularized this method of fashioning foot apparel. The sizing of bullets for barrels came from this measurement technique. Whether thinness or thickness of foot has anything to do with your breeding or character, I'm not sure, but there is a connotation of worth when something is of the "highest caliber."

calm   If you've gotten angry and someone asks you to calm down, they mean for you to cool your temper. This word came from the Late Latin for "heat of the day," which can make you anything but calm. However, their *use* of the word made much more sense in relation to our modern definition. It referred to a place of rest during the heat of the day. To find "calm" was to get away from the burning summer afternoon.

camouflage Sometimes a word's origin has a kind of head-scratching meaning. This word of French birth more than likely came from the phrase "smoke blown into the nose." This certainly would make your eyes water and cause you to mistake what you see. Or this could have referred to smoke being used as a cover or to disguise how many troops you have. The idea of being disguised is what has clung to the word as it made its way to us.

cancan This loud, sexy, high-kicking dance that we associate with certain French clubs got its name from French children who thought the exuberant dance had the look of a duck waddling about on land. Their association between the bottom wiggling of ducks and dancers gave it its name. *Canard* is the French word for a duck.

cancel When something has been canceled you can go ahead and cross it out on your calendar. This notion of crosses takes us back to the beginnings of the word in ancient Rome. The earliest jails of the time were made with a lattice-type wooden crosswork. The lattice of the prison got applied in an abstract sense to crossing out anything that was to be voided, invalidated, or annulled. So the idea of being removed from sight behind the latticework of the jail gradually gave rise to the term for stopping any activity or marking anything so it can't be used again.

candidate   This is another word from Roman times. A candidate for office wore a white toga to symbolize his straightforwardness, honesty, and *candid*ness. The original Latin root word meant "white," from the belief that this was the color of purity. There was wishful thinking even in ancient Roman politics.

cannibal   When Columbus first got sidetracked in the Americas during his attempt to find shorter trade routes to the Spice Isles, he was told of a terrible tribe of maneating natives on the islands of Cuba and Haiti. The Indians who told him about these Caribs (from which we get Caribbean) also called them Canibas. Columbus reported their name as Canabalis. What the name actually meant in the language of these feared island tribesmen was "brave."

canter   When a horse moves slower than a gallop but faster than a trot, it's moving at a canter. The English pilgrims of the 1200s and 1300s were responsible for this term, once called a Canterbury gallop. As Chaucer's *Canterbury Tales* tells us, it was a custom to make pilgrimages to Canterbury in the springtime, and the mounted travellers went at an easy pace. . . . They "cantered."

carbine   This light shoulder rifle, popularized by the cavalry, got its start with the bubonic plague. Someone had to carry the corpses of the victims of the Black Death from their homes to be laid out for burial, but most did not want to touch the dead for fear of getting ill. Since the plague was killing one out of every three

people, it was a justified fear. Those men who did carry
the bodies were given a derogatory nickname, the
"escarrabine," from the French word for the scarab
beetle, which eats the flesh of the dead. When the fears
of the plague died out, the bravery of these men was
remembered and the nickname got attached to soldiers
on the front lines and those who operated some of the
early engines of war. After the light musket was
invented for use by cavalry, the word was applied to
those soldiers. Finally, it got used for the weapon itself.

carnival   If you translated this word literally, you'd
have "flesh, farewell!" The Lenten traditions of fasting
and penitence were
always preceded by
great feasts. If you were
going to have to give up
all those goodies, you
might as well have one
big gorge before saying
good-bye to meat.
Mardi Gras is just one
example of such a
celebration. You'll find
the flesh-eating defini-
tion in *carni*vore and

the "good-bye" in *val*edictorian (farewell speaker). The
word *carnation,* by the way, means "flesh-colored."

celebrate   This is yet another Latin word, meaning
"to fill often or numerous times," which makes sense,
especially when drink was a primary means of festivity.
The idea of "a great number" is found in *celebrity,* which
refers to someone who would definitely be known by a
great number of people, if not intimately, at least by
sight.

chap   Two different meanings come from this word's usage. The English call any "old fellow" a chap, but originally it was applied to peddlers and other tradesmen in the countryside, called "cheapmen" from the first notion of *cheap,* meaning "to trade or bargain." A good *chapman* (as the word became in time) was always welcome if he was fair in his dealings. We also get our word for those small, sometimes self-published books, *chapbooks,* from the kind this merchant would sell. Now, having *chapped* lips has nothing at all to do with this English fellow. This *chap* comes from a Germanic root that has as its base meaning "to cut." From that root we get other words like *shape, landscape, scab,* and even *shave.* The word *chaps,* meaning what a cowboy wears to keep from getting saddle sores, comes from a Mexican-Spanish word, *chaparejos.*

chauffeur   That very wealthy French person who rode in the first steam-driven cars needed someone to build a fire under the boiler and keep it stoked while driving. *Chauffer* means "stoker" in French. When the internal combustion engine replaced the old steam cars, it was natural to let these driver/fire-tenders take on the new role of keeping the car in working order and filled with fuel.

check   Checking out the word *check* led me to the Persia of antiquity, where our modern game of chess got its start. The word stood for a piece on the board representing the shah or king and referred to one who controls. As the game spread into Europe in the 1200s, the attack on the king was given the term *check.* *Checkmate* also came from the Persian, meaning "the king is dead." The concept of controlling was used in banking to refer to that slip of paper that gives you control of your money. Checking out of a hotel might find you with a restaurant check to pay. *Checked* cloth came from the pattern of alternately colored squares on the chessboard. Hockey gives us a more violent way of controlling another person. When a dog pauses to reaffirm the scent of the prey he is tracking, he is said to "check," but when a falcon checks, he's leaving the proper game for a lesser bird. Those are just a few things I've checked off my check list.

cheese The Latin origin of this word is not surprising, since its root meant "to ferment or become sour." If something is "cheesy," meaning of poor quality, that comes from the slang for milk beginning to turn sour. But when we call someone a "big cheese," meaning "an important person," we go back to a Hindu word for "something." A *chiz* was a thing of importance. The origin of the old gangster phrase "Cheese it! The cops!" which meant "get out of there fast," is uncertain and could be part of a long list of words and phrases we use to avoid taking God's name in vain, from *Geez* to *Gosh*.

chow Even though we know Orientals have long eaten dogs, it's a pretty sure bet that we are not referring to the black-tongued breed of dog when we speak of food as "chow." The word for the dog and the word for eating come from two different Mandarin Chinese terms, the latter meaning "stir-fry." Some might argue that our slang word for food could have come from a Latin-derived French word for "stew pot" or "caldron," on which our word *chowder* is based. *Chow mein* is Chinese for "fried noodles," and the pickled vegetable mixture called *chow chow* comes from another Chinese word meaning "mixed."

cider Cider goes all the way back to the Hebrew and was initially an intoxicating drink of grain and honey. The word was also used to describe a drunk person. The Greeks took the word when translating the Bible and they passed it on. The non-alcoholic beer some think of as new actually has a tradition going way back, when unfermented cider was called sweet cider and was available for the young and those with more sober tendencies. Hard cider was the fermented version used to produce vinegar and hangovers.

clink   The origin of this sound-word is simple enough: It goes back to a Dutch term for a kind of brick that was made by firing clay until it was extremely hard. It was the sound that these bricks made when struck together that gave them the name. Later, when a musician hit a particularly bad note, he was said to have made a real "clinker," alluding to that brick sound. Why is a jail sometimes called "the clink"? This comes from an old London jail with this name. The Clink was well-known in England and became the nickname for any prison.

clue   When a detective traces a criminal from a telltale fingerprint, we can see a real relationship with the ancient beginnings of the word. In Greek mythology, Theseus had to travel the maze of the Labyrinth to kill the Minotaur and stop the constant sacrifice of Athens's youth. From King Minos's daughter, who had fallen in love with him, the brave Theseus got his "clew" (the original English  spelling when it came into our language in the early 1600s). This was a ball of thread that he unwound as he went in and later followed back out. After that, anything that might lead you from the unknown to the known became a clue. *Clew* was also the name for balls of thread or twine for many years.

coat of arms   These shieldlike heralds of symbols representing certain families or tribes were like flags that soldiers could rally around on the battlefield. They also helped soldiers identify their ranks from the enemy. The first coats of arms were really light garments worn over the armor with the symbol printed or woven on it. Crusaders wore only the cross as their coat of arms, showing that that symbol of Christ was their identity and symbolic "family."

cockamamie   We know that when someone has a cockamamie idea it is usually pretty worthless and second-rate. There are two varying histories of the word. One comes from *decalcomania,* which was the process of making fake tattoos or putting decals on windows, on walls, or in frames. In this sense the "art" was a kind of counterfeit. This idea seems to have gotten mixed up with a cheap molasses candy found in early New York, called *cock a nee nee.*

coin   *Coin* goes back to Latin, as you've seen so many words do. It meant "wedge," from the stamp that coinmakers used in stamping their coins. But "a penny for your thoughts" would have gotten you only a hunk of cloth in barbarian Europe, since that was one medium of exchange from which we get the word *penny*. A "piece of eight" was a valuable Spanish coin that was sometimes quartered and "eighthed" when exchanges were made and no smaller coin was available. Early colonists used these and doubloons, as well as tobacco, for trading.

comedy   The ancient Greek festival celebrating Dionysus always involved a great deal of song and story. As those events became centered around plays that told the stories through choruses of singers and groups of actors portraying various scenes, the beginnings of today's theater were seen. When the stories were lighthearted revels the singers were called *komoidos,* from which we get our word *comedy.* The choruses that sang in the plays whose endings were less happy wore goat skins to let the audience know the nature of the play they were seeing and because the wilder nature of the god of wine was represented by the goat. These plays were called tragedies, from "song of the goat." We didn't invent the musical; music invented the drama.

companion   *Companion* had a simple but nice beginning, meaning "one who shares bread with another." In olden days bread was the staff of life and to share it was to share your livelihood. Breaking bread was a major sign of welcome and hospitality. As society got more crowded, another word evolved: *company,* for "a group that shares bread." Now, in today's company the idea is also to share the "bread" the group makes, but in our free enterprise system we tend to divide the bread a bit more unevenly. By the way, *comrade* comes from a root meaning "to share the same road."

complain   The Latin root here has a very descriptive meaning. *To complain* was "to beat the breast." With the heart considered the central location of the emotions, you would literally pound your chest when describing your ills. This self-flagellation can still be seen as an almost natural gesture of complaint in many cultures.

confetti   The way we use this word today got its start in Italy at carnivals and festivals, when those parading through the streets would throw candy and bread to the crowd. Most of the time this was why the crowd gathered, to get the trinkets from the various guilds that were showing off. Later, as the clubs, guilds, and organizations decided to spend more money on the wagons and costumes for the occasion, the sweets were replaced by bits of paper thrown into the air. This wasn't as much fun for the crowd, but was admittedly safer for the children, who might scramble in the dirt for a chewy bit of candy. Goodies can still be found tossed to the crowd at major festivals such as Mardi Gras in New Orleans or Carnival in Rio. The British called them sweetmeats, their word for *meat* originally meaning just "food."

congress   A word we mainly apply to our astute governmental institutions of the House and Senate had a very different origin related to bodies. One of the earliest uses of the root of this word was for sexual intercourse. The word was also applied to a hostile encounter between two opposing forces, as in "a congress of armies," from the Latin "come together." You know, these early definitions might work when applied to our political leaders, since it sometimes seems like war on Capitol Hill. And I won't even go into how the taxpayers feel after our representatives get through with them.

cop   Why do we call a policeman a cop or copper? The word seems to go back to a Dutch word that came from an Old French expression meaning "to seize or catch." Its very earliest use seems to have been associated with practicing piracy. This was how many enemies were caught: A noble or official of the state would hire mercenaries to track down a thief or offender and bring that person back.

You couldn't very well send your army, since you might start a war. So the very first police officer, the "copper," was born. We still use the word in its original sense when someone "cops a plea" or "cops a bargain" or "cops out." A *constable,* which is another word for police officer, came from Late Latin: "count of the stable." This person started out with the very important job of tending the lord's horses and stables, and this trusted position eventually led to the constable being the person in command in the ruler's absence, the upholder of the laws of the realm.

cordial   We go back to the Latin for this word's root and actually look to medicine for part of its ancestry. Heart problems are not new, and when someone was weak of heart a stimulant like a drink of some special brewed tea or a fermented beverage might make the patient feel better. This drink was called a cordial, something "for the heart" or "of the heart." That term is still applied to certain liquors. We use the word today mainly to characterize a warm or sincere person. When it comes *from* the heart, cordiality can be very stimulating *to* the heart.

corporal   All the meanings of this word turn to the root for "body." Whether referring to the cloth that the plates for communion rest on in church or a form of punishment, anything from a paddling of the backside at school (a little rare today) to the death penalty (even more rare), this root focused on the physical. The *corporal* in the military came from the "head of a *body* of troops." This was one who was just above the run-of-the-mill *soldier* (which came from the name of an ancient Roman coin, the "solidus," used to pay the troops). The *sergeant* got his title from the Old French, meaning "one who serves." The title *captain* came from a later French term meaning "head," as in head of a column of troops, of course. *Colonel* also shares that link to the column from the Italian for "column leader." The seagoing Arabs gave us the rank of *admiral* ("amir-alt") from "high commander." The word *military* itself goes back to Roman times, from a word for "soldier." *Troops* comes from the French word for "herd." The *infantry* were the youngest of that "herd" and walked into battle; since they were so young they were the "infants" of the army.

cosmetic   We don't think much of the stars or the universe when we see the cosmetics section in a drug store. More than likely we see the *mascara* (from an Arabic word for "clown" or "mask") or the *perfume* (from Latin for "smoke," incense being one of the earliest perfumes). But the word *cosmetic* goes back to a Greek word for the universe, *cosmos,* meaning "order." A *cosmetician* is "one who is skilled in ordering or

arranging things," if you take the word literally . . . and
I guess anyone who's watched a woman put on her
make-up could see how this definition fits. Pretty
cosmic, eh? And if she is the *cosmopolitan* type, she'd be
comfortable anywhere because she's what the Greeks
would call "a citizen of the world."

covey   We speak of a group of game birds in flight, such
as quail, as a *covey,* though the term actually comes
from the French word for the act of sitting on eggs to
hatch them, basically "covering" them. But where does
the notion of a *gang* of buffalo, a *drift* of hogs, a *watch* of
nightingales, a *skulk* of foxes, a *muster* of peacocks, a
sloth of bears, a *fall* of woodcock, a *shrewdness* of apes,
a *cast* of hawks, a *kindle* of kittens, a *covert* of coots, a
cete of badgers, a *wisp* of snipe, or a *bevy* of deer come
from? These are all the official terms for these particular groups, not to mention a *pod* of seals or a *sounder*
of boars. Some of these labels are easy to figure out.
Others present a flock of questions.

coward   When some animals slink away in fear, their
tails instinctively curl between their legs in an extra
protection of their genitals. Appropriately, the old
French root of *coward* meant "with tail between legs,"
fitting for one who would rather avoid harm than
confront an opponent. Running from a threatening
situation is not always a cowardly thing to do, but we
have another expression for this, one that also refers to
animals. Deer are known to use their tails as a kind of
antenna to detect danger, and from this we get the
phrase "to hightail it out of there."

crazy   *Crazy* goes back to a Scandinavian word for
"broken." The Old Norse language described the insane
as somehow brokenheaded, with shattered minds,

which was a common-sense definition for the way a person seemed when crazy. Something was not working properly. We've softened the term somewhat in today's world, when a person can be crazy about a car, a movie, or another person, or go crazy at a sporting event or concert. . . . But the feeling of being not quite right, a little cracked, persists and we still hear the serious question "Am I going crazy?"

creosote The Germans got this word from the Greek, meaning "preserver of flesh." How did this sometimes gooey black mess that clogs our chimneys and wood stoves originate? Ancient healers tried many plants and brews of plants for medicinal purposes, and it so happens that certain tars from wood and coal make excellent, if smelly, disinfectants. In fact, tar from the beech tree was used to treat bronchitis and tuberculosis. Most creosote today is used to preserve wood, such as fence posts or telephone poles, which are painted or soaked in creosote to make them last longer.

crisscross As I'll mention later, the sign of the cross was sometimes marked as an *X,* and this *X* was called the Christcross. Through time, those that couldn't write would use this symbol to show that their intent was sincere. They were signing a document "in Christ's name." The symbol was also placed at the beginning of the alphabet in the earliest school child's *hornbook,* which was not a book but one page covered in a protective, clear sheet of horn to preserve the alphabet and numbers it contained. The name for the mark got slurred over the ages into *the crisscross.* Because many times people would kiss the *X* of their signature in reverence for its meaning, the *X* also came to represent a kiss.

crocodile   The Greeks gave us this animal's name, which means "worm of the pebbles," from the reptile's love of lying out in the sun to warm its cold blood. The expression for false weeping, "crocodile tears," came from the belief that the beast cried after eating its victims, a rather wasted display of emotion, since the party for which the tears were supposedly being shed was already undergoing digestion.

The word's "cousin," *alligator,* comes to us through the Spanish from some Latin roots meaning "that lizard." The less-used word *caiman,* the name of a related species, comes from the Carib Indians and gives us the name of a nice vacation spot: the Cayman Islands.

crotchety   We sometimes call a grumpy person, especially one of the elderly, "crotchety." What *crotchety* really means in its Old French original is "full of little hooks." The word derived from *crochet,* a term for the process in which little hooklike tools are used to fashion thread into cloth. The idea that as you get older you are plagued by little aches and pains, as if poked by little crochet hooks, and that that gives you a sour disposition, is captured in the word *crotchety,* which uses an older spelling of *crochet.* That same spelling can be seen in the nickname for a quarter note, a *crotchet,* so named for its hooked shape. Another word using the "hook" concept is the Dutch word from which we get *cramp.*

cry   The power of Rome gave this word much more meaning at one time, centuries ago. A citizen of Rome was a powerful person in the heyday of the empire and could grant many favors to the non-citizen: freedom from bondage, passage through the territories, judicial pardon, and so on. A *cry* in those days referred to a plea to a Roman citizen, a Quiris. It is uncertain if other words like *inquire, acquire,* and *require,* among others, had anything to do with the power of the conqueror. Today a cry can be anything from a sorrowful sound to a shout before battle to a street vendor's calling out.

curfew   This word, when translated from its French origins, means "to cover the fire." In medieval days it was a regulation in many of the towns of Europe that fires be extinguished at a certain hour. This did not mean that homes would be without heat. The rule applied to outdoor fires that lit the streets in the evening, fires that were later replaced by oil lamps, then gas lamps, then electricity. Everyone knew that being out and about at too late an hour could only cause mischief and that it was best not to tempt evil spirits by letting them see you on the streets. Later the word was applied to the bell or other signal that announced the hour at which people should vacate the streets.

dachshund   This long-bodied, long-nosed canine, sometimes nicknamed "hot dog," got its German name for its intelligent and ferocious hunting ability. The

Germans developed the breed to hunt badgers. A
badger could disrupt a herd of cattle or sheep, and its
carnivorous ways were a menace to the safety of a calf
or lamb. But badgers were also nearly impossible to
hunt down. Deep in their burrows, with their vicious
teeth and almost steellike front claws, badgers were
safe from people, who might risk losing a hand by going
after them. So breeders developed a dog with short,
powerful little legs to dig into the badger's hole, a long
torso to fit into the tunnel, and an equally long snout
full of teeth to fight the beast once it reached its lair.
Though most dachshunds today are family pets, their
bravery and loyalty have earned them their German
name, "badger hound." Other breeds have names not
quite as fierce: *Collie* comes from *coalie,* since many of
the breed, excluding Lassie, were black like coal. The
sometimes prissy *poodle* also got its name from the
German and was trained like a golden retriever to jump
in the water for game. Its name came from the German
root meaning "puddle dog" or "splashing dog."

dairy   Everyone knows that in today's more liberated
society both men and women work side by side in our
dairy industry, providing those essential products to
our food supply. Oh-oh . . . Tracing this word, I find it
goes back to an Old English root of about twelve
hundred years ago and that it was applied to a female
breadmaker. Not that this wasn't an important task,
but in those days this young woman also tended the
farm animals while the men hunted or worked the
fields. The dairy maid was commonly the one who
milked the cow, churned the butter, fermented the
cheese, and gathered the eggs while she waited for the
bread to rise or bake or cool. I'll say even more about
this when I get to the origin of the word *lady.*

daisy   This flower got its name over a thousand years
ago from its tendency to adjust to the light. The early
tribes of England called it the "day's eye" because it
would open in the morning, revealing its yellow,
sunlike center disk, and then close in the evening,
covering its bright center. The written form, which
started as *daeg-eseage,* changed over the years, but the
pronunciation, "day's eye," remained much the same.

dandelion   This weed, with its pretty flowers and
feathery seed ball, was once widely used as a salad
green. Its name means "tooth of the lion," from the
French translation of Medieval Latin. This had nothing
to do with whether or not the African cat liked the
plant. It was called this because of the sharply indented
leaves that looked like a row of large teeth.

dandy   If we say, "That's just dandy," we usually mean
it's fine, unless we're being sarcastic. In fact, *fine* and
dandy go together very
often. Originally,
dandy was used by the
more rural, hard-
working lower classes
to describe an overly-
dressed, foppish gentle-
man. It was probably
derived from "jack a
dandy," from nick-
names for Jack and
Andrew, and the Scot-
tish used that phrase to
refer to a foolish person. *Fop* also was used for the fool,
who traditionally dressed in wild, multicolored clothing, which included strange hats and odd shoes. Over

time, it seems that some of these dandies proved their worth and earned some kind of grudging respect. Perhaps envy for the ability to afford excess led to *dandy* becoming less derogatory. A "merry-andrew" has a similar association with a prankster or clown.

danger   In olden days you were certainly in danger if you went against the ruler of your realm, whether a king or feudal lord. In its earliest use in the Old French the word meant "power to harm," and the only one who had that power was the lord of the estate or kingdom. No one else was allowed to do harm to another except on the orders of the lord. This led to a pretty peaceful lifestyle except when your lord was a particularly brutal one or so rule-bound that you were constantly in "danger" of provoking his punishment for any little infraction. The abuse of the "power to harm" was one of the things that led to the downfall of the feudal system.

date   When you set a date for something you are going back to a tradition established in ancient Rome, when a decree or law became official from the moment it was written down in that empire's capital. The word came from a common phrase: "written or given in Rome." It later came to mean the first line of a document, which told when and where it was written, which is why letters and proclamations still use this style. The computer industry has taken over the original Latin word, *data,* and applied it to any written words or numbers. Now, the fruit known as the *date* comes from the Greek and has nothing to do with showing up on time. It meant "finger" because of the shape of the popular, sweet palm product.

daze   Once again, it is the Old Norse language we turn to for the beginnings of this word, which applies to

everything from a punch-drunk fighter to a daydream-
ing schoolchild. In olden days the root of this word
meant "to become weary," and as a result of that
intense weariness to be almost confused as to reality.
Dazzle also comes from the same word and first meant
"to be dazed continuously," being so tired as to be
blinded to the world.

deacon In days past, as today, many men would like
to serve the Church and yet get married and have
families. The old Catholic and Greek Orthodox
churches provided a role for these men as deacons,
those who would assist the priests in various Church
functions. The word comes from the Greek for "servant." The Anglican Church adopted the ranking and it
was passed on to many other reformed Churches. Even
if the deacon only led the congregation in singing or
reading verses, it was a position of respect and service.
Not everyone appreciated the notion, however. Some
felt that allowing less than ordained leaders to have a
place near the altar lowered the value of the religious
experience. That prejudice can be seen in the term used
when a grocer arranges a box of produce so that the
poor selections are hidden under the good to make the
group look better. This is called "deaconing."

dean Our colleges abound with deans of all types, and
at that level the rank is highly respected. We also use
the term for admired senior members of other groups:
"the dean of actors" or "a dean among his fellow senators." Actually, the word has its origin in the Greek
word for "ten." When the early Roman Catholic Church
was organizing its rankings from priest to pope, the
word was incorporated to mean "one set over ten" and
was the name of the priest who was placed over a group
of other priests, usually ten, in a parish. The English

got the word from their French conquerors and pronounced it in their own way, as usual.

debonair This word comes just about literally from
the French meaning "of good air." Not only did doctors
in the Middle Ages judge a person's health by the liquid
and solid secretions of the body, but also by the odors
the person gave off. In that time, to be of good air was to
be of vigorous health and, in all likelihood, of happy
disposition. Today our physicians are taking the idea of
odor and health very seriously, and new studies are
being done all the time concerning well-being and
aroma.

decoy Duck hunters are very familiar with the decoy.
The term also gets used all the time for "to mislead
another." The word came to us from the Dutch word
meaning "the cage." For a stalker of mallards that
"cage" is the pond or cove where he hides, making his
calls and watching his carved imitations float. The
leading of man *or* beast into a trap or "cage" is still
today's use of the word.

defy Today we think of defiance as rebellion or chal-
lenge: "I defy you to take me to court." "He defied all
odds in accomplishing the task." In its earliest use the
word applied to those who renounced their faith. In the
first days of Christianity, people "defied" by either
rejecting the Roman gods for Jesus or by publicly
reversing their Christianity for the accepted religion
(thus avoiding persecution).

delirious This word goes back to the first farmers.
When an animal such as an ox or mule would not listen
to the command of the plowman but instead wandered
about the field, pulling the plow here and there, it was

delirious, meaning "away from the furrow." It was generally illness that caused the deviation, and the word got used for anyone who was temporarily deranged because of drink, illness, or shock. We still use it when someone is "out of line" or babbling incoherently.

desire The Roman belief in astrology gets all mixed up in this word, which came out of the word *consider,* meaning "to examine the stars carefully." When someone wanted something very badly, the stars were thought to have some kind of influence. So the idea of a craving that goes beyond a mere want, such as food or shelter, was first associated with powerful outside forces.

dessert Any lovers of pie, cake, or ice cream might smile to note that this word originated in the Old French and meant "to clear the table." That's when the final course of a meal was served in those days: after all the other dishes were taken away, as a kind of reward, I would think, for the clean-up.

detest When we hate something or someone enough to detest that thing or person, we will probably speak out about it. The Romans used the word in a more legal sense to mean "to bear witness against," and in most cases that detesting witness probably had some hatred for the defendant. We can see the "witness" aspect of the word in other related words, like *testify* ("to protest or bear witness *for* something"), *testament* (a witnessing, whether of a will or a religious writing), and *test* (a teacher's witnessing of what a student did or didn't learn). Also related is the medieval physician's word to describe that part of a man's body that "witnesses" to his virility: *testicle.*

deuce   The devil is sometimes called the deuce, probably from a German curse used during dice games when
another player made the lowest throw. The two on the
die was not good luck, and this "deuce" got applied to
any bad event. Generally, things that turned out badly
got blamed on the devil. The "two" of the original
meaning can still be found in the name of the card and
in tennis when a game is tied at forty and one player
must win by two. *Devil* is a word that goes back to the
Greek and meant "slanderer." We apply it to Satan
because that's just what he does to God and the teach-
ings of his followers. *Satan* came out of the Hebrew for
"enemy." In naming Lucifer, "the bearer of light and
fire," the Romans may have seen a parallel with the
Greek god who brought man fire, but early Christians
seemed to remember only the fire part. *Mephistopheles*
might have gotten his name from a Latin word for
"stink," though this is uncertain, while *Beelzebub*
translates easily from the Hebrew title of insult: "lord
of the flies." To say, "It hurt like the dickens" comes
from another name for the devil, Old Nick, which got
turned about with time.

dew claw   The reason we call the little leftover claw or
hoof on animals the dew claw is simple enough: just
because it barely reaches the dew on the ground. The
dew lap, or loose fold of skin on the neck of certain
animals, got its name because as that animal forages
for grass the skin "laps" at the dew.

diabetes   The name of this disease goes back to the
Greek and refers to the tendency in diabetics to urinate
excessively. "A passing through" is what the name
means. In the Middle Ages this was the formal, polite
way of labeling this chronic illness. *Disease,* by the way,

came simply from the idea that in this condition you were not at *ease.*

diet   It is the rage of the past twenty years or so to find some way of eating or not eating in order to lose un-needed pounds or reduce fat. The word's earliest form goes back to the Greek and basically means "the way you live." More and more health ex-perts lean toward this original meaning when they talk about exercise and other habits as-sociated with a style of life as being important

along with the food you eat. The other *diet,* meaning "a day of court" or "an assembly of lawmakers," comes from the Latin for "day."

diploma   This Greek word that means so much to the high-school senior and college graduate actually comes from the root meaning "something doubled." Official documents were folded over in ancient times to keep the agreement or charter private for its bearer. The fold tended to be lost when those receiving these documents upon leaving a school wanted them to be displayed for the public. Most of them were then rolled and tied with a ribbon.

disaster   The stars have often played a role in the creation of words. In this case it was Greek astological beliefs that gave us this and other related words. This term for destruction and distress goes back to a word meaning "from a bad star." This same root gives us the little sign of the small star, the *asterisk*. An *astronaut* is a "star-traveler." Even the star-shaped flower, the *aster,* gets its name from this Greek concern for the heavens. And wouldn't we all like to be able to blame our failures on a star's ill influence?

Dixie   This name for the southern states often has a Civil War connotation, but the word had its beginnings well before the states divided and was actually a term of respect used by many northerners for the strength of the southern economy. In the early 1800s individual banks issued their own currency based on the bank's assets. One New Orleans bank was so well-endowed that its scrip was accepted far and wide at its value, the bearer knowing that other banks would honor the notes. The French cultural influence in New Orleans led to the ten-dollar bills being printed with *dix,* the French for "ten." It was mispronounced and nicknamed by the rest of America as the "dixie" note. And the wealthy South became known as the land of Dixie or Dixie land.

dizzy   The sexist term for a foolish or dumb woman, a "dizzy dame," can be found in the earliest form of the word many centuries ago. The Old English version of *dizzy* meant "foolish or stupid." We mainly associate the word with a disorientation caused by being whirled about too much, though it's also applied to those at great heights who look down and suddenly feel as if they are whirling.

doctor   In its first form the word *doctor* meant "a teacher." We revive that Latin meaning when we confer a doctoral degree on any graduate student who has gone beyond the call of duty. Our term for a rule or group of rules, *doctrine,* is related to this. A *document* was originally a lesson or a teaching.

dog   Our campfire friend's name has no real special tale in its Old English origins, but it's amazing how many different ways we've used the word. A dog can be a good or bad thing depending on whether you're a lucky dog or your date is a real dog. If a movie is a dog, we won't want to see it. If you've gone to the dogs, you're in sorry shape. But if you put on the dog, you're in for the very best offered. A  detective can dog your tail until he's dog-tired and his gumshoed dogs ache. A minister wears a dog collar, but wishes to remove it during the dog days. These sultry weeks from mid-July to September get their name from the rising and falling of Sirius, the Dog Star, during this period. When airplanes have a dogfight it's certainly not a dog's life. And if you dog-ear a book at the library to mark your place, you may be in the doghouse with the librarian. A dogface, as a World War II soldier was called, wore his dog tag with pride, but might spout doggerel in some bar after seeing a buddy he hadn't seen in a dog's age. We dog paddle in the water, drive our golf balls down a dogleg fairway, and try to avoid the dog-eat-dog world, doggone it!

domino   It is strange how this game involving little rectangles with dots on them came from a word for a

priest's robe. That hooded garment had gotten the
Latin name meaning "let us bless the Lord," and the
domino (Lord) part stayed as the name for the cloak.
Later, in French society, the domino was a hooded robe
with a mask worn to masquerades. The mask itself was
eventually called a *comino,* and here the squared
covering with the two eye holes somehow got associated
with the game of dotted rectangles. The Latin word for
"Lord and master" turns up in many modern words,
from *dominate* to *dominion.* Most people today think of
the intricate patterns of falling dominoes cited in the
Guiness Book of World Records and of the infamous
domino theory, which seems to have been reversed in
Eastern Europe, where democracy has taken hold in
one country after another.

do-si-do   Why does a square-dance caller call out
"do-si-do!" to initiate that peculiar move on the dance
floor in which the dancers circle each other back to
back? It's simply the use of a French term meaning
"back to back" that was originally used for a kind of
furniture. You see versions of the double chair, one
back to the other, in airports and bus stations but rarely
in homes, where they were once quite popular.

dote   Doting grandparents are often known to spoil
their children's children with excess love and attention,
but they never think their fondness is silly. That is,
however, the original Dutch meaning of the root word:
"to be silly." We see this more in words like *dotard,* for
a senile person, or the English *dotty,* a term for a crazy
or eccentric person, as in "She's a dotty old gal."

doubt   The Latin meaning of this word fits its present
use very well. "To move from one side to the other" was
the first sense of the word and applied to things that

vibrated as well as people who couldn't make up their minds. The skeptical aspect of the word comes from that uncertain disciple, Thomas, who just couldn't believe in the Resurrection until he touched Christ's wounds. That name, "doubting Thomas," is now used for anyone who makes a habit of being dubious.

dream   In the hard life of the early English tribes, a time to sit back and relax, take a nap, or just be frivolous was a happy time. *To dream* meant "joy, gladness, or music" and was part of both waking and sleeping states. "To dream of things" is still used in both senses today, though bad dreams are also part of our awareness. For the old English that was separate, a nightmare, which was a visitation by a goblin, usually a wicked female spirit who would lie with the sleeper for a time and maybe even have a sexual encounter. She was a succubus. Women, too, might have one of these visits from a male spirit, an incubus, but it wasn't talked about nearly as much.

duck   The bird and the shout of warning to "get down" both have their origins in the same Old English word meaning "to dive." The bird was named for its habit of diving under water for its fishy food, and the term for lowering your head to avoid an incoming object conveys the same basic idea. Now, when we say, "We ducked him under water," there's a different story. In days of old, indiscreet prosti-

tutes or dishonest tradespeople were sat on a stool that was built to resemble an outhouse bench. Then they were publicly humiliated, sometimes by dipping them underwater, to the amusement of the townsfolk. This was the "cucking stool," which came out of an Old Norse word for excrement, from which we also get the child's "caca." This same device was later used on accused witches, but by that time the more polite term for putting underwater, *to duck,* was given to the seat of embarrassment.

easel   The painter's stand has a name that certainly doesn't reflect the beauty of creation. The Dutch word from which we get *easel* meant "little ass." When carpenters and painters designed the artificial beast of burden they called the sawhorse, they kept up the metaphor by naming the smaller, more fragile painting stand after the horse's smaller cousin.

electricity   This strange energy that, along with coal and oil, runs our society, first got its recognition from a word meaning "like amber," because when you rub amber it will produce sparks. When the emotions are so highly charged that sparks may fly, especially at a sporting event, we might say, "You can feel the electricity in the air."

elephant   The Greeks brought home this word from the Middle East and changed it a bit. The original Egyptian root word meant "ivory" and, of course,

castrating these servants was a natural step in insuring their lack of interest in the wives . . . or at least their inability to intrude on the child-bearing duties of the harem.

exercise If Romans were slipping the latest exercise tape into their primitive VCRs, they'd be seeing a farmer yelling at his oxen as he drove them out to plow or to turn the millstone to grind the wheat. Originally, the word was mainly used in this context: "to drive farm animals out to work." In our modern, exercise-obsessed world, the joggers and "aerobicizers" might understand a little of the original Latin use of the word, especially at the end of a session at the health club with an overly masochistic instructor.

explode The spontaneous explosion of applause at the end of a live performance is something to make an actor or musician tingle with appreciation, but this wasn't always the case. In ancient Rome if an actor or singer were really bad the audience would clap loudly, drowning the performer out until they drove that person offstage. Somehow or other, this custom got misinterpreted and reversed by those who tried to copy imperial Rome, and applause became a good performer's reward. But back to the word *explode:* in Latin it meant "to drive out by clapping." Americans might understand how these kinds of things can get turned around when they watch an Olympic event from Europe and hear an audience whistle, only to find out they are booing.

explore   The more romantic notion of daring adventure is embodied in the original Latin meaning of *explore:* "to cry out loud." You have the excitement of entering King Tut's tomb or stumbling across the remains of a lost civilization in some jungle wilderness: *Eureka!* (which comes from the Greek for "I found it!"). The origin of the word *eureka* is not so romantic: As Archimedes sat

in the bath he realized he could measure solids of any shape by the way they made the water rise in the tub, and this would allow him to tell the king of Syracuse how pure his gold crown was. . . . As I said, not too stirring. Going back to *explore,* an even better word for someone seeking some discovery would have been *exquisitor,* since *exquisite* has the Latin meaning "to search out." If something is exquisite, it is highly sought after. And if something has a *prerequisite,* it has to be found first.

eye   Though the eye of a hurricane can't see, it would be in a pig's eye that we would think the storm is over. And if you make eyes at a member of the opposite sex with an eye to get to know them, you might want to catch their eye before they get out of eyeshot. If the blowing wind and the thinking mind is only an eye rhyme (which means it only looks like a rhyme), you'd give your eyetooth for eyeglasses when trying to fasten an eyelet. And if your friend is a sight for sore eyes, you might share an eye-opener by saying, "Here's mud in your eye." But if you don't see eye to eye, anything he shows you might be an eyesore that you'd cast a cold eye upon, whether it's the eye of a potato or the eye of a needle.

face   OK, ready for another? When your friends see you lose face, don't make a face; just face up to it. Even if you're face to face with failure, you can have a face-off with it because, on the face of it, even if life leaves you face down and you don't want to show your face, it's time to play your face cards, face out the situation, and give your attitude a face-lift, accepting everything at face value. Enough, already.

fan   "The fans are packed into the stadium for today's game," we hear the announcer say. "I'm your biggest fan," the gushing autograph-seeker says to the actor coming out of the restaurant. This word, *fan,* is associated with anyone who admires something, has a certain devotion to it, follows the progress. . . . But the word has a more intense background, shortened from *fanatic.* In Roman times a fanatic was someone inspired by a god; someone full of religious fervor, even sometimes said to be insane in their fever-pitch of spirituality. The word literally translates as "of the temple" (I'll tell you about *profane* later). I guess we've seen some sports fans going a bit overboard in their support of a team, and the screaming and fainting of some rock fans looks a little insane. The word, even shortened to make it less powerful, still fits.

farce   A good old-fashioned farce is silly but fun. The French of centuries ago used the word to describe these shows, in which the plot gets so ridiculous that no one could take it seriously. Their word meant "to stuff," and that's just how these stories are: stuffed with just about as much as an audience can bear. At one time a bird stuffed for roasting was called a "farce," but people took their food too seriously to let that term last.

farm   The origin of the modern farm came with the breakdown of the feudal system, in which the lord ruled the land and the peasants worked for him, taking some of the crops for themselves but giving most to their overseer. When this system of landholding began to be replaced by a more organized state, taxes and rent were the ways in which rulers kept their wealth and power. A "farm" was an area of land for which a fixed rental fee was paid at certain times each year. This allowed the farmer more leeway in production and encouraged private enterprise. The word actually meant "lease" or "fixed payment" and sometimes involved further divisions and taxations below the lord's agreement. Private ownership was just beginning. We saw the same kind of breakdown in the South as slavery gave way to a system of tenant farming, and we'll probably see it again in the former Communist countries as they try to figure how to balance private property with state functions.

fascinate   An amulet in the shape of a male sex organ began the journey of this word into our vocabulary. Witches would use such devices to enchant or entrance victims. The idea of being put under a spell stayed with the word as it was passed on, and today any object of extreme interest can be fascinating.

fascism *Fascism* is a term that was first applied to a
political movement that arose during the governmental
turmoil of the post-World War I period. This movement
glorified the nation, emphasizing loyalty to the home-
land over individual rights, and exalted the power of a
supreme leader, who usually turned into a dictator. In
those hard economic times facism was popular because
it protected big business and other wealthy interests
over the concerns of the working class. The word goes
back to Roman times, as you've seen so many do. In
those days there was an emblem of authority carried
before judges and other people of prestige that symbolized their power. It was called a *fasces* and was a
bundle of rods bound about an ax with the blade
sticking out. You'll see one on the back of a Roosevelt
dime. The idea that the many would be bound around a
central, powerful ruler or judge was what Mussolini
was getting when he first employed the term for his
political faction. The original Latin meant "bundle."

feeble Being feeble is generally a sign of age and
weakness and can indeed make a son or daughter very
sad when seen in a parent. The word goes back to a
Latin root and meant "to weep over." From the feeble-
minded to the feeble-voiced, seeing strength disappear
can bring a tear.

fellow *Fellow,* as in "fellow worker" or "jolly good
fellow," usually indicates a kind of closeness and
brotherhood or sisterhood. This notion of being tied to
the person who is your fellow goes back to the Old Norse
word that meant "cattle property" or "money" and
applied to a partner who put up some of his own goods
in some way for the mutual benefit of both. This idea
continued to be part of the word up through feudal

times, though it was gradually generalized by religion into a feeling of partnership in life and faith.

fiddle   The legend is that Nero fiddled while Rome burned. Though that story could be a bunch of fiddle-sticks, the word itself was not at first applied to any instrument. When Romans gained a victory it was only proper to celebrate the goddess of joy and victory, Vitula. Music and song were part of the happy occasion, and by the time the tradi-tion spread to the many places influenced by  Rome, and on into the Middle Ages, the name of the goddess was attached to the member of the violin family. "Vitula" was gradually transformed in pronun-ciation to "fiddle." This kind of fiddle-faddle happened all the time, as quick as you could say, "fiddle-dee-dee." Words always get fiddled with as they pass from one group to another, and their original meaning plays second fiddle to the new association.

filet   When most of us think of a filet or fillet, we think of a boneless piece of meat. How does this fit with the Old French meaning of the word, "made of threads"? First, these strips of meat were supposed to be as thin as a thread and, also, it was a custom to roll and tie the meat with a thread for roasting. *Filet mignon* just means a "small or dainty filet." The *filigree* uses wires instead of thread to make its ornamental work. Narrow ribbon is also sometimes called "fillet."

filibuster The first use of this word, in Dutch, applied to pirates and meant "one who plunders freely." Mercenary soldiers who waged their own private wars for gain in foreign countries were called this. The concept of waging a private battle to gain time is how the word came to be used in our Senate, when someone takes the floor and begins prolonged speaking in order to obstruct a particular bill. Though these senators aren't exactly pirates, they may be said to be plundering the time of their colleagues and their credibility in the eyes of the taxpayers.

filly This word for a young female horse or sometimes, in cruder circumstances, for a high-spirited girl, goes back to an Old Norse word meaning "small." Our word *foal,* for the mare's offspring, also had its start with an Old English version of the word. Today, comparing women to animals can get a man horsewhipped or at least *stall* a woman's interest.

fine *Fine* comes from the Latin for "the end." So how can we apply this word to fine china, or a fine eye for quality, or "I'm fine; how are you"? Really, this use of *fine* for superior in skill, quality, health, or appearance goes back to a Roman expression, *finis honorum,* which meant "the highest honor" or, literally, "the *end* of all honors." This "final honor" was later used for the very best of anything. If it was fine silk, its closeness of weave meant it was the very best quality. Even if it was fine sand, it was the smallest of grains, as small as you could find. You'd say, "I'm fine," meaning you were as good as you could be. The idea of paying a fine also came from "the end." It was the end of the legal dispute. You paid the "fine" and it was over. By the way, *fin*icky eaters have high standards. And to *fin*ance something is to settle or "end" how long you will pay for it.

finger   I've put the finger on the origin of this word, which had a Germanic birth and came into our language twelve or thirteen hundred years ago as a word meaning "one in five." Though we may not use a finger bowl when we've got our finger in the pie, we certainly like having something wrapped around our little finger. Some say we only have four fingers, but you can thumb your nose at them when you learn that the Old English meaning of *thumb* was "swollen finger." Though you'd hate to be all thumbs, it would make it easier to thumb through something, and we'd probably give a thumbs down to being under someone's thumb. Now we'll thumb our way to the next word.

fiscal   This word is used more and more every year in our economy-conscious world. Who knows, the fiscal year set up by our governmental bodies may someday be the calendar year and we'll celebrate New Year's with the beginning of renewed funding in July. The word has a humble origin. The *fiscus* was a woven basket used by tax collectors in Roman days. It came to represent the treasury of the state, and how much could be spent was based on how much was brought in in those baskets of the taxmen . . . not quite the case today.

fit A child throwing a tantrum on the floor and the proper measurement of clothes are very different uses of *fit,* but both go back to an original concept that branched out with time. In its original sense the word dealt with battle, in preparing for the fray and in the conflict itself. The very earliest use of the word also gave us *fight,* along with the child's explosion of temper and a burst of coughing or  spasms. You've probably heard the old use of *fight* in the song "Joshua Fit the Battle of Jericho." As war became more organized the word was applied to marshaling the troops, arranging them for battle in fit or "proper" ways. So when something was fit, it was the right way of doing things; it agreed with the circumstances. As time went on, the meaning evolved: When clothing was fit, it conformed to the circumstances of your body, and if the shoe fit, you wore it and didn't throw a fit.

flatter I like Hank Ketchum's "Flattery is like chewing gum. Enjoy it, but don't swallow it." We generally associate this kind of compliment with someone who is not being genuine but wants some favor. It goes back to a French verb that meant "to smooth with the flat of the hand." Just as you'd take the wrinkles out of a tablecloth by smoothing it out, you could take the tightness out of someone by caressing that person with your words. The feeling that this was a surface thing done for show gave the word its connotation of vanity.

flimflam If you've ever been flimflammed, whether by a simple carnival game or some fast-talking con man, you've probably felt like a fool after being swindled. The Scandinavian root goes back a thousand years to a word for mockery. When all's said and done, you *do* feel like the flimflam artist has made a mockery of your trust. *Con man* comes from "confidence" and means someone who gains *your* confidence and then abuses it. *Swindle* has a Germanic origin having to do with making something disappear . . . and not through magic.

focus If you are the focus of someone's attention, it can make you feel uncomfortable or wonderful. The word comes from a Latin term for "fireplace." Since the hearth was the center of the home in ancient times, the place that kept you warm and cooked your food, the word wound up being applied to all kinds of things that represent a place where people or things converge. Even rays of light coming into your eyes cause them to "converge" on the images reflected, making them the center of attention. Johannes Kepler used this word to describe the point where a parabolic mirror concentrates light to the point of burning.

fog Anyone trying to drive through thick fog knows just how judgment changes when one is blinded. . . . But would you associate fog with grass? The word originally had Scandinavian roots and was the Norwegian term for the thick, rank grass standing in a field after the first cutting or grazing. Because this grass was also associated with bogs and moist, soggy earth, the name also came to be linked with the low-hanging water vapor, which was also thick like the weeds. By the way, *bog* is Gaelic for "soft." If you are wrapped in a fog in daylight and see a yellowish arc opposite the hazy sun, you've seen a fogbow, which sailors also call a "sea dog." And speaking of dogs, watch for fogdogs. No, these aren't Hound-of-the-Baskervilles-like creatures haunting the mists. Fogdogs are clear patches in a fog bank.

fool The early blacksmith gave us our word for this person who lacks sense but doesn't seem to know it. To heat up his wood and coals for tempering metal, the ironworker would save his breath by using a bellows or windbag. When a puffed-up idiot of a person went about speaking all sorts of nonsense as if he knew what he was talking about, he reminded onlookers of that device  so full of hot air, but really empty. The earliest comedians played the court fool, mimicking the self-important but shallow nobles and generally making fun of all those in their path. Here is where we start seeing the word used for trickery and make-believe. For a time the word also applied to the feeble-minded, since some jesters came from the ranks of those who were mentally unfit for normal work but might say amusing or strange things. We still make fun of someone by calling that person a windbag.

foreign To the civilized Romans any people who still lived out-of-doors, roaming the woods or shores as hunters and fishers, as did the nomadic Vikings or savage Goths, were considered foreigners, which meant "living outside," away from the safety of the town gates. Our word *forest* goes back to that same Latin root, but was first used by the French of Charlemagne's court, since he kept a large forest area for his royal hunts. Many kings followed in this tradition, without which we'd never have had a Robin Hood.

foster Foster homes have received both good and bad publicity, depending on whether they provide a loving, caring environment or exhibit a sense of greed and lack of consideration. The primary purpose of this place for orphans is to take these minors off the hands of the state and put them in private care. That simplest of definitions is derived from the Old English meaning, "to provide food."

frown This word for a face marked with displeasure can be traced back to a Welsh word for "nose." Though we think of a wrinkled brow when this scowling expression comes to mind, these early islanders apparently placed the showing of distaste more toward the bridge of the nose. Wrinkling the nose at a bad taste or smell might have been part of the whole notion.

fruit Certainly, just about everyone has a favorite fruit, and we place that banana, orange, or apple high on our list of foods we enjoy. In its earliest use *fruit* meant just that: "to enjoy." Eating was one of the great joys of early man, and for that reason harvest time was often the occasion for celebration. People would take the fruit of their labors and delight in it. Science has done the job of separating fruits and vegetables, although there is actually no real difference between them and we can enjoy them all. That sense of producing and enjoying can be found in the expression "be fruitful and multiply."

fund   Many investors would say buying land is one of the best ways to spend your extra money. In the days of the prominence of agriculture, the best land was that which lay on either side of a river or stream. Water was plentiful; floods would occasionally wash rich silt over it; and it was generally free of rocks, flat, and easy to plow. This was called "bottom land," or, in Roman times, *fundus*. This good land was a permanent source of quality food for the families who worked it. The word later got used for any stock, or for stock of great value. It was also applied to the creation of a new source and brought us the word *found,* as in "Founding Fathers," but not "found art." Anything that had to do with that foundation was *fundamental*. The direct use of *bottom* can be seen when the natural landscape or the backside of a human is called the *fundament*. And when the literal, factual interpretation of the Bible or other religious texts is at the bottom of a belief system, it is called *fundamentalism*.

furlong   Horse racing is a sport as old as man's ability to sit on a stallion's back, but the question of the length of the race had always been an individual thing until property boundaries began to be established. This in turn required a standard of measurement; the one used in England was the rod, which was five and a half yards and probably came from a pole used to measure the stoneworks of a fortress. This was later used to measure acres. The furlong came from the length of a furrow on a ten-acre-square patch of land—that was a "furrow long," which measured an eighth of a mile.

furlough   When a soldier comes home for the holidays on furlough, he is using a form of a Dutch word that means "permission." Even to this day a soldier's time belongs to the service of his country or king (or in the past, of his lord). Historically, if a soldier wanted personal time unpledged to that service, he had to get permission. Among the English it was called *leave,* as in "by your leave." This *leave* comes from a different root than "leave me alone." The blending of Dutch and English in the early colonies led to the Dutch word *furlough* being incorporated into our military lingo, though today *leave* is the main word used for a break from duty.

gab   Someone with the gift of gab is known as a good conversationalist or storyteller, but most of the time when someone is gabbing we consider it unimportant talk. The Scottish gave us the word, meaning "mouthful." From that same basic root we get *gobble,* used for greedy eating, and *gob,* for that lump of stuff we're about to eat.

gadget   This general word for a gizmo, some mechanical thing or other, goes back to one of the first inventions that was helpful to early humans: the buckle. With a buckle we could adjust things to suit us better, whether it was the helmet we wore into battle or the harness we used to hook ourselves to a plow or the device that was part of the belt holding our pants up. From the root for *buckle* came the word *lock,* a great invention that allowed people to close their doors to trespassers and seal up their wealth in privacy. The more we accumulated, the more we needed gadgets to help us. This word from the Old French has a much more harmless sense today, when we're innundated by doodads and thingamajigs.

gait This descriptive word for the way a human or animal walks or runs goes back to an Old Norse word for a path or street. The kind of path or street you were on would certainly have a lot to do with how you traveled it. In the thick northern forests, a scraggly path might slow you to a crawl, while a good Roman cobblestone road would let you trot. As a side note, *gallop* means "to run well."

galaxy This word, used to describe large-scale groupings of stars, comes from the Greek and labels what they saw on a clear night. The word means "milky" and was originally part of a Greek expression for the band of thick stars in the heavens: "the milky circle." It was an expression that stuck even after translation. We still call our galaxy the Milky Way.

gale Any sailor or coastline dweller dreads the onslaught of a gale. The word's origin lies in an Old Norse word for the sound of the wind as it announces nature's outburst. To the seafaring Norse if sounded like the gods of the oceans singing a terrible chant, bewitching the water. That was the original meaning of *gale*. Over time, the Norwegians came to use the word to mean "bad." So a gale was a bad wind. Weather forecasters now use the term for a wind that has a speed between thirty-two and sixty-three miles an hour, not a very pleasant speed for a breeze . . . nothing to cause a gale of laughter.

gallon   It's now a standard measurement, but in its earliest form it was the name for a jug of wine. It probably came from the Celtic tribes and was then used by Latin-speaking Roman priests. The standardization of the size came with the ability to blow glass into molds. But a ten-gallon hat couldn't hold ten gallons. That term came from a French word for a kind of braid used in trim and also for hat bands. A ten-gallon hat used a wide band around the brim, and these became popular out West, pardner.

gang   *Gang* has had many good and bad uses in English. Those little rascals of Our Gang still can make us laugh. But the criminal groups that gave us *gangsters* are to be avoided. "Hail, hail, the gang's all here" makes us think of a happy, nostalgic gathering of old friends, but when we hear of street gangs we think of tough young punks. The Old English roots of this word referred to traveling in a group and meant "a going" or "a journey." It was always best to travel in a company. The *gangplank* was a board that let you travel from ship to shore or from one ship to another, unless you committed a crime at sea and had to walk it to your doom. *Gangway* is seldom heard anymore, but originally referred to any passageway.

gantry   These days the popular association of this word is with the space program, indicating the large frame structure next to the rocket on the launch pad. The word goes back a couple of thousand years, and in its earliest Greek form referred to a pack mule, or at least to a frame used for cargo and put on the back of a mule. When the Romans got hold of the word they took the idea of carrying a burden and applied it to the rafters of their roofs. This framework of support called a gantry is now used to support construction cranes or railway signals and expressway signs. The pack mule still comes to mind when we call that frame that supports a barrel on its side a "gantry."

garage The French originated this word, but it first applied to protecting a form of transportation of a different sort than we think of in its present use. The oldest form of the word referred to something that protected ships. As seaport towns relied more and more on ocean commerce, docks became the hub of a city's business community, and the "garage" was the dock where a ship could be tied up and protected from storms and high seas.

garble When someone is mumbling or in a state of mind that causes speech to be slurred or erratic, we say the person is garbling his or her words. The Arabs took the word from a Roman term for a sieve. This use of the word, meaning "to sift or sort out," was the most common way it was employed for hundreds of years. Then, somehow, it started to refer to the *unsifted,* the unsorted out, and especially the scrambled-up way a story or word can come out when spoken. There seems to be some relation to the word *garbage,* which goes back to an Italian root meaning "confusion and uproar," in other words, a mess.

garden   Anyone who has seen the damage a rabbit, mole, or deer can do to an unprotected country garden has learned the value of a good fence. That's what our word meant in its first use as the Romans took to heart the idea of growing interesting and useful plants within enclosures. They called it a *hortus gardinus,* which meant "plants in a fenced or walled space." We still call plant

experts *horticulturalists,* but instead of calling a garden a *hortus,* we picked up the word for the fence. The word *garland,* as in "of flowers," doesn't come from *garden* but from an Old French word for an ornament made with gold threads. It was first used when weavers and metal workers worked wreaths into tapestries and breastplates showing a coat of arms.

gas   A Dutch scientist made this word up to represent the mysterious substance he believed present in all bodies. Jan Baptista van Helmont, working in the 1600s, mixed magical powers with science when he theorized that within everything there was a mystical stuff that he called "gas," from the Greek word for "chaos." Though later scientists thought his ideas weren't much of a gas, they liked the word and used it for those invisible, but less supernatural occurrences. They did give him credit for discovering carbon dioxide, but passed on his gas ideas . . . thinking maybe they were caused by gas. I'm only gassing you.

gazebo   Sometimes words are made up and then catch on and become part of our language, like *movie* or *flustrate*. This word for a small latticed pavilion or roofed open gallery came from combining the word *gaze,* which is actually Scandinavian in origin, with a Latin suffix for the future tense, which we find in *placebo* (meaning "I shall please"). So *gazebo* literally means "You shall see." The Italian word for a similar structure, *belvedere,* has the meaning "beautiful view."

gazette   The origin of this word for "newspaper" has nothing to do with *gazing.* A gazette was a small copper coin found in Italy and especially in Venice. Early newspapers there were sold for a *gazeta,* and the papers themselves were called *novitas* at first, meaning "things that are new." Now, something I haven't been able to find out is why the copper coin's name is also associated with the name for a bird that we call a magpie.

geek   Many parents think of this term as modern teenage slang: "He's a real geek!" meaning "nerd" or someone not very "in." The word goes way back to a German term meaning "fool" and was applied to a particularly repulsive carnival performer. The "geek" in a carnival was usually the "entertainer" whose big act was to bite the head off a live animal, like a chicken or a snake. Recently, that act has been imitated by certain rock performers, but either way it's still a "geeky" thing to do.

genius   The idea that there are guardian angels who watch over us is one that goes back to Roman mythology. For the Romans a "genius" was a guardian spirit allotted to each person at birth. The spirit would attend that person until death, sometimes teaching and helping that person through every stage of life. Some of these spirits were allotted to places, too. The Renaissance brought the word to us with less of the spiritual influence, though there was still a feeling that the person was born with some gift. The Moslems took the idea and kept the spirit aspect with their genies, who were spirits capable of assuming animal or human form and influencing men for good *and* bad. Well, we have our evil geniuses, too.

genuine   "It's the real thing, the genuine article," say advertisers, using the word to assert the quality of something. There are arguments as to the genuine origin of the word, but I'm going with those who relate it to the knee. The knee? Back in ancient Rome the root word could be translated as "placed on the knees." In the days when a man might deny rights, lands, and privileges to a child he did not wish to claim, it was an important custom for the father to sit before the family or townsfolk and place his child on his knees to publicly acknowledge the youngster as his own. Our kneeling word, *genuflect,* comes from the same Latin beginnings.

glamor   We don't usually think of learning to read and write as being particularly glamorous, but the two concepts were originally linked. Early Scots thought that learning letters and spelling were magical activities, in part because it was traveling priests who did most of the teaching. Though *grammar* comes from the Greek for "the art of letters," the early Scots associated the word with magic. A variation of that word was *glamor,* which in its earliest use dealt with charms and enchantment. Later the word was linked with any alluring qualities or situations, but magic gave it birth. To be able to cast a spell, you needed to be able to *spell,* which is also why those two different meanings are related. And of course, the word *Gospel* comes from *godspell.*

goblin   The supernatural again plays a role in the creation of this word. There is some dispute as to its journey into English. One theory is that the Germanic people gave us the earliest version of the word. It was a tough job for the early Catholic priests to convert the many primitive northern tribesmen who worshiped a whole host of gods and goddesses, including one protective spirit in each household. By taking some liberties with the story of Satan and the fallen angels, the priests were able to convince these early converts that their gods had been forced underground by the Almighty. Those household gods were now *kobalds,* and miners even named an ore cobalt because it was believed to hurt silver ores. In the 1100s the French got hold of the word when a writer gave a ghost the name Gobelinus. By the 1300s the English were using the word as a name for any frightening spirit.

gun   How did a pet name for a woman help give rise to this word for a machine of hunting and warfare? The old Norse gave their catapults and battering rams little nicknames, just as a hunter might call his rifle Old Betsy. *Hilda* was combined with another word, *gunnr* (war), and they had *gunhild,* a war machine. Through time the word was shortened to *gun.*

gung ho   This word got into our vocabulary during World War II, when a group called Carlson's Raiders used it as their motto. It got to be associated with the extremely patriotic, dedicated soldier. Conflicts like Korea and Viet Nam gave the word a less positive connotation; it came to imply a soldier who was overly or foolishly enthusiastic. The Chinese root meant "work together."

gusto   Today when we "go for the gusto," we're trying for the best in life, living it to the fullest. The Italians mainly used the word for something that tasted good. Over time the idea of a good flavor was extended to the notion of a zest for life.

gymnasium   The building we call by this name keeps this word alive in our language, though we generally shorten it to *gym*. The Greeks used it as an active word in ancient times. It meant "to train naked," which was the way these early athletes worked out and competed, down to the bare essentials. Our modern Olympians wear as little as possible in their gymnastics, but I don't think today's  public would allow the original definition to have much play on the present-day mats.

hag   When we call an ugly or frightful old woman a hag, we're going back to an Old English word for "witch."

But while hags may *haggle* at the marketplace, that word for bargaining doesn't arise from any demonic nickname. *Haggle* comes from an Old Norse word for "cut," meaning the attempt to divide something up or cut the price. Nor does *haggard* come from *hag,* though she may look it. *Haggard* originally referred to an untamed hawk that had to be worn out before being trained.

halibut Translate this fish's name from its English-Dutch origin and you have "holy flatfish." No, it wasn't necessarily considered a sacred fish. It was so named because it was traditionally eaten on holy days; it was the turkey of several hundred years ago. Today we generally eat it just for the "halibut."

halo The Greeks first used this word, but not for any saintly descriptions. This was the threshing floor where the grain and chaff were separated and the grain later ground. It was usually circular in construction because that was the way the oxen would move when working on the crop. When an eclipse or corona around the moon or sun was seen it reminded Greek starwatchers of the circle of the threshing floor. Early Christians took the idea of the light around the circle as the radiance they felt surrounded a holy one.

handicap The origin of this word lies in an English wagering game of the 1600s in which players traditionally held their forfeits in a hat: "hand in cap." A player who repeatedly put his hand into the old cap to drop his losses there was certainly at a disadvantage. Of course, his hand might go in to take out winnings, too, but the idea of being less than even stayed with the word. Its next use, in horse racing, was to assure that advantages would be evened out. If a rider was particularly light, a horse was handicapped by having weight put in its saddle. Eventually the term was used for people who had a particular burden to bear or obstacle to overcome. Finally it became a common way of describing those with physical disadvantages.

handsome In the early 1500s this word had a very literal meaning: "easy to handle." Something that was handsome did well in the hand. Later in that century it was applied poetically to noble and generous benefactors. These men gave handsomely. With a bit of vanity thrown in, these princely souls also had to be good-looking. We very seldom use the word with women, but we still employ it when talking about money: "He paid a handsome price" or "That was a handsome tip."

harass If you've ever felt harassed, whether on the job or by the kids at home, you'll understand the meaning of the word's root in Old French: "to set the dogs on." Today it's in referring to sexual harassment that the word is most often employed, but it was first used in hunting and later in warfare to describe repeated attacks or raids. *To harry* means the same thing in a battle situation but seems to come from a different source meaning "army." Now, as far as pronunciation goes, with all the emphasis on the sexual aspect of the word in today's courts, it would probably be best to put your stress on the first syllable.

harem You'll recall the old Hollywood movies in which many young, nubile beauties are lounging about in the tapestried luxury of an Arabian palace, when suddenly the disguised young adventurer bursts in, looking to hide from the angry guards waving their scimitars. This is our view of the harem. In reality, if that young man got a glimpse of those concubines he was liable to be beheaded. The harem was a sacred and forbidden place to any but the master of the house and those few asexual eunuchs on duty. In Arabic that is the meaning of the word: "sacred and forbidden place."

harlot   Originally, this almost biblical term for a prostitute was a name for travelling entertainers and vagabonds, generally itinerant jesters and tramps who begged a meal and a night's lodging with a story, song, or foolishness. When the entertainment involved the use of one's body in exchange for food or a bed, the word began to take on more of its present meaning and eventually came to refer to women rather than men.

hash   Whether it is cut-up potatoes or chopped corned beef, we've heard of a food called hash. And when someone wants to rehash some topic, they want to go back over the details. The Old French word from which we got *hash* was a word for "ax." We also get *hatchet* from the same root, meaning "small ax." The idea of chopping something into pieces fits well with food or ideas.

haywire   When something goes haywire, whether it's a plan or a machine, we know it isn't working . . . at least, not correctly. The word is literal and came from some early loggers who kept working even when their equipment broke down by borrowing some farmer's baling wire and rigging things together "on a wing and a prayer." Those shade-tree mechanics passed on the name to us for anything jury-rigged or jerry-built for temporary operation. In those days, when something "went haywire" you knew what to blame it on.

hazard   The English got the word from the French who got it from the Spanish who took it from the Arabs, all as they passed on a game of chance. The word meant "an unlucky throw of the dice." You could hazard a guess that could be hazardous, if not to your health then certainly to your finances. Tennis players know the sporting origins of the word when they hit the  ball to the hazard side of the court, and golfers are always trying to avoid hazards like bunkers and water. These days we primarily think of the word as associated with danger or risk.

hearse   Believe it or not, this word that we now use for a vehicle to transport the deceased to the church or cemetery came from an ancient word for "wolf's teeth." This wasn't because those early Latin users thought of death as some devouring beast. It was a tradition to place a framework of lit candles over the coffin on its stand in the church, thus allowing mourners a last glimpse at their loved one. These candleholders looked like a rake or harrow and had the descriptive name "wolf's teeth" because of the close-set, triangular frame with the white candles sticking up. Later the name was applied to a frame that was hung over a coffin or tomb to hold final farewell notes from loved ones, from which we get the tradition of headstone inscriptions. Over time the stand that held the coffin began to be called the hearse. Finally, it came to refer to the transporting vehicle. The candelabrum can still be seen in a Roman Catholic church, where they are called by that ancient name, *hearse,* and used during the last three days of Holy Week.

heathen   This word is associated with nonbelievers and pagans mainly because of its use by strict religious groups like the Puritans. It had a simpler origin and referred to "those who lived on uncultivated land," or in England, out on the heath. Those who lived away from the towns and cultivated fields were likely to be ignorant of the generally accepted religious beliefs.

heirloom   Separate this word into its parts and you get the idea of the first use of the word. *Loom* was initially used for any tool or utensil, but over time that name came to be applied to a single tool, one of the most important in the household. Tools were extremely valuable in days of yore, and a loom was one of the most valuable of all, for the making of cloth, rugs, and coverings was vital to maintaining a way of life. The tradition of passing down tools and other valued possessions to family members and friends was not only practical but essential to day-to-day life. When land was later allowed to be owned, that also got passed on to loved ones.

henchmen   There are some bad associations with this word today due to its use in criminal circles. The henchmen to which the word first referred were more than likely groomsmen for the lord's horses or men who attended to the maintenance of the castle and its weapons and armory. These squires were trusted underlings, and for a very long time that is how the word was used.

hermit   With fewer and fewer solitary places there are fewer and fewer hermits, though some of us hole up in our homes or apartments and might be considered hermitlike by those in the social world. The Greeks invented the word and it meant "one of the desert." I have no idea why spicy cookies of raisins, nuts, and molasses are also called hermits, because they certainly don't last long in isolation.

hobnob   When we're "hobnobbing," it's usually with the rich and famous. But the expression from the Old English meant "to have and to have not." It was used in toasts and had a feeling of "Sometimes you've got it and sometimes you don't, but let's drink to it anyway." Today *hobnob* goes with *hoity-toity* (those who get to play).

hock   This informal way of saying we have to sell or pawn something goes back to a Dutch word for "prison." Unlike today, when debt is the normal state of affairs for just about everyone, debtors of the past were likely to be sent to jail upon that first missed payment. Overcrowded debtors' prisons led to the rapid colonization of England's colonies in America and Australia, and apparently many of us never lost the debtor's mentality. Now, a hamhock has nothing to do with the jailhouse and comes from an Old English word for "heel."

honeymoon   This word for the early harmony in any relationship, but especially marriage, comes from the literal joining of *honey* and an old way of saying month: *moon.* The idea was that the first month of marriage was the sweetest, but just as the moon is full and bright it starts to wane, and so, some have learned, does matrimony. The word later came to be associated more with the

trip taken by the newlyweds to some faraway or isolated place. We still employ the old notion of the word when we talk about Congress and the president enjoying a "honeymoon" period.

horror   From the same root that gives us the idea of shaggy or bristly comes this word that goes back to Latin and originally meant "to have the hairs stand on end." That certainly fits the state you're in when you're horrified. Later, as the word passed into French, it was mainly associated with trembling in fear.

hors d'oeuvre   These tasty treats before a fancy meal get their name from a French expression meaning "outside of work." Preparing the meal was part of the ordinary labor of the kitchen staff, and any extras for special occasions or feasts were not part of the regular chores.

how   I'm talking about the Indian greeting here, not a way of doing something. I was just interested in learning about that famous expression we've all heard in Westerns when the chief holds up his hand and says, "How." It's actually *hau* or *hao,* which comes from the Dakota and Omaha Indian tribes, and was really a way of saying "Hello." No, we don't get *howdy* from it. That came from a shortening of "How do ye do?" Similarly, *goodbye* is a shortening of "God be with ye."

howitzer   This name, which we think of as applying to World War II German mortars, actually goes back to a Czechoslovakian word for "catapult." Our version of the word comes from a Dutch version of a German version of the original, definitely revised along the way. The main fear concerning howitzers was that by using high-arcing trajectories, they could reach targets very far from their point of departure. There are those still trying to build even bigger super-guns. . . .

hubbub   When there's an uproar and a din of confusing noise, we sometimes call it a hubbub. The word goes back to an early Irish battle cry, which in its ancient form meant "Victory!" When those ancient tribesmen won a fight, whether with invaders from the coast or another tribe, there was certain to be a lot of shouting and celebrating far into the night.

hulk   Because of the amount of notoriety surrounding the huge green man known as the Incredible Hulk, youngsters probably will associate the word with "huge" or "monsterish." Greek sailors first employed it for a ship that needed to be towed. We still apply the word to wrecked vessels or those that are no longer seaworthy, but ask comic-book fans for a definition of the word and they'll more than likely relate it to something angry, green, and big.

humble That air of modesty and meekness that makes a person humble is still respected, although the word today has as much a sense of punishment as it does a proper way of behaving. Being humiliated is no fun. The old tradition of a lower-class person bowing and scraping grew out of a fear of being attacked or assassinated. It was very hard to stab someone while they were lying face-flat in the dirt. Equals held out open right hands and clasped them to show there was no weapon in them. (Is that why *left* meant "sinister"? Well, I'll say more on that later.) *Humble* meant "ground" or "soil," from which we get *humus*. The expression "eating humble pie" nowadays refers to humiliation, but the root word for *humble* here goes back to another word entirely. In this case the original word referred to the edible organs of an animal, generally a deer. These parts of the loin and innards are certainly not the most attractive nor tasty part of the animal, but you didn't waste anything when you were hunting for your food. These particular cuts of meat were best served covered up in a pie and baked until they were less recognizable. To eat humble pie, then, was to eat the lowliest parts of the kill, and this became associated with humility and forced apology.

humor We mainly think of laughter with this word: "He's got a good sense of humor" or "It was a very humorous story." But we still use the word in the old-fashioned way when we say, "She's in a bad humor." Medieval doctors believed that one's moods and mental disposition were caused by a balance or imbalance in four fluids, known as "humors." The blood regulated happiness, and we still talk of "thin-blooded" or "red-blooded Americans" as if "blood" referred to a state of mind. The doctors' word for blood, *sanguine,* is still used

to speak of cheerfulness as well as the bodily fluid.
Another fluid, phlegm, still has emotional connotations, as reflected in *phlegmatic,* which can mean "calm
or unemotional." The third fluid, choler, dealt with
solid wastes and temper. We still say an angry person is
choleric. Cholera was so named because of the diarrhea
associated with it. Finally, black bile was believed to
make one sad or irritable, and we might still use *bilious*
for a sour-tempered grump. These early doctors may
have been on target with all this, but I won't humor you
with it anymore, for it puts me out of humor talking
about blood, phlegm, and bile.

hunker   To "hunker down" these days basically
means to draw upon every resource to win some conflict.
President Lyndon B. Johnson popularized it in 1965
with this meaning in mind. It's also sometimes still
used in its ancient sense, which means "to crouch." The
Old Norse root doesn't have any relation to *hunk,* which
came from a Flemish word for a chunk of food. We hear
it a lot now for a sexually appealing man, who apparently can be food for the eyes.

hunky-dory   When everything is hunky-dory, it's
just right and you're perfectly satisfied. The word goes
back to a more practical Dutch term meaning "a safe
place or goal." To get to this place of refuge was the
object, and when you got there everything was fine.
Children kept the word popular through a game in
which the base or safe place was called the "hunky."

husband   This word, which we primarily think of as
referring to a marriage partner, goes back to an Old
Norse root and spoke to a more chauvinistic society in
which the man's word was final. *Husband* meant "the
master of the house," the bondsman of the household,

the owner. This notion of managing a home is present when we speak of animal husbandry and is still used once in a while to mean "to be thrifty" or "to budget," as in "husbanding your energy or resources." To give you an idea of what a male-oriented world it was (and some say, still is), *hussy,* which we use as a demeaning word for a woman, came out of *housewife.*

hushpuppy   This popular cornmeal filler in seafood and fried-chicken restaurants was originally conceived by southern cooks for practical purposes. In many homes in the old South, the kitchen or cookhouse was in a separate building to avoid heating up the home in the sultry summer and, too, it was safer should a fire break out. But the joy of hunting also led to a passle of dogs being part of the landscape, and here was a problem. How do you carry plates of good fried chicken and collards past the mutts without a huge uproar of yapping and jumping? What you did was cook a bunch of little balls of cornmeal with your leftover batter and throw them away from your path as you brought that food to the "big house." Then it was "Hush, puppy!"

husk   We get this word for the dry covering on corn or other seeds and fruit from a Dutch word meaning "little house." Having a *husky* voice came from the idea that it seemed dry as a husk. And usually, someone who's out there shouting and getting hoarse is likely to be a rugged fellow, so the word gets used for strong, burly folks. Now, the dog got its name as a variation on the name of its original owners, the Eskimos. The dogs were "Eskys."

hypochondria   We go back to those medieval doctors and their humors for this word, which translates as "below the breast." In those days the hypochondria was a region of the abdomen. Since the stomach was considered the seat of melancholy, those poor complaining people who had some problem or other but didn't seem really ill probably had something out of balance in the hypochondria. Today the word calls to mind those neurotics who are constantly hounded by illness or the threat of it. Perhaps we could refer such people to a medieval doctor, who might tell them about their humors being out of kilter.

hypocrite   If we used this word as it was first used, we might call Meryl Streep or Dustin Hoffman great hypocrites, to everyone's misunderstanding. The Greeks originated the word for actors playing a part on the stage. The theater has had its good and bad days throughout history, and the idea of wearing a mask or playing a role, pretending to be one thing when you are really another, wasn't always such a box-office smash. Religion in particular demanded selfless honesty, and such falseness as you might find on the stage was considered wicked.

hysterical   Most often we think of hysterical people as being out of control, though sometimes we'll apply it to a comedy or comic. When someone says, "The play was hysterical," we think of strong bouts of laughter. But when we hear about a hysterical person, we more than likely picture uncontrolled panic, weeping, and screaming. Originally, the word was always applied to women and in Greek meant "of the womb." It was believed that disturbances of the uterus caused hysteria. Of course, a *hysterectomy* is a surgical removal of the uterus, but *hysteria* today can be applied to both sexes and even a mass of people. Psychiatrically speaking, true hysteria is an almost manic-depressive neurosis, involving hallucination, amnesia, and even sleep-walking.

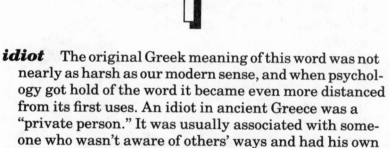

idiot   The original Greek meaning of this word was not nearly as harsh as our modern sense, and when psychology got hold of the word it became even more distanced from its first uses. An idiot in ancient Greece was a "private person." It was usually associated with someone who wasn't aware of others' ways and had his own style of doing something. Gradually, the word began to be used for ignorant and lower-class people, and in Roman times was exclusively used for the plebeians, the lower classes. From there the word went downhill as far as having any positive connotations, but we still get that sense of a private or personal way of doing or saying something in *idiom* and *idiosyncrasy*. *Ignorance* is a direct transcription from the Latin for "we do not know." *Imbecile* was originally taken from the Latin for someone very weak, "without a staff to lean on," but over time it came to be associated with senility and, finally, with anyone who was mentally deficient.

illusion The literal meaning of this word goes back to the Latin and was "to play against." The idea seems to be that you were being fooled or mocked by the gamester, and our word *ludicrous* comes out of this. Those who could move the pea about under the shells so deftly that you could rarely ever pick the right one could make you look very foolish. As their tricks increased in difficulty these marketplace gamesters became entertainers and their illusions gained more respectability. *Illustrate* comes from a different root and meant "to make bright," which colorful drawings would do on pages that the early monks copied.

imp A rascally child usually gets this almost affectionate label for his or her mischievous behavior. "He gave her an impish smile" gives you the feeling that he is boyishly cute in his expression. Way back when, the Greeks used the word as a horticultural term. It was a name for implanting a shoot in the ground or grafting it onto another plant. As the word made its way through the world and  time, it was used for both a shoot or sapling and then for any offspring. The grafting idea is still heard in falconry when a bird's wings are imped, or grafted with new feathers to repair a damaged wing or to give the bird better flying ability. Somehow or other, the notion of descendant got used to describe small demons, "imps of the devil." These mischievous pranksters could cause a person all kinds of trouble. With this connotation mixed into the batter of this word, a rowdy child was now an imp, which referred to "descendant" as well as "little devil."

impeach On the rare occasion that an official does something so bad as to be impeached, we understand that that person is going before some kind of tribunal to be removed from office. It was a worse punishment in the earliest sense of the word. It meant "to put in chains," which is a meaning that might be effectively revived for judges, presidents, and others who abuse their office.

inaugurate Speaking of presidents, we commonly associate this word with the swearing-in celebration of a new one. In ancient Rome this word meant something entirely different. Among the many things an augur would do would be to determine whether or not you should do something by the way the birds were flying. These almost magical soothsayers would tell a general not to march on one day or do battle on another by the formations of the birds on the wing. They might even catch one and cut it open to observe its entrails for omens. An "inauguration" was done before beginning any major venture. With the advent of Christianity, the only instance of divination from birds came in the story of the dove at Jesus' baptism. By the way, the word *auspicious* is one of the words that came out of this bird study by the ancients. If the birds were flying in the right way, then the day was considered auspicious: a good one in which to start some project. The word literally means "bird watcher." We all know that some of our politicians are "for the birds" and even bird-brained, but science *has* shown that birds fly lower to the ground before a storm. What birds are eating *can* give you an idea of the conditions of the land. Bird watching is still popular, but not usually for these forecasting purposes.

incentive   Many of us need incentives to do our best work, whether it's bonus pay or an extra day of vacation or just family pride. The word originally referred to singing and concerned the person who set the tune or started the song. This leader of a choir got the group going; in getting them to sing his or her song, the leader was motivating them. It's nice when the world is "singing your tune."

infant   For the Latin-speaking people of several thousand years ago this word meant "one who is unable to talk." Babies fit this meaning best in their incapacity for speech. We've already talked about the almost humorous name for foot soldiers, *infantry*. Now, an *infante* was the name given to any son of a Spanish or Portuguese king when that child was not the direct heir to the throne. An *infanta* was the daughter of one of these kings or the wife of an *infante*. Make sense?

infatuate   This word could be translated literally as "to make silly or stupid." When someone is infatuated with another person or thing we don't take their affection quite as seriously. "She's only infatuated," we say. But we don't think of infatuation as being foolish or deluded as much these days. It now has more of a sense of being a prelude to love.

infect   When germs are spread or a wound swells, we talk of infection. In Roman times the word came out of the clothmaking industry. It meant "to work in dye." These laborers would come home with the browns and reds and purples clinging to their skin, and if they were very fresh from the dye vat they might leave stains and handprints on anything they touched. When early medicine tried to explain the nature of the transmission of disease, this was the best comparison that could be made: that, like dye, the germs could taint everyone they touched.

influenza   Speaking of disease, the popularization of this word that we now commonly shorten to *flu* came in the terrible epidemic of 1743, when thousands of Europeans died. Medieval doctors gave many diseases the name *influentia,* from the Latin meaning "a flowing in," a term that also made reference to a visitation from the stars. It seemed that some invisible substance flowed into the victim and caused the disease. They were right, of course, but they couldn't isolate the microscopic organisms until centuries later. After the epidemic of the 1700s the symptoms of fever, muscular pain, and all the rest became specifically associated with the word *influenza* and later *flu.* Twenty million people died from the swine flu of 1918. Our word *influence* also comes from the same root, from the idea of some power indirectly affecting a person or series of events. It can even have mystical qualities when someone talks about the influence of the stars.

inkling   When I first saw the word *inkling* I thought it might refer to some tiny little print, as in "baby ink." I had no inkling that it went back to the 1200s, to a verb we no longer use in English: *to inkle,* which meant "to mutter," to speak so that others could barely understand. In other words, you would only get an inkling of what the person was saying.

insult   When someone insults you, it's almost as if they've slapped you with words. At one time an insult was cause for a duel or even warfare. The word originally comes from the French, who used it for someone who triumphed over another and then behaved arrogantly about it. When someone beat you and then laughed at you for it, they were insulting. The French took the word from a  Latin word meaning "to jump on or jump over." An older meaning of the word is still used in medicine when talking about "an insult to the stomach" or some other organ. We get *assault* from the same original root. And we *exult* (jump for joy) when we get the correct *result* (jump back from the edge . . . or reach the end).

interest   The conquering Norman French introduced this word into English when they imposed all their laws and regulations on the subdued British Isles. A "share" in something meant you were a part owner, and we still use the word that way when we say, "He had an interest in the business." When you were loaned money, you had to pay a certain "share" of that money above the borrowed sum: the interest. After a time, when you wanted a part of anything, whether a hunk of ham or a pretty girl, it was of interest to you. If it took a "share" of your attention or made you curious, you had an interest in it. . . . It was interesting to you.

intoxicate   When someone wakes up with a hangover after a night of carousing, that person might readily agree with the original meaning of this word from the Medieval Latin, "to put poison in." Today there are nicer meanings implied when we smell an intoxicating aroma or are intoxicated by another's looks or charms, but the fact that alcohol *is* basically a poison makes those medieval fellows more right than not. We see the root in one of today's big issues: toxic waste disposal and the use of nontoxic chemicals and pesticides. The "poison" sense of the word seems to be winning out.

investigate   This word is much-used in both law enforcement and science. Police departments have their investigators or speak with private "i's" (later changed to "eyes"), while the Centers for Disease Control investigates the latest medical problem. Once again we go back to pre-Christian Rome for the earliest and simplest meaning of the word: "to follow the footprints." After all, that was probably the key clue for the earliest crime solver and one of the only ways to trace a suspect. No, *invest* doesn't come from the same root, but meant "to put clothes upon" . . . not a bad first investment.

iota   *Iota* is used today to represent the tiniest amount, the faintest trace. It came from the Greek alphabet and was the name for what we call the letter *i*. We get the word *jot* from this same word, meaning "to write a small amount" or "a little note." Since the letter *i* is so small, the term came to stand for the smallest of things and was even used when the Greeks translated the words of Jesus in Matthew 5:18: "For verily I say unto you, till heaven and earth pass, not one jot or one tittle shall in no wise pass from the law, till all be fulfilled."

isolate "No man is an island," but when you are isolated you might feel that way. The Latin root from which we get this word meant "to make into an island," in other words, to separate from the main body. The same root gives us *insulate,* though this has more of a sense of protection than the lonely feel of isolation. It seems that in a global economy, the days of isolationism are disappearing because no country can be an "island" either.

jade The belief that crystals and other of nature's stones had healing powers goes back to ancient times, as you saw with the word *amethyst.* Jade gets its name from that part of the body between the last rib and the hip, the flank. Why? It was believed by very early medical practitioners that the stone could help cure pains in the kidneys, which are located in that part of the body. Its full name in Spanish was "stone of the flanks," but we ended up with the *ijada* portion, or "the side." Now, when someone is *jaded* by life it could well be that they have just too much jade, but that is not where the term comes from. Our contemporary use of this word, which conveys a feeling of being dulled by having too much, comes from a word from several hundred years ago for a broken-down horse. A "jade" was exhausted and worn out by its labors. The name was later applied to a worthless woman or a girl who wanted her own way in everything.

jay The noisy birds we call jays got their name from the Latin, and it was meant to express the kind of emotion these birds must be feeling to love to squawk so much. "Full of joy" was basically what their name meant, though a person described as a jay is thought of as a chatterbox. We get our word *gay* from the same Latin root, but the older meaning of that word has fallen out of use since its widespread application to those of a certain sexual preference. It was a tradition in the days when the jay was named to use names of people, like Robin and Martin, for birds, and Gaius was a common Roman name. By the way, a Kansas native is called a Jayhawk, but there is no such bird. When Kansas and Missouri were settling their border areas in the late 1850s, there were a lot of skirmishes between Unionists and those in favor of slavery. These Unionists called themselves "jayhawks" because they would swoop down on the noisy opposition who supported slavery. "Bleeding Kansas," as it was nicknamed, eventually fought for the Union and lost more men than any northern state. *Jaywalking* goes back to that earlier connotation of the foolish talker. This "jay" was a stupid person not paying attention to where he or she was going.

jazz The slaves of early America gave us the beginnings of this word. *Jasm* meant "energy, drive, and pep" and came from a word used by the African Tshiluba and Mandingo people that meant "to cause to dance" or "to step out of one's self." The "energy" definition and the "dance" meaning got mixed together in the music. Its use as a word for sex came in the twenties from American college slang. It also got the slang meaning of "meaningless talk," as in, "Don't give me that jazz!" It has survived today as the name for a powerful and unique form of American music . . . and can still be found with other meanings, like "fancy," as in "That's a real jazzy car."

jeopardy   No doubt this word that means "danger or risk" will forever be influenced by the popular game show. Years from now the quiz show's use of the word will color the meaning, and people will think of the mentally challenging game when the word is mentioned. That may not be so bad given the word's origin. *Jeopardy* comes from the French and was first a phrase used when there was a draw in chess and the next move would break the tie. It was a term for a split game in which each player had an even chance to lose or win. The word gradually got used for any situation in which there was a chance for loss. So games may start and end the word. **A:** "A book that provides an interesting look at the history of language." **Q:** *Where in the Word?* Right! And that was the daily double, too.

jewel   On the subject of games, this word we now use for precious stones actually comes from the same Latin word from which we get *joke*. The first uses of the word *jewel* made it a plaything, part of a game, a bauble. When all is said and done, a diamond is just an extra-hard piece of coal, but tell that to Wall Street, where games are taken very seriously. It is funny how words change in strength or meaning. A *jest* was originally a tale of brave adventure, but over time comedy won out and a jest became a funny story.

jiggle   When Jello jiggles or we jiggle the TV switch, we get a good idea of the movement conveyed by the word. And if someone says a businessman is jiggling with his books and later watches a dancer jiggling in front of him at the club, we can understand the different actions of these people. In its original sense this word clings more to the dancer than to any of the rest, as it comes from *jig,* which is a lively dance we associate with Ireland. Truthfully, jigs are danced in many lands and the word got its start from the Old French word for *fiddle* . . . and I've already talked about that word.

journal The French took this from the Latin word meaning "daily." Something that was recorded in every day, such as a ship's log or a book of transactions in business or government, was a journal. Later, personal memoirs and publications of news and information took on the name. *Journalism* now covers the whole range of reporting on the events of the day. Maybe a paper issued at night should be called a "nocturnal."

joust Jousting is not done much anymore except with words or at popular Renaissance fairs. The violent pastime of the 1100s took its name from the Latin word that simply meant "close together." The movies have given us plenty of these contents, and books like *Ivanhoe* celebrate the knights' practice at war. We have another word today for the kind of jousting subway riders and mall shoppers may find themselves involved in: *jostle.*

jubilation This state of happiness got into the Latin vocabulary from the Greeks, who took it from the Hebrew word meaning "ram's horn." In the Old Testament a Jubilee occurred every forty-nine years and lasted a full year. During that time, slaves were set free, the lands were left untilled, property that had been in dispute was given back to former owners, loans

were made without interest, and every sale had to be a
square deal. This was a sort of Sabbath year, the
seven-times-seven years. The blowing of a ram's horn
signaled its beginning, and the Hebrew term became
the name for the joy that was felt by most of the partici-
pants. It was a tough tradition to maintain, and by the
time the Roman Catholic Church got hold of it the year
of Jubilee was a time when sinners could gain full
forgiveness of their sins by performing certain pious
acts.

jukebox   Our common word for a coin-operated record
player actually came from a disapproving word for
prostitutes and other "bad" people, used by blacks
living on or near the Atlantic coastal islands of the
South. The Gullah people called a brothel a "juke
house," meaning "a disorderly place." Usually, drinking and loud music were part of this scene, and when
clubs, bars, and dance halls in the early part of this
century began to use nickel-a-play record players, the
Gullah word got used. The "juke box" was that noisy
little container, and the name stayed with it.

julep   The South again comes to mind when we hear
the word *julep,* especially as in "mint julep." The word
goes back to ancient Persian, and the root from which
we eventually got *julep* meant "rose water." This
sweet-smelling liquid was used for centuries in cooking,
bathing, and cosmetics. As time went by, other sweet
and syrupy drinks were called juleps. Face it, roses
weren't always available. Much of the time the julep
was used in medicine to conceal bitterness or other bad
tastes. When the southerner decided to put bourbon
whiskey into the sugar water, along with crushed mint
and shaved ice, a drink was concocted that maintained
the word's existence.

jury   The Romans had a couple of legal terms that brought us a wide range of words. *Jus* and *lex* gave us two notions of determining fairness and rules for dealing with one another. *Jus,* from which we get words like *justice, judge,* and *jury,* had to do with determining each situation as it pertained to the law. A jury was a group sworn to hear legal evidence as objectively as possible. *Lex,* on the other hand, was the law itself, and from it we get *legal, legislation,* and *loyal.* A jury can determine *injury* (which first meant "not lawful"), but must watch for *perjury* (false swearing of evidence) both of which are within their jurisdiction.

kaleidoscope   Here is a made-up word that if translated from its parts would mean "to see beautiful forms." The Scot Sir David Brewster invented the device using a prism and colored glass in the early 1800s. The poet Byron first used it to mean "constantly changing pattern" in one of his poems, and since then it's become a common adjective for swirling, changing events or scenes.

kaput   We really think of this as a German expression meaning "It's over," usually in a bad way, as if something were destroyed or no longer usable. In fact, the Germans got the word from a French card-playing phrase, *etre capot,* when a person has lost all the tricks in a hand of cards. Literally, it means "to have a hood thrown over your head." *Capot* was the name for a cape with a hood attached, and the idea of the gaming expression was that you'd been hoodwinked; you must have played that round blindfolded. It's all over for you.

karate   This is a Japanese word that's made its way into English because of its glorification in movies, combined with the self-defense craze. *Karate* comes from a combination of two Japanese words and means "empty-handed," referring to the weaponless defender who uses hands and feet to disable an attacker.

keister   Though this word is not widely used, it *is* widely understood as another way of naming that soft portion of the backside, the gluteus maximus. This Yiddish term for the derrière came from a German word for a box or chest. The Germans probably got it from the Romans, who took it from the Greeks, a common trail for a word. Jewish-Americans passed this funny buttocks word into our language, and though the hind end is not exactly box-shaped, the idea that the fanny is like a storage chest fits well enough. I'm getting out of this one before I make an ass of myself.

kerchief   *Kerchief* comes from combining two French words: *couvre* ("to cover") and *chief* ("head"). By the time it was brought misspelled into English by those conquered by these French, it had its shortened form. We took *chef* and used it for a head cook; I've already talked about the sense of covering in *curfew*. Later, we just slapped *neck-* and *hand-* on *chief* for different versions of this scarf. We left the spelling alone for the leader of an Indian tribe or the head of an organization, the chief.

kerosene   This word came from the Greek for "wax." This petroleum distillate has become popular again due to the interest in various kerosene heaters. Why "wax"? Well, paraffin is used in its creation. It's been called coal oil, and in England they actually call it paraffin oil. We've just added a chemical suffix to make the waxy word sound more scientific.

ketchup   Ketchup is also called "catsup" and "catchup," and I've even seen it as "ketsup." When we get a food or spice from another language, sometimes everyone wants a hand at spelling it in English. This Chinese word originally described a product made of brine and minced seafood. The Malay people took the word for this concoction and spelled it *kechap*. Britishers brought it home with a variety of formulas . . . and spellings.

khaki   The sturdy cotton or wool we call khaki gets its name from its color, which can range from a light greenish brown to a light yellowish brown. The word originated in the Persian and meant "dust." So dust-colored cloth, popular among the Turks, Pakistanis, and Indians, was "khaki." The Pakistani language, Urdu, is where the English eventually found the word. The name for that language, by the way, came from a Turkish word for "army," which was applied to the conquering Mongol horde. *Horde* and *Urdu* are brothers of the same root. . . . All right, they could be sisters.

kidnap   We know what they did with horse thieves in
the Old West. Stealing animals has always been a high
crime in societies
where the animal
provided a livelihood.
In its Scandinavian
origins, this word
translated as "snatcher
of young goats." When
this tactic was used to
detain a child or adult
who was valued by the
clan or family, the word
also embraced that
crime. *Kidnap* has
always conveyed the sense that the thieves weren't just
stealing, but stealing to trade for gain.

kilt   Though Scotsmen are among the few who still
wear the kilt, this form of dress was once popular in
many parts of Scandinavia. The word has Scandinavian
beginnings and meant "to tuck up." This was an easy
way to get dressed: just grab a length of woven cloth,
wrap it around you, and tuck it or fasten it up. Today
the kilt is more ceremonial, though many a Highland
laddie would as soon whip on a kilt as struggle into
pants.

kindergarten   This word for the widely accepted
preschool grade, mainly for five year olds, comes
directly from German and means "child's garden." The
concept of the very young getting a positive group
experience in a happy, exploring environment goes
back to 1837 and the German educator Fredrich Frobel.
He made up the name for this special program meant to
prepare a child for the rigors of school. The notion was

brought to England by a refugee priest from Germany, who opened his first kindergarten in 1850.

klutz   It seems these days that this word is used for more than just the kind of clumsiness with which it was once associated. Today a klutzy person represents almost a way of life: a scatter-brained, unmechanical, somewhat insecure comic figure who has trouble opening a can of soup and will be sure to knock over a glass at a fancy restaurant. The amused and forgiving attitude we have today toward the klutz wasn't shared by the Germans who first used the word. It meant "a clod of dirt," and referred to a person who was dull-witted *and* clumsy.

knight   When this word was first used over a thousand years ago it meant "a boy," a lad who usually served around the house. Over  time, as these servers grew to manhood and took on more important tasks, some requiring bravery, the word began to assume a more glorious meaning. When a powerful clan leader defeated other clans and unified the new lands, his "knights" were given titles and a share in the kingdom. Soon, the process of becoming a knight began to involve years of training and serving, and these men-at-arms became the great standard-bearers of a privileged, gentlemanly tradi-tion. Today, though sought with great intensity, there

are very few knights in shining, or even dull, armor . . .
and even the Knights of Columbus are diminishing.

knuckle   Basically, the old German word this came
from could be translated as "to make into a knob." We
get *knock* from the same root, possibly because that
action involves the knuckles. Before I knuckle under
and move on to the next word, let me knuckle down and
talk about one other use for knuckles, other than
cracking. Have you ever heard someone claim possession of something by saying "I've got *dibs* on that"?
A long time ago there was a children's game called
"dibstones," also called "knucklebones" because it was
played with the nearly useless leftovers from soup
made out of pig's knuckles or some other animal's
bones—nothing was wasted. In the game, the bones
were used as counters, and "laying dibs" on something
was claiming rights to it. Some people still use *dibs* to
mean "small amounts of money," as in "He paid in dibs
and dabs."

Ku Klux Klan   The original group was formed in part
from the old "patrollers," men who were paid to guard
the road between farms and to check the passes of the
slaves, who were allowed to visit other plantations on
certain days. After the Civil War the vigilante patrollers became secret societies, with their own mystical
initiations and pledges to keep identities secret. *Kuklos*
(Greek for "circle") was the term representing their
closed circle and *Klan* came from "clan," for their
kindred sense of racial brotherhood. This particular
organization, which had some notoriety during Recon-
struction, was reorganized in 1915 in Georgia, and over
the years the name Kuklos Klan degenerated into the
Ku Klux Klan of today. There were other secret

societies of the time that used the circle idea, like the Knights of the Golden Circle.

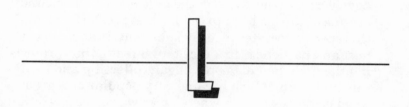

lace Many a man might claim to have been caught by a bit of lace, and some women might even lay that trap purposefully with a lacy little outfit. Before anyone laces into me for speaking of male/female relationships as some kind of hunting activity, let me say that the word *lace* originally meant in Latin "a noose or trap." The first use of the weblike fabric was to ensnare something, whether an animal in the wild or a gladiator in the arena. The netting was employed as a tool and a weapon. When a more relaxed lifestyle led to less practical uses of the material, lace became a more delicate and ornamental fabric. I'll lace it all up by saying that the warrior still gets a bit of use out of the word: The gold or silver braid on an officer's uniform is called the lace.

lackadaisical We still use this word for a lazy person, although it seems to be getting somewhat old-fashioned. It comes from an expression of regret, "Alack the day!" which gave the idea that you wished the day had never come. *Alack* came from another phrase meaning "Ah, what a loss!" So "Alack the day" meant you'd wasted the day, and who better to waste your time than a lackadaisical person!

lacquer Our modern lacquers are basically synthetic coating materials used to give protection and shine to everything from wood and metal to fingernails. Bugs, however, are where we got the first *shellacs*. The Hindu origins of this go back to the lac insect. The female of this species secretes a gooey substance that coats the nest and hardens into a nice tough resin, thus protecting the little home. People began collecting and using this bug resin, which became very popular as a great wood protector. Later, when a tree was discovered that exuded a black protective fluid, it was named the "lacquer tree." Science got even farther away from the insect with chemical imitations.

lady When we hear "She's a real lady," we get a picture of manners, dress, and elegance at their best. The earliest use of the term takes us back well over a thousand years and gives a not-so-stylish description: "kneader of bread." That's right, we get our word *lady* out of the flour-dusted image of a woman squeezing dough. But, men, don't scoff. *Lord* actually comes from "keeper of the bread."  That's how those lords and ladies got their fine castles and kingly lifestyle: making bread and then doling it out to the workers. If you had some land, got your people to work it, grew some wheat, had it ground, and made the bread, you could live through the cold winters, survive a siege by a hostile neighbor, and feed your people. . . . And in those days, food was power.

larceny   We label those who commit larceny as
thieves and robbers, and today it is a crime in its
smallest or grandest forms. In its earliest sense,
however, the word referred to mercenaries, men who
took on military service for pay. These soldiers of
fortune could be rather roguish, and when the battle
was done they might plunder a home or village for all it
was worth. These dregs of the military gave a bad
reputation to freebooting fighters, and by the time
France was becoming powerful under Charlemagne,
these *larcins* were starting to be frowned upon. Eventually, such ransacking for booty was considered piracy
and thievery, and these acts became crimes.

lariat   A cowboy doing fancy tricks with his noosed
rope comes to mind with the word *lariat*. A rope was a
vital tool for work with animals. It could hold a wild
horse, subdue a runaway steer, and fence off a herd of
sheep for the night. *Lariat* is a Spanish word and was
the name of a rope used for tying mules. The easily
sliding noose made securing the animals much quicker
than would have been the case if knots had to be tied
and untied. *Lasso* is also Spanish and was another
noosed rope used for catching a stallion or calf. It means
"to snare."

lasagna   The Italians seem to be very frank in naming
their foods. The story of lasagna takes us back to the
chilly Italian winters, when a visit to the outdoor
facilities could really chap your cheeks and was only for
the strong of heart. The chamber pot was the only
indoor plumbing of the time, and this large, sturdy
vessel could be emptied later. Whether because of a
lack of good cooking pots or a certain strange sense of
humor, *lasagna* comes from the Italian for "chamber
pot." This layered concoction of noodles, cheese, and

sauce was and is traditionally baked in large pans and pots, but the chamber pot has long since been put in the attic. OK, what of the other noodles? *Linguini* means "small tongue"—yuck! We get *linguistics* from the same source. *Manicotti* means "little sleeves." *Macaroni* looked like small macaroons, "little cookies." *Spaghetti* comes from "small strings." And worse of all, *vermicelli* means "little worms." And they love their pasta?

left   Left-handers have recently gotten some attention as an abused minority group; in fact, history has not been kind to them. You probably already know that *sinister* is Latin for "from the left," because fighting a left-handed swordsman could be very tricky for a fighter used to dealing with right-handers. A lefty might shake your right hand and stab you with the left. And the French term *gauche,* for a tactless or clumsy act, literally means "left." Well, the word itself is of Dutch origins and probably got into English with its earliest meaning: "weak or useless." Lefties were once again left out. Even intellectuals berate poor left-wingers with only the poorest of left-handed compliments.

legend   The word first meant "things for reading" in its early Latin use, but by the time medieval Latin priests had introduced the word into English, the things made of legends were the lives of the saints. These were "legends" in the first English use of the word. Later, stories of other heroic figures were also called legends. Finally, the word got applied to any popular tale handed down, or even to a person of wide acclaim. The earliest use of the word can still be seen on maps, where the "legend" is the part you read.

lens   From telescopes to contact lenses to our eyeballs
themselves, the lens is an important part of our daily
life. The camera lens brings us our news, entertainment, and home movies, and the modern surgical laser
beam passes through its concentrating lens. The word,
though, has a simple, vegetable origin. When Renaissance man began grinding the lens for his telescope, he
thought it had the shape of a lentil seed and gave it the
Latin name for lentil, *lens.* By the way, the fancy name
for a freckle, *lentigo,* also gets its name from the seed.

leprechaun   Of course, these strange little wealthy
shoemakers get their name from the Old Irish, but
actually the word was influenced by the Romans, who
came into England around the time of Julius Caesar.
The Latin word for body, *corpus,* was combined with the
ancient Irish word for small, *lu.* Over time the "lucor-
pus" got stretched and fiddled with as it was passed by
word of mouth. By the time it was written down, it was
in its present form. Well, the little people probably
didn't worry about the changes.

lettuce   Though milk is often used in some kinds of
Ranch-style salad dressings, we don't normally think of
lettuce and milk as having a relationship. But "milk" is
the Latin origin for this leafy vegetable's name. Because certain species have a milky fluid that comes
from the cut stems, the early Romans gave it the name
"milk plant." From the same Latin root we get the word
we use when mammals suckle their young: *lactate.*

libel   How do *library* and *libel* share a common ancestor? The Latin for "book," *liber,* was applied to pamphlets that spoke out against certain laws or persons in

power. *Libel* meant "little book." The powers-that-be considered these pamphlets defamatory and took their writers to task. Their formal, written response to the books in a court of law was also called a "libel." When legal minds got hold of the concept of libel, it started to get more and more complicated. A person couldn't just say bad things in public about another person or set of rules. They had to have proof or else be punished. Today, in the Land of Lawsuits, libel is still tricky fun for the lawyer.

licorice   The Greeks discovered this plant, and their name for it translated as "sweet root." The Latin-speaking people altered the word in translation, influenced by their word for a liquid beverage, since the root had to be treated to extract the flavored liquid. Around 500 A.D. we had *liquirita*. The French then got hold of the word and we got closer to our own spelling, still having the sound of *liquor* attached.

line   I'm not handing you a line when I tell you that the thread of this simple word's history traces back to the Latin for the flax plant, from which we get linen. Because of the importance of clothmaking in ancient times, this process gave rise to many words. At first, a line was a thread of linen and was also used for one's descendants because of the genetic threads that linked parents and children. *Lint* was the fluff from the flax that hung around a weaver's loom. *Lingerie,* created by the sexy French, came from "linen garments." So, to hit a line drive, or to ride in an ocean liner, or to follow a line of thought all gets you tangled up with the original thread. Even *linoleum* floors come from the processing of the flax plant's oil with cork and burlap.

litter   For the past several decades this word has gotten so associated with bits of trash that we've almost lost its earliest meaning. The litterbug has replaced the meaning from the Latin root: "bed." We still see this first use when we speak of a litter of kittens. Animals give birth in their stalls or "beds," and so the young of those animals have long been known as their litter, especially when the dog or cat has a little box that resembles a bed. The first human beds were made of coarse cloth stuffed with straw, corn shucks, cotton leavings, or anything else that was soft, including feathers for the wealthy. Because these stuffings were sometimes found strewn about the floor, *litter* also got used for the debris and rubbish it is linked with today. The kitty may still have a litter of kittens, but she's not going to sleep in her kitty litter.

loiter   These days, *to loiter* has taken on legal connotations from those signs that say "No loitering." The Dutch brought the English the word in the 1500s, when many vagrant Hollanders moved to Britain. The earliest meaning was "to totter or shake," like an old-timer who couldn't move so fast. By the time it got to England, it was more often used to mean "to be in the way," "to hang about," and, finally, just "to dawdle."

lollipop   By Shakespeare's day the word *loll* had gone from the Dutch "lull to sleep," from which we get *lullaby,* to a more exhausted-sounding use, "to hang the tongue out." The northern English used this idea of panting to describe the eating of certain hard candies: to loll the tongue, then pop it back in. We still use a variation of the word for the sucker, but we use the verb *loll* less for the tongue than for just relaxing or hanging limply. *Lull* also stayed with us in nearly its original form, as in "we lulled them into a false sense of security."

lozenge   Math experts might know that what we think of as a cough drop is actually a word for a geometric figure. The word means "diamond-shaped" and goes back to an early word for a flat stone that the Romans borrowed from the conquered Gauls of future France. Later, the lozenge was a symbol on a coat of arms in that diamond form. In the 1500s, when some of the first cough drops were introduced, their diamond shape led them to be called by that now-common name.

lunatic   I guess this word's origin is pretty well known, but when the movie *Moonstruck* came out it struck me that if we took the meaning of the word *lunatic* literally, the movie could be retitled. The early belief that the moon was the cause of insanity was widespread. There were even superstitions that staring at the moon could drive you mad. The Latin *luna* still gets a lot of use today when talking about things lunar, but the phases of the moon no longer figure in psychoanalysis. Then again, statistics show that more crimes are committed during the full moon than at other times. Is that because there's more light to commit them or because those moonstruck folk of the past were right all along?

Madam   Our formal name for a married woman and our informal name for the operator of a house of ill repute goes back to the Old French word meaning "my lady." Though today's liberated woman sometimes prefers the more matrimonially mysterious *Ms.* it is still considered proper etiquette to begin a letter to a woman that you don't know with "Dear Madam." Madonna, the name we associate both with the Virgin Mary and the pop star, goes back to the Latin, also meaning "my lady."

magazine   This word was born in the Arabic language and meant "a storehouse." Whether it refers to that part of a gun in which you put the gunpowder or bullets, or to that "storehouse" of pictures and information you'll find in the doctor's waiting room, *magazine* is still a common word. Its application to a dockside warehouse or a grain bin is not very common, but we are constantly using the word for those monthly periodicals and weekly collections of articles.

mail   Through rain and sleet and snow . . . Well, the mail does get through, though the fax may give it a slow death. You'll still see the mailbag in the small towns of America as letter carriers makes their appointed rounds. The word *mail* came from an Old German word for "sack" or "pouch."

malaria   I've already talked about the "good air" of *debonair. Malaria* means just the opposite, "bad air." Early doctors tried to pin the blame for illness on many things; the fever of this disease was thought to be caused by bad air. And in fact it was stagnant water and the surrounding rank air that bred the mosquito, and that culprit brought this chronic illness to mankind.

mall   Practically a way of life over the past twenty years, the mall has been a phenomenon. Why do we call it the "mall"? The word goes back to a street game something like croquet, which may have begun in Italy and then spread to France and later to England. The game involved using a mallet to hit a wooden ball through an iron ring. The French called it *palle maille,* for "ball and mallet." The English fooled around with the spelling. Now, you need a good, quiet street without traffic to play the game, usually an alley. Eventually, these streets became known as pall mall lanes. In London the Pall Mall became lined with clubs where players might readily obtain a brew after a good game. Soon, shops and boutiques took advantage of the audience for these games. As the game's popularity dwindled (some say golf was its next phase), the "mall," as it became known, was then just a nice place to go shopping on foot. Our large shopping centers copied the idea. And you're wondering about *croquet?* It's more than likely from the French word *crochet:* "hook," for the shape of the wickets. *Alley* also got to us from the French verb *aler:* "to go."

mammoth   The Russians gave us this word for the prehistoric elephant that we also use for anything huge. However, their word meant "earth." Why? Since the bones of these creatures generally turned up underground, and since preserved woolly mammoths were found frozen in ice in what seemed like burrows, it was believed that the mammoth was a burrowing creature. These hairy-backed elephants probably *did* protect their more vulnerable undersides by lying in gullies at the approach of icy weather, to be found frozen there after the Ice Age.

manna We still speak of "manna from heaven" for some windfall of good fortune, something needed that comes to us by surprise. For the Hebrews wandering the desert, it was a lifesaver to wake up every morning and find this strange food laying on the ground. Their word *manna* meant "What is it?" God works in mysterious ways, though some theorize that this early morning food delivery could have been a form of mushroom sprouting from the manure of the herds of sheep and goats also searching for that Promised Land with their owners. Whatever it was wasn't questioned at a time when it saved their lives, though the question was its name.

manure Speaking of manure, in the days of primitive agriculture there were things an animal could do and there were things that had to be done by the hand of man. The oxen might help with the plowing, but the spreading of the fertilizer, the planting of the seed, and the harvesting were the farmer's tasks. *Manure* was the polite way of speaking of the droppings that were collected and spread over a field. It meant "by hand," as did *maneuver*. In those days, so much of the work of growing crops was *manual* labor.

map In the days when a seafaring captain's map was as important as his sail, these precious guides were painted or woven on cloth to preserve them from the elements and to help them survive the constant folding and unfolding they would undergo on a journey. The word *map* comes from the Latin for "cloth." From this same root we get *napkin,* which means "little cloth." The best map was a *mappa mundi,* a map of the world. When good paper and printing got put on the map, cloth was wiped off the map.

maroon   We think of being marooned as being ship-wrecked on a desert island, or perhaps, in a more criminal sense, as being *put* on that island by a band of pirates: "You can't maroon me like this!" The word comes to us from an American Spanish name for runaway slaves in the West Indies in the 1600s and 1700s. When these slaves escaped on the islands, the only place for them to hide out was in the jungle wilderness of the interior mountains. The word literally means "living on the mountaintops." But in doing that, the runaways were cut off from civilization. Gradually, the word came to mean being isolated from the rest of the world, being stranded, with no hope of rescue or of finding another place to go. The French took the word and altered its spelling to give us the word we use today. The *maroon* that means "red" comes from a French word for "chestnut" or "chestnut-colored."

marquee   Today we primarily think of this word as associated with the theater, referring to the projecting, awninglike structure where we read the title of a movie or play and maybe the names of a couple of the stars. This idea of letting you know what's inside also applies to the original French word. The marquee was a special little linen tent that was pitched above an officer's tent in an encampment to let you know where he was. If you had a message to deliver to your leader, it was handy to be able to quickly identify his tent among all the others. The word is still sometimes used for the large, open-

sided tent that some people use for entertaining.
Another form of the word, *marquis,* was a title for a
nobleman below a duke but above an earl or count. How
was that connected with the tent? Well, at first the title
was one that was looked down upon. Such a person was
a "count of the frontier," out in the countryside, as if
living in a tent.

marshal   If Marshal Dillon had known his title came
from a German word for a horse groom, he might not
have gotten quite as much respect from Miss Kitty or
from the badmen he tracked down. But as we saw with
constable, these horse tenders were important to the
lord of the land and grew to be officials of the court. By
the time the word had come from the French to the
English, it was a title of some respect, like *sheriff,*
which comes from the Old English. The sheriff was the
"reeve" (steward or official) of the shire (manor), the
"shire reeve." The word *martial,* as in "martial arts" or
"martial law," comes from the Roman god of war, Mars.

martyr   We use this word a lot these days to describe
people who let others walk all over them and then
complain about it. "Don't act the martyr," we say to
such a person who whines about how awful he or she
has been treated. Well, most of us do think of the
original martyrs, who died rather than renounce their
religious beliefs. And we also still use the word for
someone who dies for a cause. The Greeks gave us the
word and it meant "witness (for Christ)." Those who
went around preaching the gospel in the early days of
Christianity were likely to suffer stoning or crucifixion
by the less-than-tolerant Romans . . . or maybe become
a snack for a lion. As a result, the word got to be
associated with suffering and death.

mascot   Most mascots today are either cute, goofy, costumed creatures like chickens; tough animals like bulldogs and goats; or symbols of conquest, like gladiators or Trojans. The origins of the voodoo doll or rabbit's foot might be the same as those of the mascot, which can be traced to superstitions of over a thousand years ago. In France, where it started (influenced by Latin), the word dealt with witchcraft and sorcery, and with putting good- and bad-luck charms and spells on talismans, which might be animals or little mementoes. Though this supernatural notion was frowned upon by the Church, people have never been able to get it out of their heads that some special little object might bring them good luck. Such objects of superstition still hold sway, everything from the rabbit's foot (because when a rabbit thumped his foot he was warning the rest of the warren about danger, and having one of these might keep danger from you) to the four-leaf clover (which became a symbol of good luck because it was so rare), to other lucky charms like coins or souvenirs. Athletes, especially, have always been a group that believed in good and bad omens. If a tiger or a hawk might fire a player up to believe he had some of the same qualities, where was the harm?

mask   The Arab word for "clown" gives us the word *mask*. And though it might enhance a woman's eyes, the word *mascara* comes from the same source. We've seen some women (and men) whose use of make-up can get pretty clownlike. The Italians spread the word, using it for the name of a costume ball, a *masque* (which the French were fond of), or a *masquerade*. Today we use the word more for a disguise of any kind, especially a pretense.

massacre This word has both serious and not-so-serious uses. It may refer to a terrible wave of killing that indiscriminately destroys everyone in its wake, or to a humiliating loss in a sporting event: "The team got massacred by its opponents." Its origin is found in a Latin word for a type of club that could be a handy weapon in the hands of wild northern tribesmen, who might use it to smash anyone and everything in their path. *Massacre* meant "knock on the head."

matador Sport can be a religion for many, but bullfighting seems to have actually started out that way. The Spanish took their word for "bullfighter," which today basically means "killer," from a Latin root that originally meant "sacred." The ritual slaying of the bull was part of a sacrificial ceremony showing man's dominance over the animal world, combined with his respect for that world. Though animal sacrifice has largely disappeared in most societies, this controversial, intense sport continues its centuries-old tradition in Spain and some Latin American countries. (In Portugal the bullfighter works from horseback and doesn't kill the bull.) To those Americans who are shocked by the sport, a bullfighting fan might point out that each year in this country hundreds of dogs and roosters die in illegal dogfights and cockfights. These fights certainly do not have the grace and drama of a bullfight, in which a man with a sword dances around a two-thousand-pound, untamed bull.

mate   Whether it's the idea of the matched pair, the
spouse, or the close friend, the word *mate* conveys a lot
of intimacy. Of course, the word has its more practical
side, too, as when animals perform their mating rituals
or sailors salute the first mate aboard a ship. All its
meanings—whether the mate to a sock or a helpmate
through life—go back to a German root meaning "the
person one shares food with." Our word *meat* has the
same origin. As I mentioned before concerning the word
companion, sharing food was an important act in
yesteryear. It might involve a choice hunk of meat like
a *steak* (from the Norse for "stick" because it was
originally roasted on a spit) or a bit of *sausage* (from the
Latin *salsus,* meaning "salted"). I'll talk more about
food when I get to *mess.*

matrimony   Marriage has a history going back
thousands of years and began for many of the same
reasons it still exists today. From the early tribesman
who no longer wanted to share a certain woman with
the rest of the males of the tribe, to the father who
wanted his daughter protected after his death or who
used her as a bargaining chip to prevent continued
conflict with a rival chief, marriage is all mixed up in
love, security, and sex. Our words for it have different
beginnings, too. *Matrimony* originally referred to the
woman's side of the union, since the Latin root meant
"motherhood." *Marriage,* on the other hand, applied to
the man's vow and goes back to a Latin root meaning
"husband."

mattress   As society gets more civilized, beds get
softer or more luxurious. Tent-dwellers might just roll
up their mat every morning and fling it on the ground
at night with a simple woven blanket on top, but a
mansion-dweller may have a goosedown pillow, silk

sheets, and a plush mattress and box springs, or maybe even a water-filled bed. The word goes back to the Arabic term for "place where something is thrown." The hunters of the desert tossed their rugs or furs to the sand and slept where they lay.

mayday This international phrase of distress has nothing to do with the labor holiday or rite of spring. The month was never part of the origin of the word. Phonetics gave us the word's spelling, but the French gave us the first use of the expression: *m'aider,* meaning "give me aid" or "help me."

mediocre No one really wants to be average. Even if you said, "I'm just an average person," we'd probably feel you were putting yourself down. So *mediocre* is usually meant as a criticism, even though we know it means "average." In fact, this word from the Latin literally means "halfway up the mountain." You're not at the peak, but neither are you at the bottom. You've climbed to the middle, but there's a long way to go to reach the top.

menopause This word has gotten a lot of publicity in our open society, where premenstrual syndrome and impotence are the subjects of afternoon television. At one time you used euphemisms for things like this when speaking in polite society. You said, "She's going through the change of life," or "the change," or even the "climacteric," which suggests some kind of ending. The word's been around for centuries and has the same root as *menstrual,* a Greek word meaning not "blood" but "month," which the Romans took and passed on as usual. It came from the monthly cycle of the woman having to pause.

mess   Who hasn't seen the pile of dishes in the sink after a good meal and heard someone say, "I've got to clean up this mess"?

The French, who love their food, borrowed the word from the Romans, but *mess* first meant "a course of food." Each dish was a "mess," which we can still hear in the old-fashioned expression "a mess of greens." We also find the original use of the word onboard a ship,  where men of rank eat in the "officer's mess." But since the piles of dishes and utensils had to be cleaned and put up after all the courses were completed, the word started being associated with the aftermath and not the meal itself, and now applies to any state of confusion: "Look what a fine mess you've gotten us into."

miniature   In the 1200s and 1300s, before the printing press, the only way to get a copy of the Bible was to have a hand-copied version from the diligent monks of the many monasteries. But how boring to sit day in and day out, copying page after page! And especially if you were a sensitive young man with some artistic ability, which was a prerequisite for copying in beautiful script. To alleviate the boredom and give outlet to these talents, the monks were allowed to draw little pictures within the text using bright colors. One of the most widely used was *minium,* or red lead. That is where our word *miniature* comes from: "to color with red lead."

The word got linked with the smallness of the drawings and not with the color and became a particular style of painting. Now anything that is of tinier size than normal is called a miniature.

mirror Imagine the surprise that early man had seeing his own face reflected in a still pool of water. The Greek legend of Narcissus has him falling in love with his image. The original Latin root from which we get *mirror* did mean "to wonder at," in the sense of something wonderful. When the Old French took this root and applied it to a glass coated in melted silver, it was less of a wonder and meant, simply, "to look at." But the sense of amazement is still present in other words derived from the same root, like *miracle* ("something wonderful") and *admire*.

miser Though we don't appreciate the spendthrift who goes into debt through foolish buying sprees, we also dislike the stingy miser who hoards his money like a bitter Scrooge. We think of misers as wealthy cheapskates who, to preserve every penny, deprive even themselves and their families of everything but the bare essentials of survival. The Latin root means "wretched or unfortunate," which would seem to fit the case of the miser, even if a "fortune" was stored away somewhere.

mistletoe   The romantic tradition of demanding a kiss from one caught under this parasitic plant has a less-than-kissable origin. Literally, the word means "bird droppings on a twig." That's just how this evergreen, poisonous plant gets high in the trees with no climbing vines from the earth. Birds eat the white berries and leave their seeds behind on limbs, where they sprout and  grow. Early tribes thought these plants had some kind of magic to live and stay so green, high in bare oak trees during the depths of winter. To have a sprig in the home during that season was considered good luck. A woman under the sprig was extra good fortune, especially for the man who caught her there and wanted some of that good luck to rub off in the form of a kiss. Don't be under it at its initial planting, however.

molar   It's obvious that our twelve molars can do the job of grinding up just about any reasonable food below a coconut shell and above oatmeal. *Molar* is Latin for "millstone," but which came first: did the ancients name the teeth after the stone, or vice versa? Either way, the word is connected to grinding and has links in many languages, from *mallet* (the hammer that can crush) to *maul* to *immolate,* which is a fancy word for something killed or destroyed as a sacrifice. Why "sacrifice"? There was a tradition of sprinkling meal or flour on the animal that was to be burned at the altar, and that's what this word originally meant.

mongrel   This is generally not a nice term for the heritage of an animal or a human; it implies that the mixture of families or ethnic groups was not of the highest order. The word comes from well over a thousand years ago and simply meant "mixed" or "a crowd." From that same root we get the word *among.* There are crowds of us mixed breeds among the *blue bloods,* who get their name from the way their veins stand out in their pasty white complexions.

monkey   There's a great deal of argument as to where this word comes from. One theory is that the little simians looked like *monks,* with their brown hair shirts and shorn locks. We get the word *monk* from the Greek, meaning "alone or solitary" (the *monos* root is attached to many single things). Now, the Spanish have a word for a female ape, *mona,* that could be the origin of *monkey.* But a favorite theory is that the famous folktale "Reynard, the Fox" gave us the word from the son of the ape, Martin, whose name was Moneke.

mortgage   Most of us eagerly await the final mortgage payment, looking forward to that day when the bank no longer has any more claim to our property. But it sometimes seems as if that day will come long after we have passed on. "Dead pledge" is what the word meant in the Old French, and it was a promise given concerning who would get the property if the owner died. When banks and other lenders got into the business, it was *they* who held the ownership should something happen to the lendee. We see the roots of the word in other terms like *mortuary* (pertaining to burial) and *engagement* (a pledge of marriage, meeting, or employment).

mozzarella   Let's get back to more Italian food. This soft, white Italian cheese means "little slices," and this was the way it was often used to melt better on the cooked pasta or *pizza* (a word most say comes from the Italian for "point," but others say may be influenced by the German for "cake"). Make that wonderful crust, spread it with tomato sauce, pop on some *pepperoni* (Italian for cayenne pepper), top with mozzarella, and "Mama mia!" that's a meal!

mucketymuck   OK, we don't use this one very much anymore, but, speaking of food, that person of importance, that "high mucketymuck," got his name from the Chinook Indians of North America. Their expression meant "plenty to eat," which a mucketymuck should have, and that would definitely make him important. (Some people use *muckamuck,* but either way they're way off the Indian original.) *Muck,* our word for sticky mud, goes back to a Middle English root for "dung." That root is seen in the slang term for those reporters of the early 1900s who blew the whistle on political corruption or questionable business dealings: *muck-rakers.*

mug   Coffee and beer are today the two most common beverages drunk in a mug, but various kinds of liquid refreshment have been sipped from these drinking vessels for hundreds of years. *Mug* goes back to the Scandinavian root word for "pitcher or jug." But why is a police picture of a suspect or convict called a "mug shot"? It was a custom to make drinking tankards in the shape of the faces of ugly humans with grotesque facial expressions. So this was a way of indicating that this kind of picture wasn't for the cover of *GQ.*

mumbo jumbo   We hear this expression used most often for someone who is confusing us with a lot of double talk or meaningless activity. If you were an

African native of the Sudan and spoke Mandingo you might be glad to have what we have translated as *mumbo jumbo*. This was actually a witch doctor or priest who would say magic spells to make the troubled spirits of your ancestors go away and keep the village from evil. When slaves brought this kind of magical incantation to the Americas, most whites thought it was a bunch of nonsense, but they took their own spelling of the African word and used it for any kind of gibberish.

muscle   In an age of body building, muscles have become the goal of athlete and housewife alike. The word began as a comparison to an animal; not that those who had too many muscles looked like animals, but that the muscle under the skin looked like something alive unto itself. The Latin root means "little mouse."

musket   Speaking of comparisons to animals, although these common rifles of days gone by are now used only rarely by hunters or collectors, the origin of the name of this weapon joins it with the name for a pesky summertime bug. Both *mosquito* and *musket* go back to the same Latin root word for "fly." The later Italians actually named the arrow or bolt of the crossbow "the little fly," comparing its speed, sound, and ability to sting the enemy to the insect. The French honed the spelling of the word even more and used it for the shoulder gun. Though we think of musketeers as great swordsmen, the name was given to royal bodyguards in the 1600s and 1700s because they carried the rifles. Now, neither the smell of gunpowder nor the common connection of flies and odors has anything to do with *musk,* which is more than likely connected to the Persian for "testicle" because of the shape of the sac containing the gland that produced the odor in the musk deer that was so widely used for perfume.

mustard   This widely used condiment has a name that comes from the Latin for "new wine." Passed on from the French to their English subjects in the 1100s and 1200s, mustard paste was originally made by mixing grape juice with powdered mustard seeds. Dijon mustard still uses wine in its tangy recipe. Grapes were not part of the once everyday medical treatment of the mustard plaster. Mustard powder, flour, and water were spread on paper or cloth and used as a poultice for various congestions and illnesses. Don't blame the terrible gas used especially in World War I on the humble plant. Mustard gas was so named because it smelled like mustard, though it was purely chemical in nature.

mystery   Mysteries are popular pastimes for reading and watching, but not much fun to be a part of. Just misplace your car keys and see how much you enjoy the search. It's as if your brain has cotton stuffed in all its memory banks as you try to trace the steps back to the last clear recollection of where you placed those keys. The origin of the word lies in ancient Greece and religious initiation  rites. Literally, it meant "to close the eyes and mouth" and was a reminder to those being allowed to learn the secret rites that they should remain a secret. We get our words *mystic* and *mystical* from this religious origin. As the word made its way through time it got used for anything that was secret, unknown, or curious in explanation.

nag   When we hear of someone being nagged, we understand that there is another person who is whining or pestering or plaguing that person to do something, stop something, or get something. You'll notice I've avoided a gender reference, being stereotype-shy, but admit it: *Nag* is traditionally a woman's title. Did it come from the name for a racehorse gone to seed: the nag? No, that horsey slang goes back to a Germanic word imitative of the sound of the horse, from which we also get *neigh*.

nasturtium   This fancy name for a common garden flower makes it sound as if we are quoting from a botany book and its list of scientific names. What you're actually saying when you name this plant is "nose pain." That was the Latin nickname for this edible, candy-colored flower and its petals. That's because plants like this (and like mustard, which we've already talked about), can cause a burning sensation in the schnozz when eaten. You who love Chinese mustard know this very well.

nasty   When you've been nasty you might have said some nasty things, maybe about the nasty weather or a

nasty fall, but however it occurred, you are like a bird's
nest if you go back to the old Dutch sense of the word.
Certainly not all bird's nests are nasty, but those that
are covered in droppings and mess couldn't be very
pleasant places to live, and it makes a good comparison
to someone or something that is foul (terrible pun!),
either physically or morally.

nausea   Those of you who have faced the first day of a
cruise staring at the water over the railing, watching
your lunch fade in the distance, can relate to the Greek
beginnings of this word, which meant "seasickness."
You'll find its root in *nautical*. The Romans borrowed
the word, as they did so many others, changing the *naus*
("ship") to navis, and you can guess all the words we get
from that. We get the word *noise* from the same Greek
word for "ship," although it was the Romans who took
the word for barfing at sea and applied it to any unpleasant situation, which is what a lot of noise can be. The
French changed the spelling to our present-day word
for din and clamor.

ninny   It used to be common to call a fool a "ninny," but
we don't hear it as much these days, not because there
aren't still one or two fools around. . . . We've just got so
many new words for the breed, from *nerd* to *nimrod*. My
last hearing of *ninny* was with someone berating
another's courage: "Don't be such a ninny. You can do
it!" The word comes from a nickname for Innocent,
which was a common first name a thousand or so years
ago (look at the list of popes). The real meaning of the
word got mixed into the batter, and *ninny* came to mean
a simple, inexperienced person, likely to do foolish
things out of ignorance.

nitpick You always seem to hear this word with three others: "I hate to . . ." You *would* hate to do what the word originally meant: "to pick little lice off someone." A nit is the egg or young of a louse and so, in saying you are nit-picking, you indicate that you're aware of the tiniest things that can nevertheless be very bothersome. Having a nitpicker could be helpful. Who wants nits?

noble In the days when a publicist's job was a nightmare, without TV cameras, tabloids, or *People* magazine, the only way to be a celebrity was by word of mouth. The best way to be talked about in the days of Roman glory was to perform daring deeds on the battlefield or make brave speeches in the Senate. *Noble* at its outset simply meant "knowable." But since doing good was the best way to be known, this meaning got attached to the word. . . . Not like *notorious,* which comes from a less attractive root meaning "to be acquainted with." Someone who was notorious was usually famous for something not so good. They were someone you might make note of, but not talk about with much honor.

noon How times change. Originally, "noon" was at 3 P.M. The word comes from the Latin for "ninth" and referred to the ninth hour after sunrise. Early Catholics reserved this hour for prayer. Spanish Catholics found this time convenient for a *siesta* (Spanish for "sixth") and moved noon up to the sixth hour after sunrise to tie in with the midday meal and a nap afterward. *Noon* soon became associated with the middle of the day, when the sun was at its highest and the sundial cast no shadow. When timepieces became more accurate, that middle spot in the twenty-four-hour day became our present "noon." I talked about the Roman calendar earlier and told that the fifteenth day or thirteenth day, depending on the month, was called the "ides." Well, the ninth day of the month was also called the "noon." Another word from the original Latin for nine is *November,* which was the ninth month in the old Roman calendar. We kept the name, even if it is in the eleventh spot. You see, times *do* change. Oh, and from that you Catholics get your *novena,* prayers and devotions said for nine days in a row.

normal   Joe Brainard said, "If I'm as normal as I think I am, we're all a bunch of weirdos." Is there such a thing as "normal"? Yes, if you're talking about the original Latin use of the word for a carpenter's square. This handy tool could make sure your walls were at solid right angles and that everything was even and balanced. If it was "made according to the carpenter's square," it was normal. That "norm" could be used to make patterns so that everything was alike and would fit together. The word began to be used for anything that was standard, usual, typical, and level. It's interesting that the slang for a very "normal" person who does nothing risky or outside the rules is "square."

nostalgia   This is a Greek combination that means "homecoming pain" or "homesickness" and was invented at a time when many *were* far from their homes and felt the ache of yearning for days past, when the family was gathered in peace. It was during the Revolutionary War that this word got commonly used for this sadness, and it was actually employed by doctors for what today might be called battle fatigue. Nostalgia was an actual illness that was diagnosed by the physicians of the day. The word has lost its medical sense today but still carries with it a sense of longing for that which is gone. We can find medical terms that contain part of this word, such as *neuralgia,* which means "nerve pain."

nozzle The end of a hose or some other kind of spraygun is called a nozzle, which means "little nose." We don't look down our nose at comparing things to the nose, but the image can be gross when we "pay through the nose." We don't like it if the market takes a nose dive, but we won't turn up our noses when someone has made a bet that is on the nose. And if a bunch of flowers makes your nose happy, you can call it a nosegay. I just wanted to lead you by the nose through a few things I nosed out.

nucleus This word is so linked with science and the atom and cell that it's hard to imagine the simple beginnings of this word, which goes back to the Latin for "nut." That's right, a nucleus was the kernel of a nut, though now it can be anything about which others are centrally grouped. It might be nice if nuclear energy came from the cracking of a pecan.

nun Originally, in the Middle Ages this was a respect-ful form of address for an older woman, though it probably came from baby talk. *Nonna* was the Latin, which got transformed into *nunne* and finally *nun.* Because there was such great respect for women who went into religious orders, the word came to focus on these special individuals. The child-oriented start of this word can still be seen in the name for the English children's nurse: *nanny*.

O

oaf This word for a stupid or clumsy person is not used as much as it once was, but its origin is full of magic and mystery. Among the old Norse tribes the birth of a deformed child was not only sad, it was embarrassing to the father and mother and their proud clan, even more so when the child seemed normal at birth and then, as the years passed, turned out to be retarded or physically handicapped  in some way. Their explanation? The elves had come and stolen the human baby and replaced it with a changeling. *Oaf* in its first form meant "elf" or "goblin." This belief also made people less likely to harm the child, knowing it was from the fairy people, though they might superstitiously avoid it.

oasis   Very few Egyptian words are brought into our language, but here is one we're all familiar with. The Greeks imported it in ancient times, and we know it as a fertile place in the midst of desolation. It meant simply "dwelling area," which certainly fits, since it's the best place to live in a desert land. Today it's any refuge from the hustle and bustle of the world.

oblige   When that cowpoke in the old Western takes that drink from the dipper of water offered by a bold beauty of the prairie and says, "Much obliged, Ma'am," we translate it as "Thank you." The first Latin uses of the word were much more serious. *Oblige* literally meant "to tie to" or "to bind." When you were obliged to someone you had a legal or moral tie to them. We get that feeling more with the word *obligation.* The word for that tough strip of tissue binding bones together, *ligament,* also contains the early root word.

obstetric   "She who is present" would be a translation of this word from the original Latin, *obstetrix,* or "midwife." Birthing babies was women's work in ancient times and the midwife was a respected occupation, many times held by a wise old woman with no fear of a malpractice suit. Death in childbirth was just one of the many risks in raising a family and was rarely a case for legal disputes, as it has become today.

odd   The Norse gave us this word for the peculiar. All it was to begin with was their name for the third point of a triangle. Since it was the third, it was the odd angle, and the word began to be used for other things besides numbers that didn't quite divide up right, from the odd sock to the oddball. Today the odds are that you'll find oddities make great tourist attractions, though having just odds and ends could leave you the odd man out.

oil With our society still dependent on fossil fuels, oil is the economy's lubricant as well as your car's. The Greeks gave us the word thousands of years ago when their precious oil came from pressing olives. The root from which we get *oil* is Greek for "olive." You wonder if the Popeye cartoonists studied their word origins. . . . Of course, today we have so many oils, from vegetable oil to *petroleum* (from Medieval Latin: "rock oil") to that old-fashioned word for margarine, *oleo* (originally "oleomargarine," from the French "pearl-colored oil").

omelette This popular way of fixing eggs comes from the French, as you probably already knew, but the word itself was taken from the Latin name for a thin metal plate. Since the beaten eggs looked like that before they were folded over the cheese, meat, or other goodies, the name stayed with the dish as the English learned the recipe.

onion It must have fascinated early Roman gardeners to be able to peel layer after layer of this bulb, finding another smaller version beneath. The name they gave the plant apparently reflected this, because the root from which we get this word meant "union or oneness" and is the same root for *union.* This was such a different kind of bulb from the *garlic,* which came in cloves and got its name from the Old English for "spear leek" because of its tall, spearlike stalks. Leeks, onions, garlic, and *shallots* have been popular foods for ages. Shallots and *scallions,* which are taken before the bulbs enlarge, were named for a place. The Romans called these "onions of Ascalon," which was a port city in southern Palestine.

opera   Of course, Italy gives us this word for the grand musical drama, but its Latin root simply meant "work." Well, anyone who's ever been through a rehearsal schedule, especially for an opera, knows it is truly a labor. Words like *operate* and *opus,* and other brothers and sisters of these, come from the same humble beginning.

opossum   These strange, tree-dwelling, pouch-packing night-roamers have an ugly-looking set of teeth and a ratlike tail that helps them hang from a limb. Even the Indians didn't think they were too cute, calling them "white beast," from the white fur on their faces. This translation from the Algonquian stayed with the critters, and you'll even find that some breeds of these  marsupials living in Australia are called opossums. Though they seem slow-witted, as evidenced by those that didn't get out of the way of cars on the highway, they have a protective behavior that's allowed them to avoid being dinner for larger beasts. No predator likes to eat something that's already dead; they want to kill it themselves. So 'possums pretend to be dead when they sense this kind of threat. Even the cartoon character Pogo was a critter who knew the value of playing 'possum.

opportunity   "Opportunity knocks; temptation beats down the door." If opportunity knocked back

when Roman sailors first used the word, you'd hear the
blowing wind at the door. This was their word for a
favorable breeze, one that was blowing "toward the port
or harbor." You wouldn't have to spend time fighting
the wind trying to get to the dock, and so it was good
fortune and something you should take advantage of.
From seafaring use it was an easy step to apply the
word to any set of circumstances that came at the right
time and in the right place.

orangutan   I first thought this name for the ape of
Malaysia had to do with its coloration: "orange and
tan." But I learned that we English-speakers took the
word from a Malay phrase: "man of the forest." These
fellows have the reputation of being the most intelligent of the simians next to man and show up as buddies
of actors in various movies, generally outperforming
their co-stars. *Orange* goes all the way back to the
Sanskrit and was the name for the fruit even in ancient
times, driving poets looking for rhymes mad then, too.

orchestra   It would look strange if you went to a
symphony hall and saw the dignified musicians in their
gowns and tuxedoes suddenly get up and begin cavort-
ing with their cellos, boogying with their bassoons, and
frolicking with their French horns. . . . The word
orchestra, in the Greek, meant "to dance." It was the
name of a part of the theater, a little semicircle in front
of the stage where the chorus danced. As music got
more refined this space was used by the players of
instruments, and the word got applied to the group
itself. When the group was shielded from the audience
by a wall, or was set at a lower level, it got put in the
"pit." The French called this area the *parquet,* which
meant "little park," and we later applied that word to a
kind of wood inlay in floors because of the way they
made the floor of this section of the theater.

orientation Thousands of college students or new employees go through a formal orientation, getting them acquainted with their new surroundings and responsibilities. If they took the meaning of the word literally, they would be learning to face east. It's actually an architectural term that was used in building churches, which were designed so that the altar would be on the east side of the structure with the church aligned east to west. This same Latin root gave us our name for the Far East, the *Orient*. And that most eastern part of Cuba where Castro had his first stronghold is called Oriente.

Ouija Though many fundamentalist religions frown on using this board, which is thought by some to communicate with the spirit world, its name has a very positive translation. It's actually a trademark name combining the French for "yes," *oui,* with the German for "yes," *ja.* For some this is just an amusing way to touch knees with a member of the opposite sex, but for others the board has been a source of intense interest, belief, and guidance.

outlandish Though we don't use this word for outrageous or odd things as much as we used to, I like it as an old-fashioned way of saying "far out" (which has also gotten old-fashioned). It originated simply from a way of describing foreigners whose behavior sometimes didn't fit the customs of the lands they were visiting. They were from "out of this land," and so were likely to be weird.

owl The bird noted for its wisdom actually gets its name from its sometimes scary night calls. The Old English term for this night hunter meant "howl." A pretty simple beginning for the name of this creature, which got its reputation for wisdom from the Greeks.

They made it the bird of Athena, who was the goddess of wisdom.

oyster   Although it's the muscle inside the shell that we mainly refer to as the oyster, the Greeks named it for its hard exterior, using their word for "bone." From the same root we get the name for the much-publicized disease *osteoporosis,* as well as many other medical "bone" words.

ozone   Speaking of publicity, ozone has probably had more written about it in the past several years than in its whole prior existence, what with the constant talk of holes in the ozone layer of the atmosphere. If you've ever smelled that strong aroma when an electrical wire shorts out, it's not just melted insulation you're sniffing. Ozone is created not only by the sun's rays and their effect on oxygen, but also by air passing through an electrical discharge. The smell gives it its name, which comes from a Greek root for a reeking odor.

pageant   Though most of us think of pageants involving pretty girls parading before judges in displays of fashion and talent, the first pageants were religious in nature and were little dramas used by the church in medieval times to explain God's ways or to tell Bible stories. The word comes from the Latin and meant "a scene in a play." Later, historical dramas that tried to show the events of a certain time period were also called pageants. Finally, the beauty pageant seemed to take over the word.

pajamas The Persians passed this name for loose-fitting trousers on to the Hindu language, where the British found it and absorbed it. Among the Persians and Indians, it was popular for both sexes to change from more formal garments into something less restrictive for casual entertaining, for loung-ing, or for sleep. The more demure English took the fashion and used it more strictly for  sleepwear. If they'd taken the word strictly, we'd only wear the pants of the pyjamas (as the British spell the word), since the original word meant "leg garment."

pal The *Gypsies* are an unusual people who in their wanderings through Europe have been persecuted as much as the Jews, and with much less fanfare. Most of us in America have only seen them in werewolf movies, when the strange wagons with the exotic women and musical but mysterious men come drifting in. Now, I'm getting to *pal,* a word they gave us, but first, where did these folk come from? They were called Gypsies because it was believed they were outcasts from Egypt. But that was not their origin. They called themselves the Romany, and some interpreted that as meaning they were from Romania. Though many did wander along the Black Sea, this was not their place of birth either. It

seems there has been racial warfare since the beginning
of time, and legend has it that when the light-skinned
Aryans swept into what is now India, they enslaved the
darker-skinned Dravidians, who were the natives of
the land. Many Dravidians fled to wander homeless for
generation after generation, scorned by those they
traded with because of their dark and mysterious past
and strange culture. *Romany* came from a Sanskrit
word for a man from a low caste of musicians, and from
the same root we get a name for a drum, the tom-tom.
Pal was a Gypsy word for "brother" or "mate." In the
tight-knit troupe of the Romany, the whole clan was
considered family as they palled around the countryside. The word has come into our language with a
gentle, endearing feeling attached to it.

pall   This word has mainly been associated with
funerals, as the cloth (generally velvet) that is put over
the coffin. We also hear it used in other ways, for a
covering or darkening in phrases like "a pall of smoke
crossed the battlefield" or "a pall of sadness covered the
congregation." In its first uses, it referred to a cloak
worn by the pope, which was given to him by the
bishops and archbishops, and it got its name from a
cloak worn by Romans. Later the Church called the
cloth that covered the chalice used in communion a
pall, and this is the sense we have when we cover the
coffin, cloaking the remains of the departed.

pamphlet   In our day the pamphlet has become a
wide-ranging publication that includes everything
from guides to vacation spots to advertising for cars,
stores, or food. These little *brochures* (and this word
comes from the French for "a stitching" because of the
way the pages were loosely sewn together) are
everywhere you look. They originated in the 1100s and

were short Latin love poems. The *pamphilus* were very popular ways of making a quick impression on one who'd caught your eye. Pamphlets were actually different from brochures because they were unbound, merely folded. Political writers found this form a quick, easily distributed and inexpensive way to speak out on issues, and the pamphleteers of later years wrote anything but love poems.

pandemonium Though the word is from the Greek language, it was actually made up by an Englishman. We use the word today for a situation of confusion, uproar, and noise, but it first appeared in John Milton's *Paradise Lost* in the 1600s and was the capital of hell. When Satan and his fellow rebel angels were cast out of heaven after their revolution failed, they built a huge residence, Pandemonium, so they could meet and plan their guerrilla action up on earth to mess up God's creation. It translates as "place for all demons."

pants I probably could have talked about *pants* with *pajamas,* but the origin of this word has many pockets, so I'll hang it in a separate spot and not wrinkle it in with another word. Unzipping the roots of this word carries us back to the early days of Venice, Italy. It was a tradition for towns, villages, and countries to have their patron saints, just as in pagan times there were  household gods and goddesses. St. Patrick was Ireland's

protector, and in Venice it was St. Pantaleone, a
physician who was killed in 305 A.D. as a Christian
martyr. This was actually a nickname for his coura-
geous character, meaning "all lion." Venetians prided
themselves on their courage, and "Pantalone" got to be
a name for any person from Venice, like a "Hoosier"
(from "Who's here?") is a person from Indiana. Now,
with the travels of that great Venetian Marco Polo the
city began to get a reputation as a merchant city, full of
traders in goods from around the world. This kind of
business focus gave rise to jokes about stinginess and
bargaining, which spread from Italy through the
commedia dell'arte of the 1500s. Here one of the stock
characters was the gullible old father, almost always a
skinny, slippered Venetian merchant, who was the butt
of pranks and about to lose his pretty daughter. His
name was Pantalone, after the nickname for the
Venetian. He wore the large, baggy trousers that we
still see on the circus clowns of today. Yes, here we are
at the origin of our word's current meaning. The
breeches themselves took on the name *pantaloons,* but
got tightened up a bit. The word got shortened to our
present-day *pants,* which gets used not just for the
trousers but also for the underpants and panties of
modern wear. This whole thing has got me *panting* . . .
which, by the way, comes from a Greek root meaning
"to show." That same root gives us *phantom,* when a
spirit shows itself. When the breath comes out in a little
misty fog, it, too, "shows."

parade   It sometimes surprises me that these displays
of flower-strewn floats, waving beauties, and marching
bands are still so popular, but it seems that everyone
loves a parade and it makes perfect entertainment
while you're waiting for the turkey to cook and the
football game to begin. The word has a military origin

and comes from the Spanish, through a Latin root meaning "to prepare." It was the place to exercise the troops, and we still hear of the "parade grounds."

paraphernalia   These days the word has gotten so attached to the world of drug busts that many think of it only in that context. It does have a legal origin, however. It was a tradition that when a woman got married she brought with her a dowry, money, or goods that became the husband's property after the vows. In some cases the size of this dowry became a factor in getting the girl married off. And if she left the husband or died, this property was legally his. All she could take with her, or that her side of the family could take if she died, was the *paraphernalia,* which was Greek for "beyond the dowry" and included clothing, gifts she'd received, and other personal goods of the household that she might have purchased. With divorce being a rarity, the man had just about all the say over the possessions of his estate. Now, if *he* died, the widow received the dower, which was at least a part of his estate. In the days when entering a convent was much more popular than it is today, the Catholic Church required that candidates seeking admission pay a sum of money as a symbolic marriage sum for Christ, also called a dowry.

parasite   The Greek meaning of this word was "fellow guest." One who was going to share your food was a *parasitos,* which literally meant "beside the grain." The traditions of ancient Greek hospitality were abused, as are many generous ideals, and it became common to see professional dinner guests roaming from household to household, exploiting the notion that you could not turn someone away from your table if there was enough to feed him. These abusers led to the word getting a less-than-friendly feeling attached to it. It later got applied to anyone who took advantage of another's generosity. When biology got hold of it the word turned scientific on us, but still carried the old connotation of taking something without giving in return.

parasol   We don't use this word for the fancy umbrella much any more, but it's interesting, since it was the first form of sunglasses. The *para* part of the word is not from the Greek for "beside" or "beyond" but from the Old Italian, meaning "a shield," from which we get a word like *parry*, the defensive move in fencing. And the *sol* part is the name of the sun in Latin. We get words like *solstice* and *solar* from the same root, to name just a few.

parka   On the subject of protection from the elements, this word has gotten a lot of use in recent years as a type of hooded coat good for winter wear. It comes from the Russians, who got it from the Laplanders of the Samoyed tribes of the tundra regions near Finland. It means "the skin of a reindeer," which was the key ingredient in making the heavy fur coats. The Eskimos got the word from them and we brought it into English from there.

parlor   It once was common to have a little room in the house where we would entertain visitors. A young man would sit with a girl *and* her mother there in the parlor, where the spider also welcomed the fly. The very first parlors were confession or audience chambers in monasteries for those outside the cloister (from the French *parle*, "to speak"). Much later it applied to any room equipped for some special purpose, like an ice cream parlor . . . and the place where conversation is a major part of the business, the beauty parlor. A "parlor radical" talked a good game.

parole   Once again, the French love of words gives us this term, which means "word of honor" or simply "word." When a prisoner is released early he must give his word that the good behavior he exhibited behind bars will continue outside the walls of jail. In our day the promise seems less a part of the release than the mere need for space. This word for "word" also turns up in the military, where a "parole" can be a password used by a guard or officer of the day. Part of this root can be seen in *parable*, which literally refers to "throwing words beside," in other words, making a story for comparison.

partridge   The Christmas carol about the partridge in the pear tree may take on a different meaning when you realize the name for this bird is a humorous allusion to the whirring sound of its wings when it is flushed from cover. Its name means "to break wind," which to the old game-bird hunter was exactly how the flutter of the birds in flight sounded . . . like someone with gas.

pave   For the Romans, making a good road meant beating down the bumps and filling in the holes and stamping them flat. *Pave* comes from the Latin "to strike or stamp." The famous cobblestones were their main pavement and there are still Roman roads in use to this day. *Asphalt* in its earliest days was a binding agent like pitch used in stonemasonry and meant in the Greek "to cause not to fall."

pavilion   Tents have been vital throughout history when armies had to be mobile and needed temporary shelter. The fancier tents especially popular at jousts and other knightly events got their name from the Old French word for "butterfly" because the ornate flaps of the entrances looked like butterfly wings. Today the word is used for everything from open shelters at parks or fairs to a summer house to a building annex.

pay   Having all the bills paid does bring a sense of peace, doesn't it? Well, that's the first way this word was used. It came from the Latin root for "peace" and first appeared in medieval France, when the economy was beginning to move in a free-market direction. To pay someone was to give that person satisfaction of some kind, whether through money, goods traded, or services rendered. The word conveyed a sense of satisfaction for work done.

peddler   In this age of abundant shopping centers and malls, the days of the roving peddler, who brought his odds and ends into town for sale, are just about over. At one time, though, these salesmen were welcome in rural regions, where they sold hard-to-find household items for the kitchen or for clothes-mending and gardening. The first of these travelling *hawkers* (which comes from a German root meaning "to bend," as with a load on one's back) carried all the goods they could in covered baskets, which they bore on their shoulders. *Peddle* comes from the name of the basket itself, used in the twelfth and thirteenth centuries.

pedigree   I think of dogs when I hear this word, though occasionally it's used when snobbishly speaking of your ancestry. It actually means "crane's foot" in its earliest French, from the shape of the first family trees that people used in showing their line of descent. That's kind of a *pedestrian* ("on foot") word for those trying to put themselves on a *pedestal* ("foot of a stall"—because it holds it up).

pelvis   Bones get named for crazy reasons, like the coccyx of your backside being so named because it is shaped like the beak of a cuckoo. The pelvis gets its name from the Latin for "basin" or "cup," once again because of the shape. Elvis made many a young girl go a bit cuckoo when he shook his. . . .

pen   This word goes back to the Latin root for "feather." For hundreds of years that was the very best material for a writing instrument. Take a quill and slice off the end at an angle and dip it in some staining fluid and you could record your marks. The word for what your baseball team wants to win, the *pennant,* goes back to the same root because these flags are shaped like feathers. *Pencil,* on the other hand, has a more crude origin and literally meant "little penis." This wasn't because of any comparison between the writing instrument and a man's sex organ, but because the Latin *penis* was the word for a tail and the first use of the word *pencil* was for artist's brushes made from fine hair, usually from the tail hairs of animals.

penetrate   In many of the temples of Rome there was a special room where food was stored for sacrifice and for the priests and initiates. To go into that room for food was to "penetrate," from the Latin root for the interior of a building. You had gotten to the inner sanctuary if you had penetrated. The word still conveys the sense of entering a defended or reserved place, whether it's referring to a running back penetrating the defense or a hypnotist with penetrating eyes.

penguin   It's believed that the Welsh gave these birds their name, from two words in their tongue meaning "white head." This was not because penguins have particularly white heads; most of them are black. It's thought to come from a white headland, a snow-covered place on a North Atlantic island where penguins were first found. The place itself gave these seabirds the name.

penny   Cloth was a valuable item to ancient man, and what was valuable could be traded and exchanged for other things. Just like the buckskin we spoke of earlier, hunks of cloth were a medium of exchange in uncivilized Europe. From a Latin word the Germanic tribes gave a name to those pieces of cloth that later made its way into English as *penny*. When money got a bit more standardized, the penny got to be a small fraction of a pound. Some think the expression "pay a pretty penny" may go all the way back to the cloth, where the most attractive was the most valuable, but pinching pennies and being penny-wise but pound-foolish refer to the later coin. These days a penny for your thoughts won't buy much. . . .

pep   We think of someone with pep as being active, full of energy, raring to go. The word actually comes from a shortening of *pepper* and first applied to someone who was hot-tempered or was a saucy soul. This type of person was likely to be energetic and lively, and eventually the word was associated with vim and vigor and lost some of its original peppery qualities.

perfume   If we talk about fumes, we usually don't think of pleasant fragrances. Instead, we think of gas fumes or fumes from a fire. But one kind of early fume that did smell nice was incense, used in temples and later in the Catholic Church. You've seen the priest waving a censer down the aisle, wafting sweet smoke through the pews. When man discovered that certain woods and resins could remove some of the awful odors from the ancient home, he had his first air freshener. These aromatic gums and plants were very valuable to early man. Consider that two of the three gifts of the Magi were kinds of incense: myrhh and frankincense. *Incense* came through the Latin to the French and meant "to set fire to," while *perfume* was "to spread smoke through." Not everything comes off smelling like a rose in the origins of these words. Heat and temper get mixed in when we say that people who are hot under the collar are incensed, while those who think about their anger are fuming. It makes "cense."

person Such a common word for any living human being actually goes back to a nonliving thing. The Latin start for this word meant "mask," one worn by an actor on stage. The mask rep- resented a type of individual in the early plays, like the hero or the villain, and the word got used for the kinds of people you'd find off the stage as well. Their *personality* was the mask they wore  when dealing with the world. I don't want to get too personal, but do we have a personality when there is no one to see us? Oh, the drama of the thing got to me.

pester "Stop pestering me!" the mother says to the insistent child. We know the young 'un has probably been pleading for that candy bar or extra hour outside.

If the mother was using the word in its first sense she might add, "or I'll pester you." More than likely, the word had its origins on the farm and meant "to tie up an animal in the pasture." The Latin root closest to this was passed into the French and dealt with handling unruly animals. I talked about *harass* already. That word went from animal husbandry to being used on humans, and so did *pester*. Along the way we've associated the word with *pest,* but that word goes back to a different root meaning "plague" in the Latin. Since many plagues were started by insects, maybe that's why we say, "Quit bugging me!" Back to grazing for a moment, the *pastor* of the church gets his title from "pasture." He is the shepherd of the flock, bringing them a Godly cud to chew.

petticoat   When the French ruled England after the Norman Conquest (1066), they brought their laws, language, and customs. We've talked about this throughout *Where in the Word?* That they gave us some of their fashions, too, is just normal since the English who wanted to survive had to try to please these French aristocrats. Wearing the "little coat" under a dress may not have actually been the tradition of these Normans, but eventually women found the notion of layered undergarments practical and attractive. These cheaper clothes were easier to wash than the expensive dress, so they could wear the dress time and time again between cleanings and just scrub the petticoats. Besides, the undergarments made their waists look slimmer and their hips look sexier . . . at least for the times. As things go, this feminine habit got to be slang for a girl or woman: "Look at this fine petticoat." And something run by women was also given the underwear label, as in "a petticoat government." So now you're saying, "Aha! They probably call a slender female a 'slip of a girl' because slips made her look much thinner than a petticoat did!" Well, a "slip" was also a slender piece of a plant used for rooting or grafting. Now I'm getting petty.

pharmacy Could the good old drug store be a place of witchcraft? In ancient Greece that's what you might have found. The "just say no" policy in those days was based on the fact that you really could get poisoned from certain plants. But you could get well, too, and certain persons made their living making potions and cures, as well as poisons and aphrodisiacs. Since trees and plants were thought to be inhabited by nature spirits like dryads and hamadryads, there was a magic associated with using plants for medicine. As we got more practice and knowledge, *pharmacy* became more linked with science . . . but beware the druggist with a caldron in the back.

philodendron Plants must certainly feel good about our habit of giving them fancy Greek and Roman names. It makes them sound so important. Because many of these pretty houseplants have kinfolk that are seen climbing trees in the tropics, they got this Greek name meaning "lover of trees." The *phil* that conveys that non-romantic love is found all over the place, from the lover of wisdom, the *philosopher* (I'll tell you about sophomores later), to those lovers of the joined and agreeing sounds of the *philharmonic,* to those that love flirting, the *philanderers* (this actually means "a lover of men or one's husband," but a mistake was made in the adoption from the Greek and a different meaning was applied).

phony No one likes a phony, whether it comes in the shape of a person or merchandise. The word has nothing to do with telephone sales pitches. It was originally *fawny,* which was a name for a kind of ring that swindlers used to trick the gullible. It was dipped in gold and made heavy with a cheap metal interior, and then passed off as solid gold. You'll still see this kind of jewelry being sold today, but with somewhat more honesty, described as "layered in gold" or "flashed in gold" and occasionally, "gilded."

piano This word for the versatile musical instrument is a shortening of its original name. The Italians called it the *pianoforte,* meaning "soft and loud." Such a wonderful thing it was to invent something that took the idea of the harp but allowed the player to strike the strings rather than pluck them, making them loud and clear or soft and quiet depending on the action of pedals and fingers. Both parts of the original name are also used as musical directions in scores, letting all the instruments know how softly or strongly a passage is to be played.

pickle There is argument as to the origin of this word for the process of preserving in brine and vinegar. Some say it comes from the Dutch for "that which pricks the nose," while others claim it might have originated with a Dutch fisherman, William Beukelz, who is credited with coming up with the recipe. We don't call them beukels, but if you've been following, you know how words get changed

along the way, so either history has some logic to it. Before I get in a pickle about this word's creation, at least we know the Dutch were steeped in it.

picnic   The French gave us this name for the pleasant pastime that has brought romantic humans together with obliging ants. "To pick a little, to trifle a bit, perhaps to nap" all seem to be part of this word's origin, and all seem to fit the tradition of enjoying the outdoors with a bit of food, a few wildflowers, and a little lying about.

pied   All right, I realize we don't use this word much, but I was curious why we called that piper of Hamelin "pied." Was he fond of cherry cobbler? No, the *pie* is related to the bird, the magpie. *Pied* referred to its color, black and white, while *Mag* was a nickname for Margaret and was also the name of a chatterbox in many proverbs. The bird's constant twitterings earned it the "Mag." Woodpeckers got their first name, the Latin *pica,* from the same root that described their patches of color. But back to the Pied Piper: Apparently his costume was one of multiple, motley colors, almost like the jesters of old.

piggyback   This word has nothing to do with little pigs riding about on your shoulders. It's a variation of *pickaback,* which was originally probably *pick a pack.* In other words, it was like picking up a pack and putting it on your back, and it makes sense that over the years it would get fooled with and put in animal terms, since little children are most often the riders in the piggyback game. The pigs are probably scratching their heads, though. . . .

pilot   We most often think of airplanes these days when we speak of pilots, though we still call the steering area onboard ship the pilot house. The sea is where the word got its start. The Greeks were well-known fishers and sailors, and guiding their boats through rough waves and reefs demanded both skill and a strong rudder. The first rudder was merely a long oar put in the back of the boat. That was the "pilot," not nearly the original Greek word, but as adapted by the Italians, then the French, then us.

pine   How are pine trees and fat related? Well, that's what the word that is now *pine* meant in Latin. The tree got its name from the resin that came from cuts and lightning strikes and looked like the fat of an animal, yellowish and flammable. Now, when we say someone is pining for his or her long-lost love, we go to another root from the Greek from which we get *pain* and *penalty* and *penal* system. And the longing lover does feel the agony of imprisoned emotion. . . . But *pineapple* does go back to the tree, this time over a thousand years after the tree got its name. Pineapple wasn't named for any reference to fat, but for the fruit's resemblance to a pine cone. In fact the first name for the pineapple was the pine cone.

pinkie   We've all heard our littlest finger called the "pinkie" and, if you were like me before I started looking into it, you probably thought it had something to do with the color, though it's no pinker than the rest. What I found out is that the tiniest digit got its name from a Dutch canal boat. In Holland it's common to see these very thin-hulled boats being poled or motored in the narrow channels of their many canals. Because the littlest finger is the skinniest, it apparently reminded them of the boat and got that nickname. OK, now you want to know why the index finger is called the index, right? *Index* was actually the Latin name for the forefinger and also meant "indicator." Later on, other things that guide got the name attached to them.

pioneer   This word that we link to the brave settlers and explorers of new lands and frontiers comes to us from the Old French and was first used for foot soldiers who were sent out ahead of the main body of troops to clear the way. If a bridge had been damaged by the enemy, they'd rebuild it. If a path needed hacking, they'd hack it. These men were low on the military totem pole but were important to its success. That they weren't highly respected is reflected in the fact that part of the root of their name comes from a Latin word meaning "one with big feet," from which the Spanish gave us *peon*.

pipe   It might carry the water or sewage, or it might carry exhaust from a car or truck. In any case, the pipe is an important part of everyday life. The origin of the word is musical and was an imitative Latin word for "chirp," like a bird. *Peep* might be a word we're more familiar with along these lines. When the first reed or cane was made into a flute, the sound it made was compared to a

bird's song, and so the imitative word was applied to the tube that made the sound.

pirate   This word has a simple enough origin. It comes from the Greek and means "attacker." Since most Greek commerce was by sea, bandits and robbers usually came on ships, and so the word was associated with seagoing thieves. Nowadays we also use the word for those who copy another's art without permission.

pity   Our modern sense of compassion that we call pity has an almost negative feeling in our use of it: "I don't want your pity!" or "Isn't it a pity?" The word goes back to the Old French and referred to an allotment of food for a monk, given because of his *piety*. It was his *pittance*. Having concern for the misfortune or low fortunes of anyone began to be associated with this pittance, and *pity* became more an emotional attitude than a loaf of bread, though most in need would rather have the dough than the pity.

plumber   Lead's Latin name is *plumbum* and the first plumbers were lead workers. Since this was an easy-to-work, long-lasting metal, the first pipes and drains were made of lead, well before the dangers of lead poisoning were publicized. These lead workers were the ones who made the pipes and later went in to repair them, and so you had the first plumbers as we know them, but not quite at $50 an hour. When we "plumb the depths" we refer back to an ancient device that was simply a string with a piece of lead on the end used to measure depths because the weight of the lead wasn't likely to be pulled as easily by a current.

polecat   In America we call a skunk a polecat, but the original name comes from Europe and was applied to the weasel. This tricky creature would sneak into the barnyard and create havoc. His love of poultry dishes got him the French name *poule chat,* or "chicken cat."

Somewhere along the line, the name was given to the smelly North American beast, perhaps because the European weasel that was called the polecat had darker fur than some weasels found here, more of the coloration of the skunk. And by the way, the skunk gets its name from the Massachusetts tribe of Indians, and it bascially meant "little mammal who urinates," derived from the awful spray of the offended Pepé Le Pew. The notion that this little character could defend itself against much larger predators was applied to sports when one team was overwhelmingly defeated by another. They were "skunked." Of course, to cheat someone, especially by not paying a debt, is also called "skunking," and here losing also stinks.

poll   This is an age of poll-takers, surveying us for our favorite toothpaste as well as our politics. The Dutch term for "the top of the head" gives us the word, and the first polling was merely a counting of heads. Now, when democracy was first getting under way, large landowners who used to be the powerful aristocrats felt angry about having to pay property tax while at the same time adhering to "one man, one vote." So there were poll taxes to pay for the privilege of casting a ballot. You may not really be interested that a pollard is either a tree that has its top (head) cut back so that new growth can come out of the trunk, or an animal, like a goat or cow, that has had its horns removed. Shearing is also sometimes called polling . . . and voters have felt sheared by the results of some polls.

pond   Ah, fishing and swimming down at the old pond. . . . One of the reasons it's nice is because you *know* what's on the bottom. You saw the space dammed up and filled. That's how a pond and a lake are different. The pond is a small, manmade enclosure for water. The

word goes back more than a thousand years to the same
Old English root from which we get dog *pound* or
property being im*pound*ed. A related word is the
animal *pen,* which is not related to our word for prison,
penitentiary, which was supposed to be a place for
repenting your crimes, or being "penitent."

pool   Here I'm talking about pooling our resources or
the office football pool. It may seem like your contribu-
tion has sunk into oblivion in this kind of mutual fund,
but it isn't related to the swimming pool. This *pool* once
again goes back to the French word for hen, *poule.* The
way a chicken keeps her eggs gathered under her in an
efficient group for warming gives us the idea of group-
ing our resources. And, too, there was a French game in
which a hen was the target, which ties in with the idea
of stakes in betting.

porcelain   An animal is also related to the origin of
this word, Italian for "little pig." A pig and this fine clay
used for china are related? In this roundabout way: The
very shiny, beautiful cowry shell somehow reminded
Italians of a sow's womb, and some varieties of the shell
were given a delicate name for that part of the body,
porcelain. When the firing and glazing of pure clay
resulted in the shiny look of the shell, the ceramic also
got the nickname without having to look like a swine's
genitalia. The pig appears again with *porcupine,* which
basically has an Old French origin and means "spiny
pig."

porpoise   There's more on pigs and wombs here. The
Latin from which we get the name for this aquatic
mammal means "pig
fish," so named either
because of its blunt
snout or its squealing
voice. Now, our word
for the longer-beaked
and larger relative, the
dolphin, comes from a
Greek root for "womb,"
probably because of the
air hole on the arched
back of this whale-kin
that opens and closes
for breathing as it rides the waves. For you flower-
lovers and stargazers, the same Greek root descrip-
tively names the blooming delphinium and the
constellation Delphinus for their shapes.

posse   We're familiar with this word from our Westerns, where the sheriff gathers volunteers to chase the
badmen, or the outlaws themselves see the cloud of dust
in the distance: "It's the posse!" The word is a legal term
but goes back well before Marshal Dillon rode out of
Dodge. In the Middle Ages (somewhere between 500
A.D. and 1400 A.D.) the Latin phrase *posse comitatus*
was used for any group given power by the count within
his territory. *Posse* meant "having the power" or "being
able to," from which we get *possess* (having the ability
or having the power over) and *possession.* The *comitatus*
was the land over which the count ruled (later to
become our *county*). Let's say a man stole one of the
count's chickens and ran into the woods with it. The law
gave the count the right to authorize a group to drag
that man out of the woods and bring him to the count's

justice. That form of vigilante law worked well in the Old West when the lands were only territories and not under federal jurisdiction. *Deputy,* by the way, comes from those same medieval days and literally meant "a branch cut off from the tree," meaning you were an arm of the law, allotted the same power as the trunk of that tree.

post   Posting a sentry on a military post who stops the postal carrier to inspect the postage all are related to the Latin root meaning "to station or place." Getting information from place to place in the olden days usually was done in one of two ways. You could "post" your declaration, law, or announcement in some special place where all could read it or hear it read, or you could send it by courier from place to place if it was meant to be announced beyond your immediate location. These couriers took the message to a series of "posts." These emplacements were generally bases of the central government with troops and officials posted there. The couriers themselves got to be known as "postmen," and important messages were delivered "post haste." Even the galloping rhythm of a horse under that courier was called "posting." But the word for the wooden post on which a message might be nailed comes from a different source meaning "that which stands before." A variation on that root gives us *posterity,* that which follows behind, which is also related to that portion of the anatomy that jiggles after us, our *posterior.*

pout   This sulky expression goes back to an Old English word for the look on someone's face when that person is blowing out air. It means "to swell" or "to be inflated," and some say it might have come from a Flemish word for "frog." Of course, it is only the shape of the lips that lingers in our modern use of the word, though some that

pout might have a swollen ego or an inflated notion of
their own importance. Just as a side note, certain
pigeons capable of swelling their breast in a mating
ritual are called pouters, from the old definition.

powwow   As we use it now, *powwow* means a kind of
conference or gathering of the powerful. It seems the
old Western is the origin of this meaning, too. To the
Algonquian Indian these gatherings were for more
than discussing the paleface's proposal for a treaty. The
phrase could be translated as "He dreams," and it dealt
with many aspects of Indian spiritual life. Dancing and
chanting religious songs was a way for them to reach an
almost trancelike state needed to call for divine aid in
helping with the hunt, with a warring tribe, or with a
sickness.

precocious   We sometimes call a child precocious as a
nice way of saying they get into everything and bug the
heck out of us. We also
use it when a youngster
is particularly talented
or gifted in mental
skills. The original
Latin term mainly
applied to plants and
literally meant "to cook
before it's time." The
ripening process of
fruits was compared to
being cooked in those
days, since the sun's

rays had to do the work, and when something ripened
early it was "precocious." This made the easy transition
to children and their development. Botanists still call a
plant precocious when it blossoms before the leaves
sprout.

prerogative   Well before the Romans had their
Caesar and an empire to rule they were a loose confeder-
ation of Italian tribes. It was their sense of organization,
rulemaking, and living by those rules that made them
rise above their neighbors. Every so often, these tribes
gathered for feasting, trading, marrying, and lawmak-
ing to settle disagreements and keep the peace among
them. One hundred men were chosen from each tribe
and they met in a great field. This equal representation
kept everyone on a par so a larger tribe might not
dominate the smaller. These groups were called *cen-
turia*. Yes, that's where we get our hundred word,
century. (The Romans later used this as a military term
for a hundred men with a centurion at their head.) They
drew lots to see which tribe's group would get to vote on
an issue first, sort of setting the agenda of the meeting.
The tribe that got to go first got the "prerogative" (our
word is very similar to the Latin original). This gave
them the edge in this gathering, and the word has since
been associated with having the advantage. Eventually, these tribes voted to centralize their government,
and this interesting democracy turned the vote over to
senators. I'll talk of them later.

press   The power of the press came on that day when
Gutenberg first lowered a set of type down and squeezed
it onto the waiting paper. The ability to mass-produce
words took power away from the Church and its
scribbling monks and gave it to the poets, bureaucrats,
and business leaders. The name we give to those
members of the news media, whether in TV, radio, or
newspapers, derives from that simple act of pressing an
inked set of letters onto a blank page. Now, the old way
of being drafted into the army comes from a different
root. At first, men were pressed into service in the

military by being given advance pay; this Old French word for "loan" signified a common way to recruit a soldier. Later, the other meaning of *press* got mixed in when soldiers were needed in large numbers, funds were low, and times were hard. Then, press gangs would forcibly grab men and *make* them soldiers, with or without their approval.

prestige   When someone has "made it" as a leader, financial wheeler-dealer, or admired entertainer, that person has a certain status in our society and is given special treatment, the best seat in the house. Such people have prestige. Most people probably don't know that just several hundred years ago the word's French parent meant "illusions brought on by magic," which came from a Latin forebear meaning "juggler's tricks." Presto chango, the word was just the crowd's way of saying something was done faster than the eye can see . . . which is what we sometimes find prestige is, too. Just a bit of *prestidigitation,* which is a fancy way of referring to a bit of sleight of hand done by a juggler. We are impressed by this and want to see more, but like prestige, presto, it's over before we figure it out.

pretty   Here's another word that's gone through some reversals. These days a girl has beauty if she's pretty, though a pretty good deal might not be the best. If you're sitting pretty, you should be satisfied, and everyone loves a pretty day. The original Old English meaning of the word, however, was "cunning, tricky, crafty." Over the centuries the notion that being very wily was bad got softened, since someone who was clever might make something useful or invent something to save time. Something finely crafted was "pretty," now in a good way, not crafty in that devious way. And when God made something rather well, whether a day or a woman, it was appreciated as "pretty."

pretzel Two different histories accompany this tasty snack, both similar. Its ancestor was German, an offspring of "arm." Either it comes from a word for "armlet," for the ring shape of the cake, or from "crossed arms," for the way the dough is folded. Give me a soft, glazed, salted biscuit and I won't wear it on my arm.

priest Most of us think of the leader of a Catholic congregation as having this name. Preachers, ministers, pastors, and reverends tend to be the leaders of other denominations, though an Episcopalian or Anglican will have a priest. The Latin language borrowed the name from the Greek word for "old man," *presbus.* Yes, you're right, Presbyterians took this ancient word and applied it to their denomination, which was not governed by popes or cardinals, but by "elders" in the Church. This fits the origin much more closely than *priest,* who, in the early Church, was mainly a young man. I'll talk a little about some of the rankings for churchmen and churchwomen in the next word.

priority   Getting our priorities straight is a major
hobby in today's busy world, but it was the Catholic
Church that did this to
us. Oh, I know, blame it
all on God or the devil.
Well, what I really
mean is that the rank-
ings in Catholic monas-
teries and convents
gave us the word and
the concept. *Prior* was
the Medieval Latin
title of the man who
governed the monas-
tery. He was just below
the abbot in rank. In the convent the prioress ruled
below the abbess. In those days, when you made a prior
commitment you were talking about doing something
the prior told you to do before anything else. These
religious leaders had "priority"; in other words, what
they said came first.

privilege   Speaking of governing something, we know
that when someone has a privilege, they can do something that others can't or aren't allowed to do. In the
broad sense we say that voting is our privilege in
America because so many countries don't give their
citizens that right (though that is changing). Privileges
in the past might have been granted by a king and gave
the individual special rights beyond the law. Taking
the word apart gives you *privi,* from which we get
private (not part of the state) and *privy* (the old-
fashioned outhouse), and *lege,* from which we get *legal*
and *legislation.* So a privilege is a "private law."

profanity   Today we think of profanity as any strong curse word, but in ancient Rome, where the word originated, it meant *anything* that did not have to do with religion. The word comes from Latin and its literal translation is "outside the temple." So the secular world was profane and the world of the gods was sacred and that was that. As times changed and priests and ministers would occasionally make God angrier, the word took on a harder edge and applied to things more wicked than merely worldly. Much of that blasphemy came in the form of curses and swearing.

prostitute   Prostitution may be joked about as one of the oldest professions, but the truth is that prostitutes were common and even respected members of religious sects thousands of years ago. The Hebrews complained about some of the temple prostitutes of competing pagan religions back in biblical times, and it was an old tradition even then. When men came to these temples their worship included a bit of fraternizing with the gods' earthly representatives. It wasn't until the 1500s, when an epidemic of venereal disease swept Europe, that governments stepped in to control this sexual merchandising. The Romans give us the word we use today, meaning "to expose publicly" or "to stand before the public." With its illegality in most states and its regulation in most nations, prostitution has gotten considerably less public.

prude   Being called a prude these days has all kinds of negative shadings. We think someone who censors or represses sexuality is a stick-in-the-mud, a fuddy-duddy who usually has no sense of humor. Well, how words change! The Old French version focused on the

female and meant "an excellent woman." Our word
came from a shortening of *prudefemme,* which was a
fine lady, indeed. *Proud* comes from the same root, and
its earlier uses meant "gallant, brave, and good." Being
proud today carries more of a reflective quality, looking
back on something done or something made, and an
excess of it is frowned upon. And being a prude, which
can now apply to either sex (though it does have,
generally, a feminine application), has a sense of
over-concern for modesty. Prudence, however, is still a
good quality to have.

psycho   This is basically a slang word, but it gets used
so much today thanks to the movie of the same name
and numerous other entertainments featuring deranged villains. The Greek original referred to "breath,
life, soul." Science relegated the word to the mind,
leaving the soul out of the picture. So a psychosis is a
condition of the mind. A psychiatrist is a "healer of the
mind." But we get a bit confused translating *psy-
chedelic,* which means "clear mind." Actually, this was
invented to explain that people were seeing things
clearly in their minds . . . things that weren't necessarily there. Though this *psycho* root has many negative
uses today, I still like the Greek myth of the beautiful,
confused Psyche, who through love and determination
wins her husband Cupid and thus represents the soul's
persistence in loving. We can still find some of this
meaning when we get "psyched up" for something.

pudgy   This is one of the nice "fat" words, in there with *chubby, plump,* and *roly-poly.* In old Scotland a chunky child was considered a healthy child, so their word for "belly" has always had a "cute" connotation. When people are pudgy they're just a bit stout, rotund, stocky . . . not fat.

pulpit   It was a tough task for the early Catholic priests to convince the primitive folk they ministered to that they should change their beliefs and turn to Christianity, especially when the services were conducted in the mysterious and sometimes unwelcome Latin. The Roman threat was gone and the strict Church had taken a lot of the fun out of living: no wild festivals, no gory plays, no sex—at least for those of the cloth. . . . But then some imaginative priests decided to bring back some of the things the folks were missing and Christianize them. We've talked about some of the festivals conveniently made to fall in the same time frame as the old pagan ones. Now it was banned drama's turn to make a comeback . . . this time inside the Church itself. The trend started in France sometime in the 900s when little shows were put on at Christmas and Easter, telling the stories in play form. The locals ate it up and the idea spread across Europe, packing them in at local churches. The scene would be acted out and the priest would explain what had happened. The first sermons were born. These dramas got to be so popular that little platforms were built all around the church, each the stage for a different scene, and the crowd would move from one to the other. Nuns and monks began writing plays on the Bible stories and mysteries of Christianity . . . even comedies. By the 1200s the crowds had gotten so great and the staging so elaborate that the plays had to be moved outside the church. Finally, the trade guilds took over, sponsoring the plays that eventually led to our modern theater. Only one of the stages was left in the church and it still bears its Latin name, *pulpit,* though now only one actor carries the load of the performance.

pumpernickel This dark, almost sour rye bread has a strange German name and its meaning is even stranger. If you translate it, it means "the devil's gas." Because it had a reputation as being hard to digest and causing sometimes embarrassing flatulence, the Germans combined *pumpern,* which was an imitative word for the sound of expelled intestinal gas, with *Nickel,* which was a nickname for the devil. The metal itself came from a word we'd translate as "copper nickel" or "copper demon." The old German miners were looking for copper, and niccolite *looked* like that valuable ore but wasn't. They blamed this on mischievous underground dwarfs and demons. Only later did they find valuable uses for nickel.

pumpkin The original Greek could be translated to apply to much in the garden, because when we say "pumpkin" we are really saying "cooked (by the sun)." The idea behind the naming of this large fruit was that it was not edible until it was baked on the vine long enough. You might be able to eat a green tomato or baby ear of corn, but forget it when it comes to trying to scarf down a green jack-o-lantern.

punch   There are several kinds of punches. The blow delivered by a boxer is named after the action of the metalworker, especially a goldsmith, when he or she stamps the metal or perforates it for ornamentation. The tool used is still called a puncheon, though that word is also used in the sawmill and in construction for "rough timber." The name *hole punch* comes from the tradition of the tool. But the punch you drink at a reception doesn't get its name from the fact that it might knock you out if strongly spiked. The word for the drink, *punch,* came from Hindi through Sanskrit and meant "five." Its name referred to its recipe: Boil some tea leaves in water, then add sugar, lemon, and liquor . . . five ingredients.

puny   Southerners have an expression for sickness, "feeling puny." The Old French gave us the first common use of the word, which meant "born later." The runt of the litter was usually the smallest and, most of the time, the weakest and sickliest. The name got used for anything that was of inferior size or strength.

pupil   How are students, little dogs, dolls, and eyes related? The Latin *pupus* was the word for "boy," *pupa* for "girl." Since most dolls have been female, from ancient ones to Barbie (sorry, G.I. Joe), they were originally given the name *pupa,* from which we get our word *puppet.* Now, in Roman times the word *pupil* was mainly used for orphans who were supervised by a guardian. Even British civil  law used the term to refer to orphans under the care and training of the state. Later the term lost its "homeless" quality and was used for any student. The *pupil* of the eye also comes from the Latin for "little orphan girl," probably from a children's expression for the tiny reflection they saw when looking into that part of the eye. Finally, *puppy* is a word that goes back to the "doll" meaning and was first used as a name for a baby dog by the French, who love their canines. "Play-thing" is what puppies were, and children and young dogs have spent forever in play. Cats are no one's plaything.

purchase   If you've ever been last-minute shopping in a mall during the Christmas rush, looking for a gift for a hard-to-please person, you'll identify with the Old French meaning of this word: "to go hunting for." We also use the word for a grip or footing, which comes from the old notion of *chase,* "to seize," what you do when you see someone else eyeing the gift you're interested in.

purple   The names of colors sometimes come to us by roundabout means. In olden Greece there was a certain shellfish from which an excellent dye could be made. The name of the creature is where *purple* came from. Because this dye was more difficult to obtain, cloth dyed in this color became more valuable and rare. Generally, only the wealthiest could afford it, and soon it became a color of kings and was even the name given to the rank of cardinal or bishop.

putter   For those who dislike golf, wasting time by puttering might be compared to using a putter to try to get that little ball in the hole. Both words are related. It's thought that the *putter* we use when someone spends a lot of time doing aimless little tasks comes from a Dutch root meaning "to put in the ground," which might have referred to fooling around the garden, clipping and ornamenting. The name of the golf club also refers to "putting" the ball in the ground, that is, in that one particular spot of ground that is the cause of such frustration.

pygmy   The Greek word for "fist" is where we get this term for anything, especially a living thing, that is unusually small. It has nothing to do with the fierce little fighting people of Africa, but with a way of measuring. From the forearm to the fist, elbow to knuckles, was a Greek unit of measurement. The Greek poet Homer first told of a race of dwarfs living in Africa that were this size, and much later when such tiny folk were found they were given this name. There is also an Asian people who are of the pygmy height.

python   This snake also goes back to Greek legend. A large dragon or serpent lived in the caves of Delphi and spoke with the priestesses there, telling them prophesies, that is, until Apollo happened along and dispatched him. When the huge snake of the real world needed a name, what better place to turn than classical Greece and the soothsaying snake? The word is still sometimes used for a person possessed by a prophetic spirit.

quack   The Dutch invented this word, which imitates the sound of a duck. When we call a poor doctor a quack it doesn't mean his head is full of feathers. It probably doesn't have a link to the duck noise at all. A quack-salver was, in olden days, what we might think of as a snake oil salesman, who traveled around shouting loudly about all the things his unguent or salve could cure. *Quac* was Dutch

for "ointment" and *salve* was "to heal or relieve pain" (usually with that ointment). Most of these home remedies weren't worth a guinea, and the same quack-salver rarely visited again, unless he wanted to be run out of town. It was a natural progression to calling a doctor who seemed not to know his business a quack,

the shortened version. Some say this shorter version
also got associated with the duck sound because of all
the noise they made boasting about the value of their
product.

Quaker   Members of the Society of Friends didn't
necessarily like the nickname they got from others, but
that name stuck and now can be found regularly on
oatmeal products. The name reflects a rather cowardly
shaking and has been used nastily to indicate a fearful-
ness to do combat. It probably came from something the
founder of the society said about how they "tremble at
the word of the Lord." This led to them being called
Quakers. Now, the United Society of Believers in
Christ's Second Coming got a much more literal
nickname when people called them Shakers, since one
of the original customs of this celibate sect involved a
shaking dance during religious ceremonies.

quarantine   This word comes from the Latin for
"forty." Why "forty"? Anyone in those days who had
experienced an epidemic or plague knew how helpless
mankind was before it. Common sense eventually
taught those in port towns that sick sailors could bring
devastation if they were allowed on shore. It became
common practice that ships had to wait forty days in the
harbor if there was any sign of illness on board. The
arbitrary number was originally based on the notion
that after forty days the disease aboard would either
have run its course and ended any chance of contagion
or have shown its truest colors. The number later
varied from situation to situation, but the name stayed
with the isolation process. Too bad the port authorities
couldn't detain the rats of the 1300s, who easily climbed
down the mooring lines from the ships, spreading the
Black Plague across Europe through the fleas in their

fur. Three-fourths of the civilized world died in its twenty-year reign. It was called *bubonic* after the name of the lymph glands in the armpit and groin that would swell so badly they would hemorrhage and turn black . . . the Black Death . . . yuck! Forty days is linked to biblical numerology also, like the length of Christ's desert fast and of Noah's boat trip through the rain. This forty-day time frame had another use in the 1600s for a widow's right to stay in her husband's house when it was seized for debt. She had that much time to find other accommodations, and this, too, was called a quarantine.

quarrel   The very earliest root for *quarrel* meant "pant, snort, wheeze," which happens a lot during a quarrel. By the time it reached the Latin, which is where we picked it up, it was simply "to complain," also a key cause of many quarrels. There is such a thing as a quarrel that was once a bolt for a crossbow or a tool used by a stonemason, but that refers more to our next word.

quarry   The idea for this word is related to the quad- rilateral, the four-sided geometric figure. The stone quarry in ancient times was a place to get shaped stones for buildings and roads, and the most common shape shipped from the quarry was the square. "Square- shaped" is the meaning of the earliest form of this word, and the stonemason's tool we talked about above also had a square head. The quarry we speak of as an object of pursuit in a hunt or chase came primarily from a word from the Middle English meaning "the entrails of a beast." It was common practice to give the dogs that had helped in the hunt this portion of the animal as a reward for their efforts. It has its earliest kinship with the Latin word for heart, *cor,* from which we get *courage.*

quiche   Whoever said, "Real men don't eat quiche" didn't talk to the Germans who invented the word. Its root means "cake" and is related to that word and to *cookie*. It was when the French got hold of it and put in the custard and vegetables that "real men" began to wonder about it. That plus the fact that it seemed to be most popular in a region that France and Germany traded back and forth and argued about in the late 1800s and early 1900s: Lorraine.

quick   I always wondered about the expression "the quick and the dead." It seemed to me as a child that any speed must be considered quick compared to that which didn't have the movement alternative. I have since learned that the Old English root for the word came from well over a thousand years ago and dealt with anything alive. If we are cut to the quick we have the emotions closest to our lives exposed. The phrase came from the idea of opening the very core of our being. In days past, to be quick with child was to be pregnant. Today it tends to indicate a parent who is fast at keeping an infant from turning over a potted plant. And a "quickie" certainly doesn't have as much life as a "slowie," if you know what I mean. Through time, *quick* began to refer to the one with the most life, and the liveliest seemed the one who could move the fastest.

quintessence   This word for "the ultimate," "the purest form," has its origin in ancient philosophy. The early Greeks believed there were five elements, four you could see or feel and a fifth that was more mystical. Earth, air, fire, and water were the basic reality groups, but the Greeks also believed that a spiritual element was present in the heavenly bodies and latent in all things. The Romans translated their word for this element: it was the fifth (*quint* . . . you know, *quintup-*

lets, quintet) essence. This was the highest and purest of all things that made up our universe.

raccoon The Algonquian Indian name for this animal means "scratcher," from its ability to use its handlike paws to get at just about anything it wants. The raccoon is well-known for its appetite for almost any kind of food available, including the remains of a meal that the Indians might bury and the coon scratch up.

racket If you've ever seen a very hot game of craps where the stakes are high on each roll of the dice, then you've probably heard the shouting of the gamblers, calling to the roller or exhorting the dice themselves to roll the way they want them to. In the Middle Ages a dice game was a racket. These kinds of activities have always been frowned upon by the ruling powers (unless they happen to love gambling, too), maybe because of the noise and violence of those involved and the energies spent frivolously in rolling spotted squares. Whatever the reason, in the 1800s, a racket was any illegal activity. By the Roaring Twenties the racketeer was the target of the Untouchables of the FBI and mainly dealt in prohibited beverages. Today a cynic might ask about any occupation, "What's your racket?" If you're talking about tennis and the tool of the court, you go to another root that comes from Arabia and meant "palm of the hand," which is where the racket's handle goes. Just to keep it straight, the dice game was called craps from the name for the lowest throw (a two or three) and was originally called crabs. The loser may have felt like the rubbish or chaff from which we get our more vulgar word for excrement or nonsense, but the game's name doesn't seem to be related.

radical   What do a political activist and a pungent salad vegetable have to do with each other? Well, a radical is someone who wants to tear up the very roots of government or other institutions, and a radish is a cherry or white root of garnishment. They both come from the same Latin source word for "root": *radix*. You'll find radicals in science and math, but these are certainly different than the vocal extremist. Some would like to *eradicate* the radical elements, pull them out by their roots, but we have to remember our Founding Fathers were radicals, and most who call themselves radicals would claim they want to go *back* to the roots of the most effective social arrangements.

rag   The Old Norse beginnings for this word referred to a tuft of hair. A hunk of fur was certainly not very useful to these folk; scraps like this might be used only as stuffing for something else. When cloth became the primary basis for garments, the little scraps of weaving kept the ancient name. Since early paper also was made from useless pieces of cloth, a newspaper got the nickname "rag." But *ragamuffin*, our word for a rather messy-looking kid, didn't come from his clothing style or his love for breakfast cupcakes. Ragamoffyn was a wicked little demon in the dreamlike tale of a Christian's journey, *Piers Plowman*, written in the late 1300s to help explain the mysteries of religion.

raid   The earliest Old English word from which we get *raid* meant "road." Roads marked borders in the English countryside. They allowed free passage through the various lands ruled by feudal lords, acting as little corridors for travel. If you got off the road, you could be accused of trespass and face the wrath of the duke, earl, count, or baron. Now, the Scots were well-known for a lack of respect for this kind of imposed boundary and would ride across these roads on horse-back for a little hunting or rowdiness, or even to do battle. Their pronunciation lingered as this word for a surprise attack.

ranch   Most of the time, we consider a ranch a pretty big place where herds of cattle and horses are managed by a group of hands under a foreman working for an owner and named for the brand on the cattle: the "Bar S," and so on. The Spanish popularized the word, which basically means "a group that eats together."

rankle   When something irritates us to the point that it rankles, it really gets under our skin and festers there to persist in our thoughts. The Latin from which we got the word meant "little dragon." The French used the word as a medical term to describe an ulcer or infected sore that just didn't seem to want to heal, comparing it to a snakebite. This notion was later applied to the

more emotional feeling of resentment that twists up
our gut like a serpent writhing around inside us.

rascal   Poor folk of the Middle Ages certainly weren't
a clean lot and they weren't nearly the cream of the crop
of humanity. The French seem to be the ones who
originated this word, and it probably was applied most
often to the scruffy English they had conquered. The
idea of both "scrape" and "itch" seem to have been part
of the insulting first use of the word. It referred both to
the dandruffy and muddy underlings the French saw
around them, scratching themselves vulgarly, and the
feeling that these were the scrapings from the bottom of
the barrel. *Rash* seems to have a kinship with *rascal,*
which today has much less scorn attached to it. Today's
rascal is more of a playful scamp. The other *rash,* by the
way, the one describing the foolishly bold, goes back to
a Dutch word for "nimble or quick."

real   This very unartificial word goes back to the
French law I've mentioned that was imposed upon the
English through the Norman Conquest. What you had
that was real was your property: your lands, animals,
tools, buildings. From this we get *real estate,* and this
legal concept gives us the more abstract use of the word,
meaning anything that is genuine and actual, from real
leather to realism. Today the word can even apply to
behavior, as in the expression of mockery addressed to
a dreamer: "Get real!"

ream   Just as the Arabs gave us *magazine* for the
storehouse, they gave us *ream* for what's packed in
there. "To bundle or pack together" is the first meaning
of the word. Later this was used for a quantity of paper,
480 sheets. 480? There are probably reams of reasons,
though now a ream is 500 sheets, except for a printer's

ream, which is 516 sheets. . . . But to ream something out—anything from a ring to a barrel to other more crude applications—goes back to an Old English word meaning "to widen."

reed This grass, which has given us so much pleasure when it vibrates on the end of a clarinet or saxophone, got its name many centuries ago from another kind of vibrating it did in a stiff wind. *Reed* meant "to shake or tremble." This trembling was made by manmade wind very early on in reed flutes and pipes, giving us some of our first songs.

reek This word is mainly used for terrible odors these days, but the word still also means what it did in its Old English form: "to give off smoke." In fact, an old term for smoking meats was "to reek" them. The offensive odors got to be more associated with the word and that became the primary meaning.

referee Without them our sporting events might turn into free-for-alls of unsportsmanlike behavior. Referees may be booed, argued with, mocked, and disbelieved, but their decisions are almost always final and mostly right, even in light of the instant replay. The word has a simple, logical origin. The referee is the person referred to for a decision or a ruling.

regret It would be nice to go through life without regrets, but there is always something that could have been done better. The Old Norse meaning of the first form of the word dealt with mourning the dead and signified weeping and moaning. From this same root for the sorrowful farewell to the departed we get the word *greet,* which has a sense of joy in its implied shout of welcome, though some greetings we've later regretted.

rehearse   I already described how *hearse* came from the name of a candelabra shaped like a rake, and from a word for "wolf" because of the likeness between a rake's teeth and a wolf's fangs. OK. *Rehearse* did not come from practicing for funerals or from repeated wolf hunts. This word that is the actor's pain and pleasure alluded to the rake and came from a French parent-word meaning "to rake over again" and, over time, "to repeat."

religion   Politics and religion may not be polite dinner table topics, but they have surely given us a lot of words to play with. The word *religion* itself gets its Latin meaning, "to tie," from the idea that religious practices were ways to bind people and gods together. The religious man *relies* on the belief that his god is there and is at the heart of the meaning of life, and this makes his world just a bit more *reliable*.

renegade   Staying with religion a little longer . . . A renegade was at first someone who abandoned his or her religion. The Spanish Inquisition popularized the word. After making Jews and Moslems either convert, leave, or die, the Spanish kings, under the auspices of the Church, began to punish those thought insincere in their conversion. These *renegados* had *reneged* on their commitment to the Catholic Church, or so the inquisitors claimed in many cases, and their insincerity was punished in many cruel and wicked ways from the late 1400s up until even the early 1800s, when fear and loathing finally abolished this, the cruelest of "Christian" practices.

reptile   No, I'm not going to this word as a further way to describe the religious persecution above. That would be too insulting to our lizard friends. Though we might call someone who is treacherous or sly a reptile, these egg-layers get their name from the Latin root of about fourteen hundred years ago that meant "creeping or crawling."

restaurant   A good restaurant leaves you feeling ready to go out and enjoy the rest of the afternoon or evening with renewed energy . . . and a bad one leaves you with indigestion. "A place to be restored" is the translation of this French word that stems from the same Latin root that gave us *store,* which originally meant "to build," as in a storehouse where food supplies might be built up. We also get *rest,* meaning "remainder," from that root, though the resting we might do after the meal at the restaurant comes from an Old English word that's been resting as is for hundreds of years.

retina   The Latin of the Middle Ages gave us this name for the membrane of the eyeball that is the light-sensitive inner lining. When medieval physicians were describing parts of the body, they used the fancy Latin but made common comparisons. *Retina* meant "net," from its weblike appearance. *Iris,* which gives us the color of our eyes, came through the Latin from the original Greek word for "rainbow," also their name for the goddess of that phenomenon and later given to a colorful flower as well. The word *cornea* also came from the Middle Ages and meant "horny (tissue)," like a little plate of horn covering the soft center.

retire   What has become the goal in life for many gets its start with an Old French word meaning "to draw back." The idea in the word was to have something removed from circulation or drawn back from battle, as we see when a team retires a player's uniform. It got used for resting or retiring to bed for the night, and this sense of retreating from the rat race is the main one we find today.

revere   This word has much of the sense of love surrounding it in our present use, but in its Latin origins it had a feeling of respectful fear as part of its meaning. We use the title *reverend* without much thought to the fact that what we're saying is that the minister is someone of whom to be in awe. And while reverence is a quiet kind of regard, it was once a much more intimidating position of worship. After all, in the early Church, God would put you in hell for some pretty trivial crimes, from eating a mammal on a certain day to not coming to church on Sunday, so there was plenty of reason to be just a bit fearful of this powerful being. These days we focus more on the loving aspects of reverence, and its meaning has softened considerably.

riffraff   Worthless types get this name, which comes from a combination of German and French. A riffler is a kind of file used for scraping, and a raffle started out as a Dutch dice game but later changed to another game of chance dealing with drawing lots. The French used the word to describe snatching something, so *riffraff* could be translated as "snatching the sweepings or filings." It was used for trash and rubbish that was swept from the house, and later for people who represented the rubbish of society.

rifle In the 1400s arms makers took the old musket, which was basically a hand-held cannon that sprayed its shot rather freely, and added one important feature to the barrel. They cut spiral grooves on its insides, which caused the metal projectile to spin as it left the gun. This spinning action caused it to cut through the air with much greater accuracy, just as you'll see with a football when the quarterback puts that perfect spiral on it. This new manufacturing technique used that file I talked about above to scratch the grooves and was called rifling. The technique became the name of the weapon. Rifling through something in a mad search comes from the same root, which also referred to scratching through.

rival You may have a rival in romance or at work and not be anywhere near water, but water was the primary focus of competition when the word was first born. For early man, rivers were vital, not only for drinking but also for fishing, hunting and, later, farming. When two families or tribes were too close to each other on a stream, they ended up competing for all its benefits. They were *rivals,* a word derived from the Latin, which literally meant "one using the same brook (river) as another."

robot A Czech science-fiction writer took one of his language's words for drudgery and manual labor done by servants and used it in a play as the name of his mechanical men and women. Karel Capek's play *R.U.R.* (Rossum's Universal Robots) gave us the first automatons in human form with this name, and gave us a word that is now used worldwide. From Robby the robot to today's automated factory machines, the writer's dream has become nearly a reality.

rodent   Our rats and mice, squirrels and beavers get their Latin name from their teeth. "To gnaw" is the meaning of this family's name, and this chewing action makes for fascination as we watch the nibbling chipmunk, and for annoyance when we find the field mouse nest in our storage closet, filled with chewed cloth and nutshells.

rodeo   Still a popular pastime in many areas where animals are part of the people's livelihood, this entertaining display of roping and riding skills got its name from the Spanish for "surround." A rodeo originally was a cattle roundup and also the name of the corral where the cattle were kept after the roundup for marketing. *Corral,* by the way, probably came into the Spanish from an African word for "enclosure."

rogue   The word we use for a scoundrel today was once merely the plea of a beggar. It comes from the idea of stretching out one's hands in supplication, asking for favor. Rogues were street beggars looking for handouts and, as is many times the case, some of these turned out to be of less than noble intent. Soon, rascals and vagabonds of all kinds were called rogues. These days the playfully romantic and the unprincipled trickster can both be called rogues, as can a solitary, rebellious animal, like a rogue elephant.

romance   Ah, romance! The passionate love affair is what we most associate with the romantic in our modern use of the word. Its beginnings were literary, though, as the name of a work written in French. It basically meant "in the Roman manner" and alluded to the fact that the French and Latin languages were very close. Most of the stories called romances were tales of knights in shining armor doing brave deeds and rescuing distressed damsels. The romance novel later became any tale of a great hero going through wild adventures. Generally, there was some great love affair involved, and the word *romance* began to be linked with these kinds of bondings. In the intellectual world, however, the movement called Romanticism was aimed more at allowing the heart more leeway in producing art rather than just copying what the Greeks and Romans had done. In the 1700s this philosophy affected art, music, and literature.

romp You might relate this word to romance if you have a loose interpretation of the word. In the Old French it was used for a hussy or vulgar woman, but the scorn implied in this meaning seems to have given way to a sense of the fun this kind of girl may have been having. *Romp* took on a much more merry and frolicky feeling, whether in sport or as a romp in the hay.

roost Whoever rules the roost dominates the doings and is always the top rooster in our flock of domestic chickens. Before the advent of the henhouse, chickens would roost in trees or in other high places like their wilder brethren birds. In its Dutch origins the word referred to a roof, woodpile, or timberworks of some sort. All birds are basically roosters, but the adult male got the name because of his cocky dominance of the roost.

rostrum   This word we use for a public speaker's
platform goes back to the height of the Roman Empire
and meant "beak."
Beak? Naval warfare in
those days was a pretty
suicidal business, and
the primary way to win
a sea battle was to ram
your opponent's ship
and thus sink it. Ships
were constructed with
various beaklike
projections on the prow,
many times carved in
the shape of some bird

or other creature. These projections were the rams that
oarsmen tried to jam into the enemy's boat. After a
victory the winners retrieved the prows of the defeated
ships where they floated among the debris and brought
them home to display them to the cheering crowds. One
such famous place was at the Forum in Rome, where
many of these "beaks" decorated the area of the
speaker's platform. In this roundabout way the platform itself got the name for the ship's prow and so did
every speaker's platform afterward. The habit of
having a carved figure at the front of seagoing vessels
continued, though as modern weaponry transformed
battle strategy these carvings were more for decoration
and luck. Another tradition of placing a ship's prow on
a pulpit or other speaker's dais was found in many
seaport towns.

rude   "It's rude to point," you've heard the mother
instruct the child as the rudiments of manners are
relayed. Latin again is the language of origin, and the
primary use in days gone by was for something rough or

raw, not carefully worked out. Rude logs or stone had not been carved or cut properly and a rude hut didn't talk back; it just didn't have much that was fancy associated with it. When someone lacked the refinements of courtesy, he, too, was rude. He hadn't had much of civilization's carving done to him. From the same rude beginnings we get our *rudiments* of social behavior that any *rudesby* should know (that's Scottish for an insolent person).

ruffian Was it advanced syphilis that caused the filthy, scab-covered pimps of Italy and later France to be called ruffians? In its early stages the word was applied to scabs and filth and later to the pandering activities of olden-day prostitution. As time passed, any rough or rowdy fellow engaged in some questionable activity was called a ruffian, as the English merely linked into the sound *rough,* which was like their older word for that coarseness.

rum The name for this liquor comes from what it sometimes causes. *Rumbullion* was the name for an uproar or tumult, and since drunkenness could be cited as a factor in a lot of rowdiness the popular drink got the shortened name. There also might have been a relationship with the distilling process, as the word can refer to something that is boiled up. Now, *whiskey* has a much more pleasant Irish beginning meaning "water of life." *Vodka* gets its name from the Russian, of course, meaning "little water." *Gin* came from the Dutch, short for *genever,* which was their word for the juniper berries from which the brew was made. *Beer* goes back to a Latin word simply meaning "to drink." And *wine* goes back to Latin also for the vine where the grapes are grown. A *rummy* we think of as a drunkard, but this fellow might have gotten his name from a Gypsy word for "man," *rom* (from which we get *Romany,* remember?). The word was used for an odd person or someone a bit off, daft, having had a nip too much. . . .

rummage   Our modern use of this word refers to searching for something, rummaging through a drawer or desk, trying to find that missing item. The French gave us the word, but its primary function for them was as a shipping term. It meant "to arrange things in the hold of a ship." Apparently, it wasn't always such a neat arrangement, because when the English adopted the word a rummage was a confusion of odds and ends, and we still use the word in this way at the "rummage sale."

sabotage   Spies and mystery seem to follow this word around as undercover agents blow up secret installations. The intrigue goes out of the word when you discover its French roots. It comes from a word describing the clopping about of peasants in wooden shoes. Not just the Dutch but farmers in parts of France wore those kind of clodhoppers and, apparently, when these field hands began to come into the cities to work they wore their traditional carved *sabots,* but had to learn a whole new way of life among the factory machines. The name of the shoes got to be disdainfully applied to clumsy work that sometimes led to damage or to having to redo the labor. From *sabot* we also get *boot.*

sack   We all know that when we "hit the sack" we're not talking about some vicious attack on a paper bag but about going to sleep. The expression refers to our head striking the pillowcase, though in its first use it meant the bed itself, since the early ones were just coarse cloth bags stuffed with something soft. The word *sack* takes us all the way back to a Hebrew word, *sag,*  which was the name for a kind of cloth. This rough camel or goat-hair garment was usually worn for mourning and splashed with a generous amount of ash to symbolize both the wearer's humility and the ending of life's fire. The Greeks took the word and passed it on to the Romans. When looters or pillagers needed to carry off their booty, this kind of clothing was perfect, since all you had to do was put a knot in one end. The term for plundering a captured town became *sack.* Getting "sacked from your job" is a mainly British way of saying you've been fired, taken from the tradition of workers carrying their tools in a sack. When the boss brought them their sack, they were going to be carrying the tools home a little early. Before we sack out on this word, there's *sachet,* from the French for "little sack," which usually contains scented powder. Now, the Spanish wine we hear called sack in some of Shakespeare's plays has nothing to do with a goatskin bag. The word came from Latin through the French and meant "dry," as in "triple sec."

sacrifice   Although the batter's sacrifice fly may not have much religious significance to any but the most intense fans, we usually think of this act as a helpful thing done at personal loss. The player at home plate gives up his chance to punch out a hit for the sake of moving a base runner into scoring position. Moms and dads constantly make sacrifices for their children, and many of them constantly tell us about them. If you think about where you first heard the word, you'll probably go back to a Sunday-school lesson or church service when you were told about Abraham being asked to sacrifice Isaac, killing him as an offering to God. Animals and humans were offered up regularly in those days to please the deities, and the Latin meaning of the word reflects this religious origin: "to make holy." *Sacred* comes from this root, as does *sacrilegious,* which didn't mean stuffing the church in a bag but "one who steals things from the church." Sacrilege today is just a kind of disrespect or irreverence for the Church, but this term began with those who robbed valuables from the temple. Speaking of sacrificing living things to the gods, that combination of backbones we call the *sacroiliac* gets its name from a particular part of the animal that was given in sacrifice. It was called the "sacred bone" by the Greeks, and the Latin translation gave us our name for the area parents worried about their children damaging when the "twist" was a popular dance. The Greeks were no dummies. Give the gods a bit of the rump and you keep the rest.

sad   In its first uses well over a thousand years ago, this word had a similar meaning to *satisfied*. It was used at the end of a day of work to say that you'd done enough; you were weary and sated. Somewhere in the 1200s or 1300s it started to be used for the way a person sometimes feels when he or she is worn out from hard work. Eventually, it got associated with woe and sorrow.

sage   I'm mainly going to talk about the plant here. The wise old sage, the person, comes from a different root, the Latin *sapius,* from which we get *sapient,* which really means "to have good taste." That always makes you seem wise. Good judgment is worth a lot. But the plant comes from another Latin word, *salvus.* From this we get *salvation,* "to be made safe"; *to salvage,* which is just "to save"; *safe;* and *save.* Sage was known as the healing plant and basically meant "healthy and safe." A lot of plants weren't, in ancient times. It got its reputation not only for its flavor but also for its use as a tea for stomach ailments and cooling fevers. The Roman legionnaires spread it throughout Europe on their campaigns and it became a valuable export spice. The Latin family name, *salvia,* gives us that earliest use that links it to the other words I've mentioned. Even though it was prized for its aid to the aged, from quickening the brain's function to being used as a dye for greying hair, it wasn't related to *salve,* which I've talked about before and will speak of again. There's a little more about sage in the next word.

salary   We might not like to get a box of salt from the boss at the end of the workweek, but a Roman soldier would have been plenty satisfied. In fact, that is what his pay went to buy. The troops either were given their *solidus* (a Roman coin from whose name we get *soldier* and *solid*) or were actually given bags of salt. This valuable seasoning was prized and was used in preserving food like

sausage, which meant "salted meat with sage." The first part of that meat word gives us *soused,* which was used for things preserved in salt, like pickles. Now it's mainly used for someone a bit pickled by strong drink. *Salad* also came from the Latin word for the white crystals and just meant "to salt," while a *sauce* was simply a salty broth to accompany your food and was kept near your plate on a little *saucer,* which is what that dish was first used for. These days our *salary* ("salt money") goes for more of the spice of life than merely that saline substance, but we couldn't live without it and that's no *salami* ("salted pork").

saloon   The word *saloon* got its new spelling on shipboard, where the dining hall and social gathering place for the officers was called the saloon, from an earlier French word, *salon,* which meant "hall or room" but was eventually applied to the drawing room where guests were entertained. When passenger ships became more popular the lounge area got the old seafaring name, and immigrants used it later as a name for a bar or tavern. Its early elegance has been lost and now it's used when the joint doesn't have much class.

salute   When a soldier snaps his hand up to the brim of his hat as an officer passes by, he is making a ritual gesture that goes back thousands of years. This brief bit of sign language was a greeting initiated by the subordinate and returned by the superior, and symbolized a wish for good health. Romans often placed the hand on the heart, and other societies have varied the placement also. *Salute* meant "to wish good health," and a wide range of folk have developed a sign-language hand movement out of this Roman courtesy, from the snappy British heel-clicking salute to the infamous Nazi slanted stiff-arm (*Heil* is German for "Health to you"). A *salutory* weather pattern or speech is one that tends to be beneficial. The *salutatorian* opens graduation ceremonies with a greeting to the audience. The *salutation* of a letter is its greeting, "Dear Sir . . ." And you may have heard the foreign toast *Salute,* which means "Here's to your health."

salve   We're back to this word for a healing substance, usually an ointment. The balm of the Old English origins of this word was "fat or butter." That was where our root for this word came from. Butter has long been a popular remedy for a small burn, tending to soothe the wound and give the wounded the memory of bakeries. Science today tends to disapprove of this substance for medicinal purposes. No one wants a rancid-smelling blob on their wound, nor does the brief relief hold any promise of healing. But for early man a hunk of fat or butter was the only thing in the medicine chest.

sarcasm   Oh, sure, I can see you *really* want to know where this word came from. Wait, I'm just being sarcastic. Two notions were originally part of this word that mocks by emphasizing the opposite. We get the word from the Greek "to tear the flesh," like dogs ripping into a carcass. If you are the object of sarcasm, you might feel just that way: that you are being torn into and ripped up with biting words. Another comparison associated with the Greek genesis of the word is "to bite one's own lip in rage." Feeling anger or contempt toward someone or something might provoke sarcasm, and the idea with this second flesh-tearing is that you either can't bite your tongue any more or you make someone else so mad that they chomp into their own skin.

satellite   An Old French word that was taken from the Latin brought this word into our vocabulary. Someone who waited on others, following them around to protect and serve, was a satellite in days of yore. To be an "attendant, escort, or bodyguard" were the duties of these first underlings. With the planets representing various gods, the little moons seemed to be like servants who were bound to their masters. Today we mainly think of communications, with our satellite dishes being locked on the orbiting broadcast slaves rotating the planet, or of a smaller country dominated by a larger, more powerful one.

satire   Now, this is much nicer than sarcasm, though it still can hurt its target. *Satire* has a strange translation: "mixed fruits." *Sated* or *satisfied* are words that are kin to this witty way of exposing foolishness, but why "mixed fruits"? The first satires were speechlike poems covering a wide range of subjects, a mixed bag of topics of the day. The most humorous and witty of these were the most popular and got away with making fun of the powers-that-be with irony and lampoon. The name took on some of this feeling. Satire, starting out as just a "mixture of things," began to apply to those works that laughingly ridiculed the stuffed shirt and drove that person "bananas."

scandal   Many people may secretly do things that could ruin their reputation, but only those that are caught suffer from a scandal. The Greek root of this word meant "snare, trap, or stumbling block" and was first used more in the hunt than in describing public disgrace. Warfare is probably where the word began to get its moral tone, when the commander was trapped by another force in a situation where he had to surrender. This was dishonorable and brought disgrace to his name. Later the word got more broad-based, and anyone who got tangled in the net of public shame suffered a scandal.

scar   In ancient times the fireplace was the most likely place to get a scar, whether from a blister you got while stoking the fire or a burn you got when moving a hot crock. The word goes back to early Greek and first meant "hearth," but it quickly took on another meaning, "scab caused by a burn." The Romans used their translation of the root that way and passed it on to the French, who altered it and passed it to us.

scarlet   This word made a circle, going from Latin into Persian and back to the Latin of the Middle Ages. Those early Persian rugmakers loved the bright red dye that is still seen in beautiful old handwoven tapestries and floor coverings. The Romans had cloth of this color and passed on the secret: crushing up the females of certain types of bugs. Something was lost in the translation, however, because the early Latin equivalent of *scarlet* was used for something adorned with tiny images, little *signs,* a word related to *scarlet.* The red cloth, embroidered with little figures, was attractive to the Arab peoples mainly for how it was colored, and that's what they took the word to mean. The Persians borrowed the word and changed it, and a thousand years later medieval traders picked up the Persian word, now firmly associated with the color of the bug-stained threads.

scavenger   The Flemish people of that area of northern France and Belgium we call Flanders gave us the parent of this word. In their tongue the root meant "to look at," and usually to look at closely. The French used the word for "inspection" and applied it to an import tax on foreign merchants. When the Norman French conquered England, they brought the word over the channel. Under their tight rule of the British Isles they set up toll places along many roads to both insure that rebels might not pass too freely in large numbers and to collect extra money for their treasury. Now, the "skawagers" were toll collectors. After several hundred years this occupation turned into the street cleaner, as toll-taking was phased out when the French left (though tolls are still widespread in Europe). This is where the word started getting the kind of meanings we give it now. Since the birds that eat road-killed animals serve to keep the place clean, they were called scavengers. I'm unsure where the tradition of the scavenger hunt came from, though it had to do with finding useful things among refuse, with a prize for the most collected.

scene For the Greeks, the first *scene* referred to something more protective of the actors and their costumes and masks in the early dramas of their outdoor theater. The word was used for a tent where the actors could change to become a new character or show the progression of time. They could enter and exit from three different doors in the tent, and later a platform was built in front of this structure to create more of a sense of place for the action of the play. Today we call this the *proscenium,* our name for the stage, which actually meant "in front of the tent."

school Kids would probably totally disagree with the Greek meaning of this word. For Greeks the word meant "leisure," a time when you could relax with no chores, no crops to plant or harvest, no war to fight or business to conduct. Those who went to school had leisure time and were usually the sons of the wealthy. When what these students learned helped them to become better leaders, wiser  soldiers, more deeply religious, and better at business (using written records and mathematical bookkeeping), many people wanted their young to have this opportunity. As a result, those first easy-going gatherings grew into our worldwide quest for knowledge. Now, the word

when applied to a group of fish came from a Dutch word
having nothing to do with learning to swim. That word
was used for a troop or throng.

scold   The Old Norse roots of this word applied to a
poet, one who might sit around the campfire and tell
tales of heroes like Beowulf and stories of the gods and
men. Of course, a little comic relief was always popular,
and many of these men had a tale or two of a more
risqué nature, the first dirty jokes, you might say.
These stories would expose the faults of others and
amuse at the same time. It seems that the finding-fault
part got passed on with the word as it made its way into
English. A lewd, vulgar, or abusive person was called a
scold in the 1200s and 1300s, especially a woman who
constantly railed against another. This sense of the
word eventually led to its use in referring to criticism of
children, and it still tends to be used in that way.

scruple   There are two thoughts as to the origin of the
word as we use it today, meaning "a principle or point of
conscience." The word got its start as a unit of measurement used by early pharmacists. The French used
small stones as weights on a scale, and their name for
these came from the Latin *scrupus* (small stone). When
the word was applied to ethics, the person with scruples
was one who carefully weighed the points of an argument, trying to reach a balanced decision. Others say
that the ethical sense of the word had a different source:
that the hesitation to do something because of your
scruples came from the idea that your conscience was
like a small stone in your shoe constantly nagging you,
making you uneasy in taking a course of action.

seamy   Those seamy parts of the city with their dives
and lowlife types are usually on the wrong side of town.

This word comes from the garment industry, where the seamy side of clothing is the inner side, with its rough hems and stitching. The raw and unattractive parts of urban areas got this same nickname.

secretary   Whether you know it or not, our country is ruled by secretaries, and generally they're what keep things together and running. In medieval times this word, from the Latin, meant "one who is entrusted with *secrets*." In the days when writing was a skill of the minority, it was important to have someone who could take down a ruler's orders and correspondence. This person had to be confidential, since there were many plans a leader made that had to be private until the time was right. The title of secretary today is much more common, though it still hasn't lost its value. Many a boss trusts her secretary with more than she would anyone else. And in government the name still carries its old power, as in secretary of state.

senate   Continuing with government . . . While only bitter opponents might consider certain senators senile, the two words are related. The Latin root for "old man" is where both get their kinship. Most cultures respect age, and Roman society was one of those. I talked about the gathering of the tribes in the early days before the Roman Empire. The representatives from these clans were usually the elders, whose experience led to wiser, more thoughtful deliberation. When the empire flourished, the tradition of the council of elders continued in the Senate, literally "a gathering of old men." To this day there are age requirements for our Senate. Many of these *senior* men and women are granted the respect of their age. When we say our "Yes, *sir*" (from *sire,* meaning "senior") or "Yes, Ma'am," we're going back to ancient titles of respect still given formally in England. Seniority concerns the length of time you've been with a business and often means a more secure position on the job. This can make younger workers act *surly* (which comes from *sirly:* "acting lordly and arrogant").

sequin   The *zecchino* was a small coin of Venice that got its name from an Arabic word for a coin stamp. It's not that rich Italian women wore gold coins on their clothing, but when the sewing on of tiny bits of shiny metal became a popular fashion, they thought these spangles *looked* like the coins. When the word got passed to the French its spelling was changed.

shabby   When something is worn out or dilapidated we say it is in shabby condition. We've heard the British call rudeness "shabby" treatment. The word goes back to an old word for "scab or scale." In the Middle English of the 1200s and 1300s it was usually the very poor who had the skin problems that led to boils, eczema, and psoriasis, and they were the ones who wore the threadbare clothes and lived in the seedy houses. Somehow, this lifestyle of the unknown and impoverished kept the name that originally applied to the dermatologist's nightmare. Now, living in a *shack* wasn't a bad thing in its original sense. It was the Spanish conquistadors who gave this Aztec word for "thatched cabin" its poor connotation.

shambles   Here's another word that goes with deterioration. How many times did my mother say, "Your room is a shambles!" She might have been right in the sense of our modern meaning of disorder or ruin, but if she'd been using the word as an English citizen of the 1200s, she'd have been describing a place where meat is displayed for sale at the market. Tables where the game birds hung and the cuts of beef, pork, and lamb lay waiting for selection were called "shambles." Sanitation being what it was seven hundred years ago, the day's-end scene at the shambles could be a messy, fly-covered mess of scraps and entrails. The word was later used to describe the aftermath of particularly bloody battles where bodies lay en masse. After a time, it got used in a less violent sense for places like my teenage bedroom.

shampoo   The Hindu language gives us this soapy word. The wonderful, lustrous hair of the men and women of India was massaged and squeezed with water and cleaning agents, and their term meaning "to press or massage" was taken up by the British colonists.

shed   A shed can be a shelter, but mainly for tools and equipment. It gets its name from the Old English root for *shade,* getting something out of the sun, from which we also get *shadow,* the shade created when something blocks the sun. When you say an animal sheds hair, however, or that you shed tears, this word comes from another Old English word meaning "to divide." The leaves shed or divide themselves from the tree, and the water is shed from the rocks into the watershed.

shelter   Food, clothes, and shelter: our basic needs, though the last one comes to us from a word for an Old English battle formation. When attacking a castle or fortress the first wave of soldiers would lock their shields together, forming a wall that deflected the arrows from the enemy on the ramparts. This was the shield troop, whose earliest name gives us *shelter*.

shilly-shally   Well, you don't use this phrase all that much if at all, but I thought this word for hesitating, wavering on a choice, being indecisive was one for the book. There was once a much longer phrase that the procrastinator used: "To stand or go, shill I? Shall I?" This *shill* was just a reduplication of *shall* and not the shill of the con man who uses a fake customer to get the person he's going to con to have more "confidence" in him. *Wishy-washy* and *dilly-dally* are weak sisters.

sign This Latin-formed word was used especially for a distinctive mark or seal of an official or family that appeared on written proclamations or letters as the symbol of this person or clan. To sign a document in those days was to put your seal on it. When a soothsayer read special signals in the way birds flew or in the entrails of animals, these events were considered supernatural signs, marking the future. In olden days, businesses were marked with a sign indicating the merchandise: a large shoe over the shoe store, the three gold balls of the *pawn* shop (which gets its name from the Old French word for a piece of cloth, since garments were often left as security for loans), or the large eyes of the glasses-maker. When a business began to distinguish itself from its competition through service or prices, its individual name was put on the sign. Time to sign off on this one.

silly If it's the world of business or politics, we don't think too much of someone who acts silly. It's important to be *serious*. Yet some of our most beloved entertainers based their careers on making us laugh by being just plain silly. The earliest form of the word dates back to well over a thousand years ago and meant "blessed." It generally referred to a simple soul, perhaps someone born with a mental deficiency, who, in those days it was believed, was touched by God's hand in some way; the things of this world were not important to them. It referred to the innocent, happy state of this type of person. Nearly five hundred years later, the word took on the feeling that this type of person was to be pitied: "the poor silly man." A blow on the head could put you into this state if you were "knocked silly." As the word was dragged through the halls of time it lost its aura of religion and pity and came to refer merely to that foolish, frivolous kind of behavior that is frowned upon unless you're entertaining a small child or can get away with what Robin Williams or Steve Martin can get away with. . . . Otherwise, silliness is associated with stupidity, as in the parent saying to the child, "Don't be silly!"

sincere   The origin of this word has become pretty famous, but I'll present it here anyway because it is so interesting. "Without wax" is what the word came to mean, though the original Latin word referred to the goddess of agriculture and to something grown in one piece. Even in Roman times business-men might try to make an extra shekel or two by cutting corners on a job. As the empire grew  the construction industry boomed, as the demand increased for finer Forums and prettier Pantheons. The column was one of the major elements of construction, but some builders would try to conserve precious marble by filling hollow columns with wax or by using a wax seam to join smaller pieces together so that they looked like one piece. Well, this wasn't up to Roman standards and could be a problem if the columns had to bear too heavy a weight. Columns guaranteed to be made of solid marble were sincere . . . that's right, without wax. The word came to be applied to anything that was pure, genuine, and honest.

sinus People with sinus problems have days when they wish they could pull off their noses and hose out their foreheads. It's the bent and folded-over shape of this cavity that causes the problem, and that shape is conveyed in the original Latin word. The root has found its way into other words, too. We refer to the *sinuous,* curving body motion of a snake or belly dancer, and when people in*sinu*ate that something is not what it appears to be, they are taking a winding course to the truth. Likewise, they adopt a winding approach when they insinuate themselves into a conversation.

sissy As far as we've come in the liberation of the sexes from long-standing roles and stereotypes, some people still don't want to be completely equated with those of the opposite sex. Women still wear dresses and cer-tainly don't want to be called "chairman" or "sir." Many males also avoid appearing too feminine, though they can get away with an earring and a perm these days. How many ex-football players have heard the coach scream at halftime, "You guys are acting like a bunch of girls out there!" *Sissy* comes from *sister,* and no red-blooded man wants to come off looking like his sister. The effeminate or cowardly still get this nickname, even in this age when the sisterhood has gotten pretty darn tough.

skimpy This word has two senses, one harmless and the other negative. If someone comes back from Las

Vegas and says the dancers there wore skimpy costumes, or returns from the French Riviera and com-
ments on the skimpy bathing suits, they might not be
criticizing at all; but if they talk about going into a
restaurant and getting a skimpy serving, they definitely weren't satisfied. The word is probably derived
from *scrimp,* which has a Scandinavian origin, more
than likely from the Swedish for "shrink." Though most
of us don't mind when the bathing suits shrink in
fashion styles, we don't like it when the host reduces
our portion of the meal. Most of us have had to "scrimp
and save" at some time in our lives, but we don't want
to be called a *skinflint.* By the way, this miser's
nickname comes from the idea that such a person is so
cheap that he would try to skin the valuable stone, flint,
to conserve it, or sell the shavings of this rock used in
starting fires.

sky Most of the time when we say we can see the sky,
we're talking about the blue above the clouds, but the
Norse, who gave us this word, were talking about the
clouds themselves. Maybe it was because the skies were
cloudier in those northern climes, or because these
were primarily seagoing folk and the patterns of clouds
were important to sailing. Whichever, for them *sky* was
cloud.

slapstick This kind of comedy, which we think of as
involving a lot of physical gags of the kind the Three
Stooges were famous for, gets its name from an actual
device that was used in the early farces. This implement
was made of two flat wooden sticks that would smack
together when struck against something, making a
loud noise. Actors in these comedies used these
"slapsticks" to swat each other, producing loud pops but

doing little harm to the actors themselves. This kind of violent but harmless farce took the name of the tool itself.

slob   The Irish gave us this word for an obnoxiously messy person. It goes back to a word for mud and referred not only to the fact that encountering mud in an intimate way can quickly turn you into a slob, at least in appearance, but also to the idea that mud, which is a looser form of dirt, is much like a person who is looser than the norm and doesn't quite hang together as tightly. The idea of hanging loosely is also found in the word *slobber,* from the Germanic tongue, and in the Norse *slump,* and even in the Old English root for *sleep.*

slur   Speaking of mud, this word goes back to the Dutch and meant "to trail in the mud." If you slur your speech under the influence of drink or sleepiness, it is as if your words get blurred and muddied. If you slur someone's character or good name, you drag it through the mud of shame. At one time, another name for a sluttish woman was a *slur,* which referred to her moral dirtiness. In the printshop a slur was a smeared impression on the page, while in music this was a run of notes that you would almost try to blend together. Finally, if you were making a papier-mâché creation, the loose mixture you dipped your strips in would be called a slurry because of its resemblance to thin mud.

smorgasbord   This once was a popular name for the type of restaurant where the buffet table was laden with a wide array of foods. The word is used much less than it was, replaced by the simpler, self-explanatory "all-you-can-eat." The Swedish took the word from the Old Norse. For the Swedes the name meant a place where you piled things on an open-faced sandwich. The original meaning has two interpretations: "table for bread and butter" or "table of the fat goose." My visits to the generous smorgasbord encourage me to accept the second interpretation.

smuggle   In keeping with the tradition of some of the messy words above, I give you *smuggle,* which derives from a German root for "slimy or slippery." It made the comparison that these illegal exports or imports were slipped through the hands of the law like a slime-covered stone slips from your grasp. Now, *smug,* on the other hand, once had a sense of being all dressed up in your very best and "adorned" in jewels, in our rural expression's sense of "getting all slicked up" to go out. Being sleek and well-dressed probably gave the impression of conceit, so the word got associated with a self-righteous attitude, and sliminess got back into the word's meaning.

snob   On the subject of being stuck-up, snobs have been disliked ever since the common man won his freedom. Originally, the term was used in an opposite manner for a "boy," a person of no rank. When the working class began to be a force with the rise of the city, and the uneducated guildsmen began to accumulate wealth, these nouveau-riche types began to look down on the commoners. The old term was now used for them by these same lower-class workers, indicating that these "snobs" thought they were more than they really were in rank.

snoop   Someone who tries to find out about the private lives of others is definitely a snoopy person. Detectives even get this nickname. But the Dutch root of this word had more to do with a rebellious dieter than with a spy. "To eat snacks on the sly" was what a snoop did. That sneak who gets caught with his hand in the cookie jar or that refrigerator raider of today would have been called a "snoop" in yesteryear.

snuggle The first form of this word saw the light of day as a Norse term for short-haired or "close-cropped." If it was a field of grain or a sheared sheep that was snug, then it was neat and trimmed. This notion was taken as a sailing term later on to describe the lashing-down and battening preparations aboard a ship about to weather a storm. When everything topside was snugged down, you'd go belowdecks and nestle into your bunk. Particularly cold and nasty gales might find the crew snuggled together for warmth or comfort. Much later we began using the word as a cozy way of describing cuddling with that special one.

sock I'm not talking about the punch that's called a sock, but the footwear that slips inside the shoe. The first socks actually *were* shoes. Actors in early Roman comedies wore a light, low-heeled shoe as part of their costume, just as actors in tragedies wore the knee-length, thick-soled boot called the buskin. As usual, the Romans took the idea from the Greeks, and we eventually took it from them, later making this a part of day-to-day garb. Over the centuries the light shoe was transformed into a cloth foot-covering that fit inside the boot. Our other name, *stockings,* probably came from a humorous comparison to the hose that tied the feet and ankles to the instrument of punishment called "the stocks," which also imprisoned the lower legs.

socket   After learning the origin of this word, I looked over at the electrical socket on the wall and realized that the word's early creators were more right than they knew. That wall outlet *does* look like a pig's snout, doesn't it? The early Celtic clans who used their version of this word applied it to a plowshare, however. To them, this device was like the swine who rooted through the soil, and the amusing comparison was passed on to be used for anything that had something inserted into it.

sofa   The Arabs give us this word for something we now think of as a couch. The first sofas were more like benches with cushions thrown upon them. The French took the word and changed it, just as they did the construction of this piece of furniture. Another less-used name for our modern couch, *divan,* also came to us through the French from the Persian. The earliest form of this word referred to a bundle of sheets and was used in an administrator's council room, where he might do his accounting and hold audience. The word began to be used for the room and his comfortable cushioned benches, and when these backless couches with pillows began to appear in the coffee houses their name stayed with them. They were much like the trendy *futons* of today, but we get that design from Japan.

sophomore   If you've ever been a teacher, you know that something comes over the sophomore. He is no longer the nervous, novice freshman. He's learned some of the ropes of the school and now swaggers about the newcomers with a knowing look and teasing gesture. He thinks he's got it all down pat, but there is still much to be learned, and by the time he's a junior a bit more humility sets in as he sees that these years are just one more stage in his education. We'll all be freshmen constantly if we grow in this life. But the sophomore definitely fits the original Greek word. He is the "wise fool": *soph* meaning "wisdom," from which we get words like *sophisticated* (wise to the ways of the world) and *philosophy* (love of wisdom), and *more* meaning "foolish," from which we get *moron*.

speed   When someone says, "Godspeed," we get an idea of the original meaning of this word: "success, prosperity." In our society quickness is equated with success. Whoever can get the job done fastest is the best, from our computers and mail service to our athletes and factory workers. Swiftness and acceleration are our modern concepts of speed, though there are certain activities, such as art and writing, where the rate of completion isn't the yardstick of success . . . unless you're working toward a deadline.

spigot   How many of you use this old-fashioned name for a faucet or tap? With this word you go back hundreds of years to the name for a tap on a cask of wine. The word is still used in this way. It got its start here as an ear of corn. This was called a spike and was the first form of corking for these barrels of booze. *Faucet* goes back just as far and was not a positive term in its origin. It meant "to break into" or "damage." The plug that sealed the place where someone broke into a cask or barrel came to be known as "that which stopped the damage." The *tap* has been a tap for over a thousand years.

spoil   The idea of the "spoils of war" gives us this word that is used so differently by most of us today. The first Latin use of the original word was associated with taking the hide off of an animal. When the hunters brought down the prey, the meat was divided, but the valuable hide went to the hunter most responsible for the kill. When one tribe fought another, this tradition of the victor taking the valuables of the defeated continued (their "hide" was their armor). Sometimes wars were fought solely because one group wanted the things another possessed—from lands to riches. Was it because these things were obtained unearned that they would be misused and sometimes wasted? That's one theory about why the word applies to damaged goods.

sponsor   Though the sponsor of a TV program is not married to the show on which its commercials appear, *sponsor* and *spouse* both go back to the same ancient Latin source meaning "to make a solemn promise." The word seems to go back even farther to a Greek custom of pouring oil or wine onto the ground as a sacrifice to the gods. Today's sponsor promises to pay for the tale on the screen of the tube, while the spouse hopes that what's under the veil won't make him feel like a boob. That was low, I know, especially when talking about promises.

spring   The season and the coil both have an Old English beginning dealing with quick movement. When the plants and flowers burst forth from the ground, when the trap is sprung, and when the doe springs from cover, all go back to the same early word.

You'll spring to your feet and run down to the spring and worry that you're no spring chicken anymore.

spunk Someone with a lot of spunk can certainly get you fired up about getting involved with something. The Irish gave us the word, which was first only applied to tinder used for starting a fire. Over time the metaphorical flames lit by a spunky person gave the word our meaning of courage and spirit.

sputnik This word really hit the English language in the late fifties, when the space race was in full swing and the Russians beat us into the heavens with their little satellites. This Russian word means "co-traveler" and indicated it was journeying in space with Earth. Now, the *-nik* gets to us from the Russian through the Yiddish and can be found in *beatnik,* someone who followed a different drummer, and in *nudnik,* someone who might bore the beatnik to death.

stadium The ancient Greek Olympics gave us this word, not for the stands where the audience cheers its heroes, but for a standard length used for measuring the track. Six hundred Greek feet or 607 English feet (did those Greeks have bigger feet or what?) was the length, and the tiers of seats were built later when all those armchair athletes flocked to the games. Surveyors still use a method of measuring with an upright rod (a stadia rod) observed through a little scope with sighting crosshairs (stadia hairs or wires), which goes back to ancient but accurate ways of judging distance.

staff When a businesswoman talks about her fine office staff and a hiker calls his walking stick a staff, they are both referring to the same Old English root word meaning "pole, rod or stick." On a field of battle or atop a castle, the banner of the lord of the land was the gathering point for his loyal followers. This banner was placed on a lance so that it could be held high or on a pole that could be mounted on the fortress tower. Those who honored the authority represented by that flag got to be known as the "staff" because of the flagpole itself. Today's teaching staff or newspaper staff is linked to those early military staffs. In the days when food was the ultimate cause for loyalty, bread became known as the staff of life.

stereo In the late 1950s, when this splitting of re-corded sound first began to be marketed, some people said it would never last, that monaural sound would be with us forever.... Those same people probably backed the eight-track tape to its grave, too. The word was pulled out of the Greek to describe the new hi-fi (high fidelity) music and meant "solid." The idea was that there was a three-dimensional effect when listening. *Stereo* had been used for the stereoscope, which was a way to make pictures look three-dimensional, so the new sound was first called "stereophonic." When the southerner is portrayed as a bigoted redneck or the stockbroker is shown as a greedy, amoral backstabber, or the yuppie is depicted as a shallow materialist, we're talking about a *stereotype*. This term came from an old printing process in which a one-piece plate was used to print ads and pamphlets. The letters couldn't be changed and the layout couldn't be rearranged, so you got the same thing over and over again. This notion was applied to types of people that were seemingly all alike.

sterling   When silver is called "sterling" it seems to have more value than just regular silver. This *is* a standard name for silver alloys that are at least 92.5 percent silver, but its connotation of worth goes back again to the French conquest of England. The silver coins of those Normans were called "sterlings" because they had little stars on them. Sixteen ounces of them gave the British that unit of money that is still used, the quid or pound.

stew   Basically, the Greek root for this word meant "to cook until the steam comes up." Of course, the recipe that forms the definition has been used for thousands of years and usually involves simmering a dish a long time to blend the flavors. When because of heat, crowds, or worry we feel that we're figuratively steaming, we say we're "in a stew." "Quit stewing about it and do something!" Centuries ago the term also was used for a public facility for taking hot baths. And, speaking of heat, an old slang name for a house of prostitution was a "stew." This has nothing to do with a stewardess being called a "stew." This goes back to the Old English word for steward, which meant "keeper of the hall." Besides, they're "flight attendants" now because they got in a stew about the sexist job description.

stingy   This word is derived from the same root that gives us the bee *sting*. The Old English word came to refer to very selfish people because such people feel as if they have been stung whenever they have to spend a bit or share some of their goods. Now, if you were in a pub in England and a man took a sip of ale and said, "That's stingo!" he wouldn't be referring to a bartender who didn't pour enough in the glass. This slang means that the brew is very good. It's also applied to other things with a lot of energy and zest.

stocky I talked about *pudgy* and now here I go with *stocky,* a word that can be complimentary when you talk about a solid and sturdy man, but can indicate a squat, chunky type when describing a female. The word goes back to the Old English root for "tree stump," which is definitely thickset, short, and heavy. Our word *stock* comes from this. Unless you were clearing the land for cultivation you let the stump rot on its own, since it was a huge job to remove it. Many times you made use of these stubs of trees as markers for your boundaries, and in towns they made excellent tables for outdoor merchandising. You might use a group of stumps near your home to fashion a corral for your animals for the night. The animals inside this fenced area became known as your *livestock,* and later just "stock." *Stockade* comes from a similar German root meaning "stake," and this got linked in English to the tree-stump word. When tables made of stakes were also used for selling goods, the merchandise became known as "stock." Not only was a stump a good place to make a speech (as in "going stumping"), it was also a good place to display a ne'er-

do-well . . . in the stocks (and they, too, were later built from stakes). The stump comes up again in just a few words, so I'll return to it.

stooge   The exact origins of this word are unknown, but several hundred years ago the word was used as slang for a student. In those days many students were apprentices to craftsmen or assistants to other skilled professionals. Since these novices were sometimes inept and so inexperienced as to look foolish, *stooge* got a derogatory connotation. Later, in comedy acts, actors portrayed these bumbling assistants, feeding straight lines to the comedian playing the role of boss (many times a doctor). The word was relegated to the straight man of the comedy act until the aforementioned Three Stooges gave it a new shade of meaning. Larry, Moe, and Curly each played the straight man and stooge for each other and took the word to new heights of idiocy for several generations of fans. It's hard now not to think of *stooge* without an image of the nutty trio.

stop   The very simplest words in our language have a story in their travels. This word that we read every day on the red octagon at intersections started out in ancient Greece. A supply of hemp or flax was kept aboard ships in case small leaks occurred on a trip. You could take this fluffy fiber and cram it in the crack, paint it with pitch or resin, and resume your cruise. It was also a perfect seal for homes on windy winter days. Both *stuff* and *stop* were first associated with this caulking substance. Eons ago, mothers probably were comparing a messy house to the scattered unraveled rope and combed-out flax used in early repair jobs, saying, "Clean up this stuff!" "To pull out all the stops" doesn't refer to some mad sailor yanking up all the plugs onboard ship. This was a term an organist used when wanting the instrument to play full blast. The musician would pull all the levers or stops to let all the pipes be heard.

strange   For the Romans, anything that was foreign was considered strange according to their definition of the root word: "on the outside." We now think of something that is peculiar or odd as being strange, and that *can* include some foreign customs. A stranger is no longer just a foreigner, however, though to be *estranged* is certainly a feeling of being put on the outside.

strawberry   This delicious red fruit gets its name from the little hairs or bristles sticking out all over it. These "straws" reminded the early English of a field of hay, which got the name "straw" from the way it was spread out to dry before being bundled up. After it was cut, you had to "strew" it across the field to parch it so it wouldn't mold through the winter months.

stress   This is our word of the era, the cause of heart attacks, ulcers, and mental difficulties. The word comes from the Latin and went through changes in both French and English, but it basically means "to draw tight or compress." The same root gives us *strict,* and when you're under a lot of stress someone is probably being too strict or rigid with you (maybe even you yourself). The cure for being stretched tight? Relax. Otherwise you'll cause yourself *distress,* a word used by the early French to describe a narrow passage.

stubborn   Here we are back with the tree trunks again. This was the early farmer's most difficult job: getting those stumps out of the cleared land. He might dig around them, pull them with his oxen, chop at them, or burn them, and still those stumps might not budge.

Stub was an Old English word for a tree stump, and the word *stubborn* comes out of the above description. When someone was stubborn they were as hard to move from their ideas as a tree stump. The idea of a small remaining piece of a larger object was used for many other "stubs" and "stubby" things.

stun   Lightning and thunder have inspired awe in man and animal since the dawn of time. The fury and destruction that nature can unleash in its violent moments strike terror into the hearts of children and adults alike. Latin is once again the starting point for the word *stun,* and its earliest use meant "surprised or dazed by thunder." *Astonish* and *astound* both come from the same root word.

Stun's stronger sense of being stupefied, conveying more than the mere amazement of *astonish,* probably came from an even closer lightning strike. We still use the term *thunderstruck* to express a similar kind of shock and consternation.

style   Everyone has his or her own style, however wonderful or terrible that may be. The earliest use of the word as describing how we all express ourselves differently goes back to ancient writing. The Roman *stilus* was a pointed stick or rod first used as a cattle or sheep goad. From this we also get the word *stimulate,* which is, crudely, what the herder was doing with the prod. Sometimes the staff would be tipped with iron to make its point last. Smaller versions of this were used in writing. Man has tried to record his deeds on everything from cloth to clouds, and one way was to scratch on wax tablets with the stilus. It was quickly seen that every person had a particular way of marking letters, no matter how standardized those letters were, and the idea of individual style was born, meaning how you wrote with the stilus. Somehow or other in translating the word, early writers got a Greek word mixed up with it and added the *y*. The stylus of recent years was the needle early record makers used to cut grooves into a wax platter as a master disc for production of copies. A record needle is still called a stylus, so the Roman notion of wax writing has survived into our technological age, though this, too, may be forgotten by another generation raised on CDs and digital audio tape.

stymie   We don't use this word for frustration as much as we once did, but old-time golfers may be very familiar with it. Today, as a courtesy, a golfer will put a marker down on the green when his ball might be in the way of another's shot to the hole, but in the past this wasn't done. The player lying away who was obstructed by another fellow's ball was "stymied." The tough Scots love their golf and took the word from their old tongue that meant "a person who is partially blind." Some golfers would actually try to stymie their opponent as a strategy, but as golf grew more gentlemanly players would graciously mark their balls and remove the impediment. Since then the word has drifted out of widespread use.

subtle   We use *subtle* today for many things: the delicate flavor of a spice or seasoning in a meal, the clever hint concealed in a conversation, the ingenious crafting of a color into a painting, or the ability to make fine distinctions in thought. The word came from Latin and was used for a closely woven fabric. Subtle cloth was made of fine threads precisely pressed together so that it would be hard to see an individual strand. Literally it means "under the web." *Subtile* also used to be used but is now rare. That spelling does give us more of a feeling of "tex*tile*," a word I'll talk about later.

sudden   When something happens all of a sudden, it's generally unexpected and surprises you. The Latin from which the word sprang gave it a sneaky meaning. "To go stealthily" is basically what the word meant. This secret approach of something stealing up on you was applied to any unforeseen happening. *Surprise* has a similar sneakiness, meaning "to take while napping," getting someone while asleep. *Flabbergast,* on the other hand, had a sillier start as slang in the 1700s and probably derived from the way a fat person looked when taken unawares, combining *flabby* and *aghast.*

suds   Suds today have a pretty happy life in the world of words. They show us that the clothes or dishes are getting a good washing or that the ale or root beer is properly carbonated and rich. The Dutch origins of the word were not so pleasing. The root of this word referred to swamp water and the foamy sludge of the marsh. The bubbly dregs of the bog were around long before soap was widespread, but the lather of detergent reminded early bathers of the froth of the swamp, and the word hung around to be used in laundry advertisements.

swab   The cotton *swab* is our main use of this word these days, unless you're in the navy with an old-timer who calls you a "swabbie." Both terms reflect the Dutch roots of the word, which meant "to do dirty work." Certainly, the cotton ball or fluff-tipped stick does a lot of messy jobs, whether you have to have your throat swabbed or your arm sterilized before a shot. One of the sailor's important jobs in the early days of the wooden ship was to keep the deck clean, and swabbing it was a regular chore. Another swab you may be familiar with is the long-handled device used for cleaning a rifle barrel. *Swab* also has been used as a slang word for a clumsy person.

swamp   The Old English roots of this word referred to a mushroom or other type of fungus. Since these grew abundantly in the spongy soil of the bogs, the name for the plant got attached to the place. A marsh got its name for land that was overcome by the sea, which is where most marshlands reside. *Bog* was an Irish concoction from a word meaning "soft" or "moist."

swan   We think of swans as graceful birds with curved necks and white feathers. Every ugly duckling wants to be one. But the early Germanic root word referred to the bird's voice, not its beauty. *Swan* comes from a word meaning "sound." No, being way down upon the Swanee River wasn't for the birds. It's supposed to be *Suwanee,* from an Indian word. And if you've ever heard an older person, especially one from the South or certain parts of England, give an exclamation of mild surprise by saying, "I swan," they're not calling themselves birdbrained but are harking back to an old British dialectical expression meaning "I'll warrant" or "I swear," used much like "Well, I'll be!"

swap   The hand-slapping high and low fives that are common today in sports and among the young are as old as the handshake. Before currency (and even after it), people traded all sorts of things, from services to goods.

A common practice to show that each party was satisfied with the deal was to slap hands with each other. Six or seven hundred years ago this was the way Englishmen closed a bargain. After this the exchange was over and you couldn't take it back. You'd "struck" your deal.

swastika The hated Nazi symbol doesn't have its roots in Germany at all, and terror is not at all what it was meant to inspire. The word comes from India from the Sanskrit, meaning "to wish well-being or good fortune." The symbol was ancient when the Germans decided to adopt it as an auspicious emblem of their new fascism. The flag of the National Socialist Party today carries with it terrible memories of Nazi bigotry and atrocity. Whether by design or accident, the Nazis used a mirror image of the Indian religious symbol and good-luck sign . . . ironically foreshadowing the "bad luck" of the Third Reich.

swelter In its earliest use this word meant "to die" and, later, "to faint." Admittedly, on a humid summer day when the temperature is cracking the century mark you might *want* to give up the ghost. For the early English who gave us the first form of this word, heat and humidity were something you had to bear with. There was no fan or air conditioner to bring relief. Sometimes animals and people died in that oppressive atmosphere, and fainting from the heat was common. That's when it was sweltering. The word was once used for exuding poison or venom, from the sweat-covered body, the heat-crazed rabid animal, or the angry snake seeking cool shelter. One form of this word, *sweltry,* changed over the years to *sultry.*

swerve Our most common use of the word refers to the scary but sometimes necessary tactic of avoiding something as we travel in our car, swerving out of its way. It might be hard to figure, but at first this word referred to sweepings or litter. This was the litter of the workplace, where a bit of metal might be filed or scoured into a sword or spearpoint, or a shield might be hammered and polished. From the Old English of the first thousand years A.D. to the Middle English of the next three or four hundred years, the word evolved to mean the circular motion of the polishing and filing and no longer applied to the litter below.

swindle   This word comes from a German root that had a variety of meanings, from "disappear" to "wither" to "weaken" to "become unconscious." All of these hint at the reactions a person might have to being cheated by a swindler, but my favorite is "to be made dizzy." The word was coined to explain how you felt when you'd been swindled. While you were being tricked by the fast-talking  swindler you felt as if you'd been made weak and dizzy by his scam (an alteration of *scheme*), that it almost seemed like you were unconscious as your money vanished before your eyes.

sympathy   The ancient Greek meaning rings true when you have sympathy for another's condition. You are "feeling together"; you share an understanding of what the other person is going through. Some husbands get so involved in their wives' pregnancies that they actually feel an ache in their stomachs; they have "sympathetic" pain. *Empathy,* on the other hand, is not sharing feelings, but getting so involved with some thing or person that you actually seem to be feeling what it is feeling. This Greek-based word is actually a translation of a German word meaning "a feeling in." Another of these "feeling" words is *pathetic,* which once had only positive aspects but now is used often in sarcasm or as a critical description: "He made a pathetic attempt to entertain us." "Liable to suffer" or "full of suffering" is the idea of the word as it was first used. It was used for things that moved a person to pity or tender passion. Later, the idea of suffering was taken by science to describe diseases or conditions, from the pathological liar to the psychopath. Being *passionate* can be intense and wonderful, but it can cause suffering, too. The first uses of *passion* dealt with enduring pain, and the early Catholic Church used the word to describe the suffering of Christ. The Romans gave us this word from a translation of the Greek *pathos. Compassion* was their term for sympathy, and being *passive* was its opposite.

symposium   We think of symposiums today as a group of experts leading a discussion on a particular intellectual or social topic. Though these conferences can be valuable, they can also be pretty dull. Not so with the original Greek symposiums. They were drinking parties. The translation of the word is "to drink together." It was a tradition among the Greeks to have these parties where men (yes, stag parties) got together and ate, drank, listened to music, and talked, generally focusing on one subject. When Socrates formed his school in Athens this was one of the favorite pastimes of his many friends. Plato records one of these parties in his *Symposium.* Here all the men tell of how they drank too much the day before and agree to drink only as much as they want and forego the tradition of "drinking deep." They tell the flute-girl to go off and play to herself, and then proceed to talk about the nature of love until they are interrupted by revelers, who get them all drunk anyway. This kind of speechmaking party became the basis for our more sober symposiums.

symptom Here's another Greek-born word, meaning "fall together" or "happen at the same time." The idea behind the word is that when certain conditions all happen at the same time these are signs of some larger occurrence. For example, if a fever, sore throat, and aching joints all happen at the same time, you can probably diagnose flu or some other virus. If your exhaust begins smoking and you hear the clattering of your valves and the smell of burnt oil, you'd probably better get ready for a mechanic to smile that secret smile that means you will help his kid go to college. If your symptoms indicate a *syndrome,* you go back to a Greek expression for "things that run together," from which we get the fancy name for camel, *dromedary* (Greek for "he that runs").

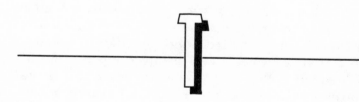

tablet The writing pad and the pill you swallow both have the same ancestor. A board used for writing or painting was the first tablet. When these were supported so that you didn't have to prop them on your knee, they were *tables.* In the late 1500s English doctors began to press their medicines into flat pills that they called tablets because they reminded them of tiny tables. By the late 1800s one company actually gave its medicine the brand name Tabloid. Today we use the word for the grocery store magazines not because they offer any curative power, but because, like the pill, they are condensed . . . and sometimes hard to swallow.

taboo   The Polynesian people of the Tonga Islands, near Fiji, had an expression for something that was marked as sacred. It was *tabu,* which meant you could not touch it or speak of it without causing the gods to get angry with you. Almost every society has something that you just don't talk about in public. Our attitude about where a woman may expose her breasts would make a Frenchman walking down the beach at the Riviera have a good laugh. Just a short time ago it was a big taboo for a Russian, Pole, or Czech to have a free and critical discussion of his government's actions. British sailors were impressed by this South Seas prohibition and took the word with them to pass it into our language.

taco   This word for the Mexican staple came from the Spanish, of course, and meant "a wad or plug." It wasn't because these stuffed corn-meal *tortillas* (Spanish for "little twisted cakes") were used as stoppers or stuffing. You could say they plugged hungry bellies, but actually the name comes from the tradition of rolling meat, beans, or vegetables in the tortilla. Folding over these goodies made the taco look wadded up. The dish was (and is) especially popular as a light lunch, which was another translation of the word.

tact   When your daughter brings home a three-hundred-pound bearded biker with tattoos under his leather jacket and you can later say, "He seems well-traveled and has a zest for life," you definitely have tact and could be a candidate for the diplomatic corps. The art of saying the right thing in a difficult situation takes a delicate touch, and "touch" is just what the word means in its Latin original. The early English first used the word to mean "to stroke," which fits our social use of the word today. The root for the sense of touch gives us all kinds of words, from *contact* to *tangible*. When you are *contagious* you can spread what you have by touching another, which will *contaminate* them (or make them impure through contact). When you have *attained* your goals, you've certainly gotten hold of success, but you'll want to *contain* yourself (hold it in) just to be tactful. Now, that hardest of all touches, the *tackle,* doesn't come from the same root. It goes back to a Dutch word for a pulley and rope used to rig ship's sails, and that later referred to any equipment including your fishing gear. Just as the pulley setup would seize and move large objects, so certain football players perform that useful operation. But I've gotten off on a *tangent* (a line that touches a curve). Though tact may require *tactics,* that word comes from another Greek root meaning "skill in arranging." While I'm touching on this subject, some say that *tango* might even come from this same root, from the idea of touching the strings of a musical instrument, and touching your partner while dancing it.

tadpole This word has been around for several hundred years and literally translates as "toad head." Derived from the Middle English, this descriptive term for the larva of these amphibians was based on the idea that a tadpole was a toad made entirely of the head, with the legs and body to grow out later. I already talked about *poll* and all of its "head" meanings, and

here is another. That other name, *polliwog,* is also
related to that root, coming from about the same time
period and meaning "wiggling head."

tang   Because of this word's common modern use in
describing flavors and as a brand name for a tasty
drink, most of us think of the word in this light. The Old
Norse beginnings of this word referred to the point of a
dagger and gave the idea of being pricked or stung. The
part of the knife or chisel that fits into the handle is
called the "tang." When the taste of something was so
strong that it seemed to stick you in the tongue, it was
"tangy." *Tag* also came from the same root and described a little hanging end or point of cloth hanging off
a larger piece of clothing. The action of "tagging"
someone might have come out of fencing practice,
where the touch of the rapier represented a wound.
"Touché!"

tank   You already heard about the strange way a
bazooka got its name. The military vehicle we call a

tank also has a strange
story in its christening.
In India it was and is a
common practice to
divert water from a
river into small storage
ponds, called *tankhs.*
This was one of the
influences on the
modern word. Another
came from the Spanish
and Portuguese word
for something that
stopped the flow, *tanque.* Now, back to the weapon. The
battles of World War I were bloody stalemates of men

trading trenches in death-dealing charges at one another. A weapon was needed that would break through these entrenched lines and plow into enemy territory. A mobile armored cannon was designed by the British under the most secret of conditions. Spies were everywhere and the Brits wanted to be first with this new device. So that no one outside the project would know what it was about, it was given the code name "Tank." Anyone at the French port where the crated combat machines were unloaded would only see "tank" as its identification. The tank did play a role in changing the course of the war, but the Germans were able to get in the game quickly and manufacture their own. The fear of future tank warfare caused France to build the Maginot line on its eastern border. These heavy fortifications were supposed to stop any tanks from ever crossing onto French soil. Of course, Nazi tanks just went neatly around this wasted effort.

tattoo Permanently marking the skin with a tattoo is a tradition that sailors brought us. This word is Tahitian in origin, and the exotic skin art was a sign of manhood for the islanders. But if you've ever heard a boxer described as beating a tattoo on his opponent, you're hearing a word that comes from a totally different source. Military veterans might be familiar with the drum or bugle signal that calls the soldiers to their quarters for the night, also called a tattoo. This comes from a Dutch phrase that described the signal to barrooms to close for the night. Drums or horns were used to proclaim the "last call," either beating a certain rhythm or playing a particular tune. The "taptoo" literally meant "shut the taps," which is where we get the title of the evening bugle song when the day is done or, at military funerals, when a life is done.

tax I left out *tax* when talking about *touch* awhile ago. Most of us would like to leave out taxes altogether. This word does come from the same Latin root that means "touch." It might seem that the government is "putting the touch" on you when it requests taxes, but the idea originally came from paying a percentage on everything you had that could be touched: your property. The word *task* comes from the same root. If you couldn't give a portion of your goods in taxes, then you might perform some job or service for the powers-that-be.

tease When you are first learning this mysterious language and you hear that a woman has had her hair teased, you may think that someone has been making fun of her coiffure. When you learn that this word originally had to do with sheepshearing and was a term for raising the nap of the wool with a comb and untangling it after it's been cut, then you may wonder why we call mocking someone "teasing." Apparently, sheep are not always fond of the shearing process, just as we don't enjoy having our dignity sheared from us by someone's teasing. Also, the plucking and combing out of the cut wool before dying and spinning can be compared to someone picking at you by poking fun, or to plucking the strings of desire with unfulfilled sexual overtures.

technical Speaking of wool, the Greek root of this word applied to a weaver or a carpenter. In that more primitive past some of the most technical things you could do would be to set up a loom to make fabric and use primitive tools to craft furniture or a home. Over time, the word came to be applied to any art or craft that required skill, from musical technique to computer technology.

teetotaler   When I was very young I thought this person who abstained from alcoholic beverages probably got his name because he toted tea wherever he went. The rage for prohibition in the early part of this century sparked a major "just say no" campaign that actually changed the Constitution. During this period it was common to say the first letter of a word with that word to emphasize it strongly. "S-special" things were *very* special, from which we get *especial*. If you were "T-totally" against alcohol, you didn't even want to see it in your perfume. Teetotallers went out and tried to convert those who still took a nip, either by taking an ax to the beer barrel or a sermon to the barroom.

temperance   All right, I'll stay with those prohibitionists just a little longer. The temperance movement sometimes had a reputation of fanaticism, but the followers of Carry Nation and Susan B. Anthony, among others, accomplished a lot. They got the government to regulate the sale of booze as far as age limits and hours of sale, and they brought an awareness of the dangers of alcohol. Some prohibitionists did get rather carried away in their violent opposition, and the disgruntled reaction of many people to Prohibition in 1919 led to the movement getting a rather prissy reputation. The idea of these organizations went back to the Latin notion of "temperance," which meant "to mix in the proper proportions." The original idea was that if you used alcohol in moderation you were a *temperate,* well-balanced person. Extremists among this group lost their *tempers* (Latin: "to observe proper measures") and became *temperamental* about any kind of drinking at all, and that caused *temperatures* to rise on Congress's hot seat. The whole issue became a *tempest* (unbalanced weather) of emotion, *tempered* only much later by an inability to enforce such *temporary* restrictions.

tenant   We're back to touching again with this word. A firmer kind of grip is involved here, though. The Latin for "hold" is the basis of this word. When someone has "holdings," land or buildings that they own, and they let others have hold of them, those others are the tenants. When you hold a position in education or government because of length and quality of service, you have *tenure,* which allows you to keep that job. If you can hold a tune, you may not necessarily be a *tenor,* but this word also goes back to that Latin forefather. The tenor voice was the one that carried the melody in early compositions. Why do the British call their lieutenants "leftenants"? The idea in this rank is "you have my leave to hold authority while I am not here." Englishmen didn't like the French *lieu* and used a more Anglic form of "by your leave."

territory   The Latin for "dry land" gives us many words in English. The area of land called a territory might have *terraces* in it that, at their outset, were mounds of earth. Plants may be put in *terra cotta* pots, a term meaning "cooked earth," from the baking process they go through. The *terrain* (lay of the land) of your *terrarium* (place for earth) might contain plants or animals. And our most popular encounter of the third kind, E.T., gets his name from *extra-terrestrial,* meaning "not of this earth."

thank   It's thoughtful to thank someone and its nice to know those two words are related. For the early English clans, gratitude was something given mainly to God and, on occasion, to a kind neighbor. Both *think* and *thank* come from the same source and give us the idea that when you express appreciation to someone you have taken time to think about it.

thigh   Everyone out there who is jogging, "aerobicizing," dieting, and herbal wrapping to shrink that section of the body from the kneecap to the hip will identify with the Old English origin of this word. Its earliest meaning was "to swell." As time passes, a thigh does seem to do that, doesn't it? From the same basic root we get *tumor*.

thimble   Just about any seamstress or seamster worth a darn has been thankful for that thimble. That little cap has saved many a finger from having to push a needle through tough fabric. Translating it from the Old English you have "thumb stall." Only you sailors would know that the metal rings on a sail where the rope is put through are also called thimbles. And very few would know that a thimblerig is another name for a swindler's shell game, using you-know-what instead of shells.

thing   This overused word got its start in English from an Old Norse word for a public assembly. A "thing" was a court or council, a time when people gathered to discuss a controversy. As the word marched through time, what was under discussion became the focus rather than the gathering itself. *Thing* came to be used for any matter of concern, and eventually had the honor of representing a creature in a horror movie.

thousand   Before we organized our numbers to stand for certain amounts, the Germanic *thousand* just meant "many hundred." There just wasn't much use for a precise word for ten hundred, since there were so few things that amounted to that much and hardly anyone who could count that high anyway. Today we would say "a zillion" for an imprecise but huge quantity. We think a little bigger.

thug   This word for a hoodlum comes from a Hindi term for a religious organization that followed the goddess of destruction, Kali.

"Thugs" carried out murder and robbery in her service, as if putting a tithe in a collection plate. "He hides" is the direct translation of the Hindi, based on this group's practice of ambushing wealthy travelers and stran-gling them. These choirboys of Kali practiced their missionary work for nearly six hundred years, from the 1200s to the 1800s, until the British put a stop to their rather violent worship. OK, *thief* comes from an Old English term meaning "to cower or lurk." *Hoodlum* comes from a Swiss word for "miserable fellow." A *gangster* is a member of a gang. *Burglars* get their name from the Latin for a hired servant. *Crooks* don't just follow the straight and narrow: They're morally bent.

ticket   How is your sense of manners linked to a pass to a ball game? *Etiquette,* now our term for the rules of proper behavior, was derived from the French word that also gave us *ticket.* At the outset, any note or memorandum was an etiquette, but as the rules of government became more specific, passes that gave you the right to go into certain parts of the city or even enter the city itself began to get the name. Soon, labels and tags that showed ownership were also called tickets, and even lists of candidates and summonses to court for small legal violations got the term applied to them. So tickets made sure things were right and proper and in order, and the English came to associate the French word with correct ways of behaving. Good etiquette: That's the ticket!

tidbit　This is kind of a silly word, but we hear it all the time for a small piece of food or news or gossip. *Tid* came from a British dialect and meant "small object," while *bit* came from *bite:* a piece big enough to take in a bite. Why is *tad* used for a small amount, especially in the South? We go back to *tadpole* here, which was once used as an affectionate term for a little child, usually a boy. It *would* sound weird to say, "Could I have just a tadpole of sugar in my tea?"

tiger　The Greeks probably took this name for the animal from a Persian word meaning "sharp." Claws and teeth were what impressed them about the big cat, whose fierceness has drawn respect and fear through the ages. We compliment aggressive people with "He's a real tiger." Tough situations are ones where you've got a "tiger by the tail." And a romance is going to heat up when she says, "Come over here, Tiger."

tingle　You kiss that special person and you hear bells and tingle all over. Well, in the original meaning of this word the bells might come out of the tingling itself. *Tingle* comes from *tinkle,* which was a word made up to echo the sound of a bell. If you've ever touched a large bell after it has rung, you'll get that tingling sensation from its vibration. And if your leg falls asleep, you might wind up shaking it as if you're ringing a bell, to get that pins-and-needles feeling to go away.

tinhorn   In a Western, when a gambler is called a tinhorn you know there is probably going to be a fight. A tinhorn is usually a cheap kind of gambler or businessman who puts on more show than he really can back up. A particular type of metal dice shaker called a tinhorn was used in small dice games like chuck-a-luck (chuck the dice and hope you have luck), where players put down money on the throws of three dice. In fancier gambling houses these games were considered small-time and were made fun of. A "tinhorn" gambler was one who was too cheap to play real games of chance like faro (from *Pharaoh,* who was on one of the cards), where high stakes were laid on the turn of a card.

tire   Here I'm not talking about getting worn out or finding yourself bored with something. I'm speaking of that set of four expensive hoops the blimp advertises, or at least one of the blimps. . . . Several hundred years ago the name was invented for a hoop of metal put around a wooden wheel to make it last longer. This was the wheel's attire and was not only practical, but fancied it up a bit. For a very long time a woman's headdress or headband was also called a "tire," from the same root. When rubber wheels became prominent, ladies quit using the word so as not to be mistaken for a battle axle.

tissue   Once again we go back several hundred years to Middle English, influenced so greatly by England's French overlords. At that time, tissue was a kind of rich cloth, a finely woven gauze prized for its delicacy. This cloth was used for perfumed handkerchiefs, scarves, and other decorative purposes. When the fine, soft paper we know as tissue was put on the market, the term was applied to it as a compliment to its smooth and gentle quality.

toast   Heated breakfast bread and good wishes offered with a raised glass of wine have an interesting link. An early tradition was to place toasted, spiced bread in the wine glass to give the drink better flavor. When a person was honored with a shared sip and a bit of sentiment, it got to be called a "toast" from the notion that just as the bread added to the taste of the wine, the admired person added charm to the company. And there was a wish for spice in his life as well.

tobacco   There is disagreement as to the origin of this word that may be only a bit of history in a few more decades. Some believe the Spaniards took the word from the West Indian term for a pipe in which they smoked the dried leaf. The name for the pipe got transferred to the plant. Another idea is that the word may have come from an Arabic word for a euphoria-causing herb that got applied to tobacco because of its relaxing qualities. Here again, it was the Spanish who borrowed the word, so either way they are the ones who introduced the word into English. Sir Walter Raleigh might have gotten credit for popularizing the herbal drug, but the Spanish had the name for it.

toddy   A little hot toddy can be a nice concoction to put you to bed. This age-old recipe involves brandy, whiskey, hot water, sugar, and spices. But an even older brew gives us the origin of this word. The Hindu people took the sap of various sweet palm trees, especially the palmyra tree, and fermented it to make an intoxicating drink that the British colonials also seemed to enjoy. They took the word with them, but used it for non-palm products.

toil   This word for difficult labor goes back to the Roman Empire and derived from the olive press. This mill used to crush olives for their oil took some effort to use, but was quite a cut above beating them with mallets. During the olive season, however, it was a long, hard job keeping up with the harvesters. When the French took the word into their language they used it for strife and turmoil as well as exhausting work, so there was toiling on the battlefield as well as in the vineyard.

toilet   Our modern use of this word mainly centers on that ceramic basin where no one washes but everyone rests. There is almost a bad connotation to the word, leading to its replacement in the phrase "I need to use the _____" with everything from "powder room" to "gents" to "little girl's room." Actually, the French parent of this word referred to a small cloth that was used to cover a shaving or hair-dressing table. The word was soon used just for the dressing table or grooming area, and finally for the water closet itself. Its original use can still be heard when we speak of toiletries, referring to soap, lotion, or after-shave. And antique collectors will show you fine examples of toilets where no one may sit. *Commode* has a similar origin in furniture as a chest of drawers sometimes found in grooming areas. In the early 1700s there was even a ladies' headdress called a commode. After a kind of chair with a chamberpot also got the name, however, the headdress word went the way of the tire we talked about earlier.

tomfoolery You might still hear someone say, "Stop all this tomfoolery!" The word goes back to a time when the insane and mentally handicapped were not always necessarily treated with dignity. Tom Fool, Tom O'Bedlam (Tom of the insane asylum of Bethlehem in England), and poor Tom were all names given any Tom, Dick, or Harry who might not be mentally sound. Acting like them was tomfoolery.

tomorrow This time that never comes originally referred to morning in the Old English *to morgen* and meant "when the morning comes." During its centuries of giving man an excuse for putting things off, it has also come to mean some unknown, undefined time in the future, "the world of tomorrow."

ton Before the 1600s this word's ancestor referred to a large cask of wine, beer, or ale. The "tun" is still a measure for 252 gallons of wine. When measurements began to be regulated for fair trading and accounting, the two-thousand-pound weight became its value. Latin gives us *pound,* which just meant "a weight." It was another word, *libra,* that told us how much weight, and this still gives us the abbreviation for a pound, lb. A common liquid measure, the pint, comes from a Latin root meaning "paint." Paint? This probably comes from medieval measurers who painted marks on containers used in gauging amounts. Of course, *quart* comes from the Latin for "a fourth," from which we get *quarter, quadrant,* and *quartet.* But the gallon that the quart comes out of got its name from a wine jug of the Middle Ages, which I've already talked about. I'll take the measure of measurements again later when I get to *yard*.

torch   Carrying a torch for an old flame can be torture. Both of those "t" words come from the same Latin root meaning "to twist." What was first twisted in the torches of the Middle Ages were lengths of straw, tied around a stick and dipped in tallow made from animal fat. *Torture* involved twisting portions of your anatomy to cause pain, obviously. *Torque,* which we now find mainly in physics and automotive talk, came from the same Latin root and was the name for a twisted metal collar or necklace worn in England, France, and Germany in ancient times. Some wonder if this was a "thumbing of the nose" at former Roman rulers, who made slaves wear leather collars, or just a fashion to display valuable metal and protect the vulnerable neck at the same time. Just a few more twists on the root of this word: When a contract gets twisted away from the original agreement, you can become involved in *tort* law (twisted); and the rich cake of nuts, eggs, and flour, the *torte,* got its name from twisted bread. I'm not through *contorting,* but I'll go on to the next bit of vocabulary to continue.

torment   On the subject of torture, torment is something we all wish to avoid, from the discomfort of the smallest bellyache to the anguish of severe illness. We go back to the twisting of our last word and a war machine of ancient times. Early catapults would wind a rope attached to a sapling trunk until it bent the thing totally back. When released, this device could fling stones or even bags of hot oil a good distance; it was the first artillery. Later, crafty torturers saw other uses for the winding device and would use the handy tool as an instrument to cause pain on the rack, where bodies were slowly wound out from their joints one notch at a time. The torture machines themselves got the name *tormentum.* It is easy to see how people began to compare a variety of agonies to that devilish object of suffering.

tornado We keep spinning through a twisting vocabulary here with this word for the most dangerous of all land storms. Actually, though, the word started out in the Latin as a name for thunder. The Spanish adopted it and altered it to *tronada,* and then swirled that with *tornar* ("to turn") to create what we know as *tornado.*

torpedo We think of torpedoes as slicing through the water at great speed toward an enemy vessel, but the first wartime use of this underwater missile was different. First, though, let's go back to the word's birthplace. If you guessed Rome, you've been reading along pretty thoroughly. The root meant "numb or stiff" and gave us *torpid.* When olden-day fishermen discovered what we call the electric ray, the fish that can stun its victims with a shock, they called it the "torpedo." That name is still used in the fish's scientific genus and was a widespread common name before we associated the fish's numbing power with electricity. When Robert Fulton, the genius gunsmith, painter, and steamboat popularizer, came up with a device to use in naval warfare to sink enemy ships without having to be close by, blasting cannons, he called it a torpedo, based on the notion that it would definitely stun the enemy. These first torpedoes were more like mines that might be laid at the entrance of a harbor or towed into the path of an enemy vessel.

toupee   Various kinds of hairpieces have been around for centuries, but it seems that in the 1600s and 1700s they reached a kind of social peak. Men and women wore wigs of all kinds; the bigger the wig, the wealthier or more respected you were. The man's periwig would be dyed and powdered, tied with a ribbon in the back and worn on many social occasions. Sometimes a little forelock or curl would be attached to the top. This was the first *toupee,* coming from the German through the French meaning "top." Today we're not as wigged out about hairpieces. Though hair replacement is a booming industry and baldness cures abound, these days you don't flaunt your toupee. Instead we work hard to make it blend in with whatever head fuzz remains. Wigs of prestige can be seen only on formal British officials, such as judges.

town   The same Germanic root that gives us the friendly little town also gives us the hill called a *down* and the pile of sand called a *dune.* Protection was important in days gone by, when invaders or even nearby clans might make a raid on your livestock or home. A hill with an enclosure like a fence around it was a perfect place to locate your living quarters and animals, since it could be easily defended and you wouldn't be wasting good, flat farmland. When neighbors became less hostile and villages might locate more conveniently near water, the variation on the original root referring to a hedged-in area or a fortified camp stayed with us to become our *town. City* came from the Latin root for *citizen,* which first meant "a member of the household." *Hamlet,* the small town, not the play, goes back to an Old French root for "home." And *village* got its start in Latin as a name for a country house, from which we get *villa.*

toxic   Earlier, I talked about *intoxicate* and its poisonous meaning, and now I'll take you back to the earliest
use of that poison. The word is actually from the Greek
for a bow. Particularly
deadly bows used
arrows dipped in poison,
and their name was
also part of the Greek
root, just as "bow and
arrow" seems a set
phrase today. The
Romans took the Greek
word for the poisoned
arrow, and over the
ages it got used for the poison itself.

toy   These days, toys are mainly things for children,
though you sometimes still hear the old-fashioned
"Don't toy with my affections." That is actually the
older use, going back to the Middle English of some six
or seven centuries ago. Toying was flirting—amorous
playing—and generally had sexual shadings. However,
the Dutch also had a word for finery and ornaments
that seems to have gotten mixed into English sometime
later and took some of the romantic sport out of the
word. And the Scots had a name for a woman's headdress (another headdress?) with flaps hanging down to
the shoulders that they called a "toy."

tractor   This word for our widely used farm vehicle
has a simple Latin origin in the root meaning "to drag,
draw, or pull." The late-1800s name was "traction
engine." Many other words come from this same source.
A *trailer* is something that is dragged behind. A *trawler*
drags its nets for fish. Getting *traction* on a steep hill

means your wheels are able to grip to pull you. The railroad *train* and the train on the bride's dress are both things that are pulled. Even *treaty* comes from the idea that both sides are drawn toward a common goal. And *portrait* also comes from this root as something that is drawn forth, onto canvas in a painting or on the screen, in a portrayal of a character.

trapeze   The man on the flying trapeze didn't start by flying at all. The first "trapeziums" were small tables or benches. The Greek means "four-footed" and described this table or bench. Certain gymnastic activities could be done here for the crowd to see, but there's nothing like getting way up in the air for dramatic effect. These aerial artists took their names from the way the ropes formed a square with the crossbar and the roof. Maybe it *looks* like the greatest of ease, but I'll stick to the table.

trash   The old Norse didn't have fast-food wrappers, pop tops, plastic bottles, or disposable diapers to make up their trashpiles a thousand or more years ago. Their word, from which we get *trash,* meant "broken twigs." That term is still used for plant trimmings, but our age has its overabundance of other kinds of leavings that give the word its garbage-dump meanings. Today, everything that is judged worthless, from books to movies to people, gets the name applied to it. And only a trashy kind of person would trash a place through vandalism. Oh, if all we had were broken twigs to worry about!

travel   If you're like me and are basically a homebody, then you'll agree with the Old French meaning of this word. The word comes from *travail,* which in its first use described an instrument of torture made up of three stakes. Travel in the old days was a dangerous proposition. It took forever to get to that beachfront resort on foot or on horseback and you had to carry food, water, and clothing, let alone looking after the screaming kids. And the best rest stops you'd find were bushes. Perhaps a friendly inn along the way would bring you rest from this agony, but on your journey you'd have to watch our for highwaymen, tollgates, beggars, and wild animals. No, travel then was pure trouble ... much like it is for me today.

tribe   You've probably noticed the prominent place the Roman Empire has in the vocabulary of our language. That empire would probably never have come together without three tribes that fought, bickered, and eventually united to form a republic. One tribe, the Etruscans, were invaders, some say defeated Trojans from Lydia. Their language was strange, but their military prowess was great and they conquered the Latins and ruled Latium and Rome in central Italy for several generations, hundreds of years before Christ. They also fought with another tribe, the Sabines, to the north of Rome. After a time, the Etruscan kings became cruel and domineering and the common people overthrew the monarch. Now, the tribes tried to treat each other with more equality and they would meet and vote on laws, eventually forming a *republic* ("for the people"). Rome was still the most influential city, and the language of the populous Latins was predominant. Despite greater equality, there was still a class system in which the *patricians* (Latin for "of the fathers," because they were of the original tribal bloodlines) made the laws and the *plebes* (Latin for "common people," derived from "to fill," from which we get *plenty*) obeyed those laws. The plebes eventually demanded more rights, just as people did in our civil rights movement, and *tribunes* ("chief of a tribe") were appointed to make sure the rights of the plebes were protected. They sat on benches called *tribunals,* from which we get our word for a court of law. When Rome was sacked by invading northern Gauls, probably Celtic tribesmen, the groups were galvanized into a military democracy that began to sweep the Mediterranean, absorbing the Greek and even Egyptian cultures and religions into their own. Still, they had a continuing habit of favoritism toward older bloodlines and had to learn more democratic lessons as a result of the slave wars of Spartacus and the social wars that extended that precious Roman citizenship to almost all of Italy. The lessons came too late, however, as military leaders eventually took over and formed the empire, which, after some civil warfare, produced several hundred years of good roads, cultural development, territorial expansion, legal codes, and everyone trying to learn Latin so they could fit in. Things seemed good, but a few tyrants like Caligula and Nero had many people searching for more value in life than more material wealth, and religious exploration away from the gods of state led to a climate that later welcomed persecuted Christianity. OK, I got carried away and didn't even get to the Dark Ages. *Tribe* basically means "three growing groups or beings."

trinket   We call a little ornament, toy, or inexpensive piece of jewelry a "trinket," from an old Norman French word for a small knife.
As metalwork advanced, knives could be made smaller and smaller, which led to even better craftsmanship in jobs where accurate cutting was needed. Shoemakers first used these trinkets, whose root translates as "small cutter," from an earlier root

that also gave us *trench*. Later, little knives were given to ladies to use for paring fingernails or even for protection. These toy knives might be worn as ornaments and became popular gifts. After a time, any miniature piece of jewelry or metalwork became known as a trinket.

triumph   For the Greeks the first "triumphs" were songs sung at festivals honoring the god of wine and fertility. Dionysus, or Bacchus, seemed to love a parade, and processions honoring him had special hymns sung to please him. This eventually led to our modern drama, as the Greeks toned down the drinking and orgies that sometimes accompanied these festivals and turned them into more civilized parties. Well, the Romans (yes, back to the Romans) honored their victorious generals as if they were gods with big parades and special songs written just for them, and maybe even an arch to commemorate their conquests. They took the Greek word and applied it to their tunes, and in time the word got associated with the victory itself.

trivia I like trivia, as you can tell if you've read this far into the book. This word really got its start with the gossip and storytelling of people who came to Rome to market and visit in ancient times. It literally meant "the place where three roads meet" and referred to a public square or crossroads where folk gathered to share the happenings of their day-to-day lives. So trivia was commonplace information and usually not very important in a life-or-death situation, just interesting and possibly enjoyable. In the Middle Ages scholars divided the liberal arts into seven branches. The highest and most important were arithmetic, geometry, astronomy, and music, and they named these the *quadrivium*. The "lower" arts were grammar, which in those days meant the study of Latin; logic, which was the study of reasoning; and rhetoric, which was the art of speaking and writing. These were the *trivium,* from the Latin, because there were three and because they were considered less important, reflecting the older idea of trivia being facts and knowledge that are less vital. Children studied their reading, writing, and maybe a little arithmetic, while adults explored the mysteries of music, higher math, and the heavens.

troll Remember the story "The Three Billy Goats Gruff," in which the goats tried to get by the ugly troll under the bridge? Many a child wondered about these scary creatures and whether they might just come popping out with their demands around the next corner or over a bridge. The Scandinavians told tales of these supernatural monsters and described them as either giants or dwarfs, always ugly, and generally liking caves or underground living. The Norwegian root came from an earlier word that meant "to walk or run with short steps." This is where we get the idea of trolling in fishing. The fisher isn't trying to catch trolls, but is dragging the lure for short distances. *Trolley* also comes from this root because its route was a series of stops and starts. The old-fashioned word for a prostitute, *trollop,* also comes from the troll. The early use of this word was for a dirty, lazy woman, and this later got applied to streetwalkers. Lusty singing was once also called trolling. "Sing we now our Yuletide carols. Tra-la-la-la-la-la-la-la-la."

trophy   When the Greeks beat someone in battle, they took some of the enemy's weapons, maybe a little of their cloth and foodstuffs, and perhaps some of their gold and other metals and put them on display for everyone to see. Their primitive ancestors had displayed the heads of beasts they had hunted and killed and even the noggin of a tribesman killed in conflict. Looting and plundering the enemy was the tradition of the victor. With civilization came less rude ways of gloating over the defeated, and the Greeks instead built memorials to the victory on the battlefield or in the city. Later they made representations of this memorial on medals given to the bravest soldiers. *Trophy* means "a token of the enemy's defeat." Though we mainly think of trophies as silver cups and tiny statues mounted on wood, many World War II veterans will show you a Luger pistol or Japanese sword and tell you it's a trophy of war. And you've certainly heard the proud hunter describe his mounted deer's head as a "trophy."

trouble   Put a mass of people together without some kind of entertainment and you'll probably have trouble. The Latin word that gives us our *trouble* also spawned *turbid,* which is that cloudy, stirred-up state of troubled water, but which actually came from a root meaning "noisy crowd." When something is troubling you it can be like a mob of voices all shouting at you at once. Car trouble can *disturb* you (Latin, originally indicating a disorderly mob), and when no one takes the trouble to help, it can *perturb* you. *Trouble* gradually began to refer to the stirred-up state of the crowd and was used to describe many bothersome things. *Turbid* began to take on the sense of something spinning and gave us *turbine, turbocharged, turboprop,* and more. And when the wind, crowd, or emotions are in a state of turmoil, we talk about them as being *turbulent.*

truth   In trying to find out where in the world a word comes from, it's sometimes difficult to learn the exact truth, since there's a lot of conjecture about the changes, additions, and subtractions that have gone on for the past millennium or two. *Truth* itself probably comes from the same old Germanic root that gave us *tree.* The idea was that if a thing was firm and solid as a tree then it wasn't imaginary. If your words had the solidness of a tree trunk and would take on the reality of action, then you spoke truth. A door can hang true, a direction can be true (when using a compass), and so can a love.

tuition   The dreaded word for all parents with college-age children: *tuition.* Originally, this was money or goods paid to someone to protect or guard another, usually younger, person. The guardian was called the "tutor," and as I already talked about with *pupil* the charges were usually orphans, perhaps of soldiers or conquered royalty.

tulip   As a child, I thought they might have named this flower because of the big, cup-shaped mouth of the blossom that had "two lips." Boy, was I wrong! The French got the name from the Turks, who compared the flower to a turban because it reminded them of that headdress.

turnip   Apparently, the early English tribes got their name for this plant from the Romans, who called it a *napus*. The English added the *turn,* borrowing it from the French, who got it from a Greek root that meant "made round." The rutabaga, a near relative (but, to me, not nearly as tasty), got its name from a Swedish version of an Old Norse word meaning "baggy root."

tutu   I talked about how the dance called the cancan more than likely got its name from child's talk, and here is another similar example. Children tend to like repetition of sounds as they learn language. They give many things a double name, from papa and mama or dada and momma, to boo-boo and no-no, to poo-poo and wee-wee. The name for the short ballerina skirt comes from French children, who reduplicated a word for "bottom."

twelve   Numbers have wide-ranging origins and often mix with many other words. The Germanic root for this word means "two left." It was a way of describing a certain number of things you had when you took away ten. Our names for numbers were pretty ingrained before the French conquerors imposed their terms, so although we did take that language's name for twelve, we only applied it to certain measures in business dealings. Their *douze* became our *dozen*.

twilight   Seven hundred or more years ago this word became a widely used compound, literally meaning "the light between night and day." This word for in-between light was used both as the sun set and as it rose, though we don't think of morning light as twilight any more. The word gets used now for any condition of waning intensity, such as "the twilight of his years," "the twilight of their civilization," and that place between the real and the make-believe, "the Twilight Zone."

tycoon   The wealthy and powerful man (or woman) of industry gets this name, and it's ironic in today's world that it goes back to a term of honor for the Japanese shogun, meaning "mighty lord." The Japanese took the name from the Chinese for "great prince." Give our friends from Nippon a few more years and the name may be totally theirs again.

tyke   This rather affectionate word for a small child didn't have as tender a beginning. The Old Norse language used it to describe a she-goat or bitch-dog. The Scots used it to name an uncouth man or rude person. Other British dialects called mongrels by this name. Rascally, mischievous children were first called "tykes" in the same way the baby-goat name, "kid," also got used. The word has softened considerably since its start.

ugly   Getting up in the morning and looking in the mirror can be a good wake-up jolt. I say, "Yah! Who is that person?" Maybe Old Norse speakers had a similar experience when they gave us the root for *ugly,* meaning "fearful" or "dreadful." The very earliest base of the word seems to have meant "pointed" or "sharp," like a nose or chin or ears on someone who might be called ugly. This Scandinavian sense comes through when we talk about an ugly storm approaching or an ugly fight brewing in Congress.

ukulele   I'm sure you don't associate this four-stringed instrument with fleas, but in Hawaiian it means "little jumping flea." That wasn't the original name for the small guitarlike contrivance. In the 1800s a British officer, Edward Putvis, became intrigued with the instrument and apparently got very good at playing it, because he would delight natives and fellow seamen alike with his vigorous performances. He got the Hawaiian nickname as the "little jumping flea" and popularized the musical instrument in Western circles. This nickname got applied to the little guitar itself, and Arthur Godfrey and Tiny Tim kept it alive. OK, the word *guitar* went from Greek to Arabic to Spanish to French in its travels around the world and was born from the root for "lyre."

umbrella   The Italians seemed to have popularized the umbrella, giving it its name from the Latin for "shade." That was the most popular use of the device in its early form, protecting someone from the sun. *Parasol* was also an Italian name for the instrument that ladies mainly used to "parry" old Sol's light. *Bumbershoot* originated more as a joke, a combination of *umbrella* and *parachute.* The word for the color pigment we call *umber* probably came from the same root; this yellowish-brown, reddish-brown color was called *terra d'ombre,* "earth of shade." Some say that the color might have gotten its name from a district in ancient central Italy and was actually "earth of Umbria." Those people and their language are no longer around to push for that origin, however.

umpire   I talked about the referee, so why not the umpire? This graduate of the school of hard knocks and hard calls gets his name from the French for "uneven." Now some of you may think this was a joke on the quality of this person's decision-making powers, but actually the name comes from the idea that a third party was needed to settle disputes. There may be two sides to every question, but that odd man out, the umpire, acts as the arbitrator and final word. Most of us grudgingly respect the job this man or woman does, though not many of us would say we're friends with one.

unicorn   *Uni-,* meaning "one," gets used in many words, but none more fascinating than that for the mythological creature the unicorn, which gets its name from the Latin for "one-horned." The wondrous horse assumed most of its legendary qualities in the days of knights and damsels and, much to my dismay, only appeared in the King James version of the Bible, in Deuteronomy 33:17, as a mistranslation by the monks of a Hebrew word for wild oxen. Even the friars seemed to have wanted to propagate the story of the unicorn. Able to kill dragons and heal stricken kings, the horn of the unicorn was a prize beyond compare. This wasn't like the cornucopia, however, which has three or four myths connected with it. It was either the name of the goat that fed Zeus, the nymph who owned the goat, or the horn of a river god who turned into a bull to fight Hercules and lost that attachment in the battle. In any case, the horn of plenty always gave the owner an abundance of fruits, flowers, and drink.

vaccine The terrors of epidemics of disease still haunt us and the hunt for vaccines will probably go on eternally. The name for this method of preventing an illness comes from the Latin and means "cow." Why "cow," you ask? Here's the story. Smallpox was one of the terrible ravagers of humanity for hundreds of years, scarring and killing millions until Edward Jenner found that taking a preparation made of fluid from the lymph gland of cows infected with the cowpox virus and injecting it into humans would prevent the similar smallpox. The practice of taking a dead virus and letting the human immune system develop its own antibodies to fight it is today one of the standard ways of combating diseases ranging from flu to polio. By the way, cows also benefited from this medical advance that bears their Latin name. The vaccine also prevented cowpox in their breed.

van   The vehicle of the modern family, this replaces the station wagon in its ability to transport a heap of kids and their massive amount of belongings. Its name goes back thousands of years to the Persian and came from those desert expeditions, the caravans. *Caravan* in its original form meant "company of travelers." A van driver may think his machine got its name because it is in the *vanguard* of modern driving, but that term comes from a different source, the one that also gives us *van* for the lead troop in an army. That source is the French *avant-garde,* a term usually applied to those in the forefront of artistic endeavor.

vandalism   Angry or irresponsible youth are our most common vandals, but fifteen hundred years ago they would have been ruthless and violent tribesmen of what is now eastern Germany. These wild and ignorant brutes came down out of the North and pillaged, raped, looted, and generally turned the civilized world upside down in their destructive sweep through France, Spain, and finally Rome, which they sacked in 455 A.D. The western Roman Empire had lost its military might and the Vandals took advantage of it, probably bringing on the Dark Ages in their bloody assault on organized society. After that, those who maliciously destroyed property, especially something of artistic or religious value, were called by the tribe's name.

varsity   Playing on the varsity team is the dream of every freshman athlete, male or female. Today the word has more of a place in high schools than at the college level, since most college teams have just the one competitive group, and those who might play in the future can only be "red-shirted" (from the tradition of the scrimmage team wearing red shirts that allow them to practice but not play) to keep their eligibility.

The word *varsity* comes from a contraction and altera-tion of *university*. If you made it big in a sport, you were playing on the "'versity" team.

Vatican   Maybe it's odd or ironic, or maybe it's fitting, that the name for the pope's residence comes from a pagan word for a place where prophesies were made by ancient priests. Before Rome even organized its religion full of Italian versions of the Greek deities, the hill of the Vatican, one of the seven hills of Rome, was known as a place of oracles and prophesy. In fact, the transla-tion is "hill of prophecy." The early Christian popes took this hill as their own holy place, probably as a way to sway the heathen, and absorbed their predecessors' mysticism into their own, as they did with many pagan sites and rituals. Vatican City didn't become the official residence of the pope until the late 1300s, when Gregory XI tried to bring the politically powerful papacy back to Rome from the wine country of Avignon, where it had been for nearly seventy years. That started the great religious soap opera of the time, in which there were as many as three popes—in France, Rome, and Pisa—all claiming to be the true Holy See (this *see* has nothing to do with prophecy, but came from the Latin for "seat"). These various claimants connived with kings and princes until the early 1400s, when everybody got pretty tired of the mess and a council of the cardinals got one pope to resign, deposed two, and elected Martin V. Some think the Reformation got its real start here in the midst of this petty bickering for power, when some rebels within the Church thought it would be better to have a religion with no pope at all, or at least one who didn't claim to be the supreme religious authority. This is one of the first proper names I've used in *Where in the Word?* If you've been enjoying this look at the some-times strange ways everyday words got their start, I've got a whole book's worth that deal with the names of places and people.

venison   Here's another example of how a name gets tied up in a number of words. This term for deer meat goes all the way back to Roman mythology and the goddess of love, Venus. It seems that part of the game of love for the ancients was the chase, and the love of the chase itself got the goddess's name tied up in hunting. At that time the meat of any game animal was "venison," the reward of the hunt. To strive for a goal and win it were the objects of the hunter as well as the lover, they believed. *Win* has a link with Venus's name, too. Attitudes toward love can shape a society, and the Romans had a much less romantic view of their goddess than did the Greeks. Venus could be very practical and very tricky. She was jealous and could be malicious. The more stoic Romans honored Venus, but were also wary of her charms. We get *venom* from her name, based on the potions and spells she and her son, Cupid, used to enthrall lovers. On the good side, we get words like *venerable* and *venerate,* which convey the deep feelings of respect and reverence for age, dignity, and character. Then again, we get *venereal,* as in the diseases caused by sexual intercourse. Even the name of the city of Venice harks back to the root for "beloved."

vermin   Though we mainly think of vermin as rats and weasels that bring disease or a sneaky destructiveness, the earliest
vermin in the original
Latin were worms. I've
already talked about
the noodle vermicelli,
meaning "little worm,"
and if you paint you
probably know that the
color *vermilion* first got
its name from the use of
the tiny cochineal
worm to make a red
dye. Tapeworms or
other intestinal worms are still treated with a *vermicide,* and the *vermiculite* you might see mixed with the soil in a greenhouse to sprout seedlings or used as insulation gets its name because of the way this mica compound expands when heated like a worm coming out of its hole. But back to *vermin* and how it changed from bugs to little animals . . . In old Britain the word's application to pests was expanded to include any bird or animal that killed game in the forest preserves. Poachers who acted like these creatures were also called vermin, giving rise to the word's more nasty connotations of thievery and vileness. *Vermouth* has a connection to the root also, though it is Germanic in origin and comes from a name for wormwood, which contains an extract used in making absinthe and other liquors. Wormwood was so named not because the wood was wormy but because the strong-smelling plant has an oil that can help in the treatment of intestinal worms.

vicinity   If you said, "The university is in the vicinity of my home," we would know it was nearby. In Roman times, when this word was born, the word referred to your neighbor in a village. When people began to group their houses together for protection, trade, and extended-family purposes, their neighbors were suddenly important; the people in their vicinity or neighborhood could make for happiness or irritation. *Neighbor,* by the way, comes from an Old English word for the fellow who is "nigh," or near to you.

victim   We go back to the primitive religions for this word's origin. A person or animal sacrificed to a god was what we now call a victim. The Old English *witch* and *wizard* come from similar beginnings dealing with strange sacrifices before an idol. We get our first taste of victim's rights when God stops Abraham from sacrificing Isaac to Him.

villain   The wicked Snidely Whiplashes of this world are generally booed off the stage for their devious plots against innocent but beautiful young heiresses. The villain of the Middle Ages was the lowly serf, the farm laborer who gave his all to his lord and liege. Unfortunately, these field hands could sometimes be a brutish lot and could cause quite a bit of trouble if there was a mean streak mixed in with their ignorance. "Of the villa or village" is the first meaning of the word, but since the role models of the feudal world were the lord and lady and not the rude farm worker, the word took on a less-than-complimentary tone.

vinegar   This wonderful condiment and preserver has a simple enough beginning in the Latin, from which the French borrowed the word. "Sour wine" is the translation. It can also be used to describe a person with a lot of

spunk or, on the other hand, someone with a sour
attitude, like Aesop's fox who couldn't reach the grapes.

virgin Because of our sexual associations with this
word, it can have an almost socially unacceptable and
even shocking connotation. It can also convey a sense of
holiness when applied to the mother of Jesus. The Latin
root from which we get the word applied to plants. It
was used for a sapling, shoot, or twig. The slender
branch that is the new growth of the tree is much like
youth, untouched and pure.

virus Originally, this word was used for poison,
specifically the venom from a snake or spider. When it
seemed that filthy, slimy places with foul water or
refuse also caused people to become sick from contact,
then *virus* was also applied to this. As medicine and
diagnosis became more refined, physicians speaking of
an illness tended to stay with the word that the masses
were familiar with.

volume In a typical progression the English took this
word from the French, who took it from a Latin root. A
volume was a scroll of parchment, and its earliest root
gives us the simple word *walk,* as both of them were
related to *roll:* one a roll of information, the other
rolling along the avenue. *Waltz* is of similar birth. Since
I tried so diligently to forget how to figure out the
volume of a cone in my calculus class, I'll just remind
you that mathematicians have written scrolls of
formulas for this purpose and there is great value for
the many who unroll them.

vulgar The Roman aristocracy had a pretty low
opinion of the common crowd. The masses were generally of mixed blood, could have once had ancestors who

were slaves, and had poor manners. They were vulgar. The upper class called anything of the masses, and especially their language, vulgar. Over time it came to mean crude, uncultured, and coarse.

wacky   If you're a wacky kind of person, you probably act a bit zany and off-the-wall, and generally are amusing in a silly sort of way. In the word's first sense you'd be considered someone who might have taken one too many licks upside your head. If you acted foolish in those days, it was likely you'd been stunned by a blow to the head. A "whack head," from which the word probably derived, was a person who was a little *slap-happy,* another term for knocked silly.

waffle   We took this word from the Dutch, who got it from the German for "honeycomb." The pattern of the griddle is an obvious comparison, and that pattern holds syrup and jelly so nicely that these battercakes have stuck around the breakfast table for hundreds of years. To waffle on an issue, meaning to be indecisive, came from a different, British root imitating the sound of a yelp, a "waff!" Someone who was vague or couldn't make up his or her mind was like a foolish dog barking at the moon, unsure whether it might be an enemy.

waist   "Waste not; big waist." Well, that's not how the expression goes, but I have noticed as I get older that this word fits its Old English roots more and more. It meant "growth," in reference to the size and thickness of the body. When the body quits growing upward, I guess we can certainly measure its growth outward. Men can nearly always understand the measure "waist-high," though women may have more difficulty, since the fashion waistline can be anywhere from just under the bosom to a place low on the hips.

walrus   This name for the giant, seallike mammal also came from the Dutch and meant "horse whale." Since the walrus seemed so large and blubbery and yet could move about fairly well on land with its strong flippers, the word was a good enough description. The mustached critter shows up in some of our more unusual literature, from Lewis Carroll to John Lennon . . . Goo goo goo joob. The word  *seal* came from a German word describing the animal's awkward land movement: "to pull or drag."

wampum   OK, here's another Indian word famous in the old Westerns. We know it refers to money and that the old Indian usually used bits of glass and beads as his cash. Actually, the early Algonquian used the name for strings of white shells, which were considered valuable. Not only did their shiny, mother-of-pearl finish have a natural beauty, they were also rare and thus precious. Face it, the Indian probably wondered at our fascination for gold.

warden   How are the chief official at a prison and your taste in clothes related? It's definitely not connected with liking stripes. The early Norman French passed this word into Middle English, this time mixed with the original Germanic root. The Norman word *warder* came out of the Old French *garder* ("to guard"), and the Old English word for "protect," *weardian,* got blended in. To get a *reward* reflects both excellent *guardianship* and high *regard,* and all deal with keeping sharp eyes out, whether for attackers or when attacking. *Awards* are also related to this watchful protectiveness of the guard. A stay in the maternity *ward* means being watched over by dutiful nurses and doctors, just as a *warden* watches over the inmates. The *wardrobe* was first a place to put clothes for protection. Since cloth was so valuable, looking out for your robes was important. On the other hand, many words with *ward* as a suffix, like *inward, backward,* or *afterward,* are derived from another Old English root indicating direction.

wasp   This flying insect gets its name from its nest. In the first Old English descriptions, it was the "weaver." Because of its cocoonlike, papery home and the labor it expended building it, the wasp was named after an ancient word for weaving. To be wasp-waisted was a goal for many women around the turn of the century, aided by the whalebone corset and not necessarily by genetics or dieting. *Hornet* also has an Old English beginning and means "little horn," whether from its feelers, shape, or stinger, I don't know for certain. *Bee* has an equally antique Germanic origin and might have been a description of the insect's buzzing sound. Though spelling bees or quilting bees may resemble busy congregations of honey-gatherers, *bee* in this use was derived from another word. A bene was an extra service given to a feudal lord above and beyond the regular duties owed. This came from the Old Norse, akin to a "boon," which was more of an offer you couldn't refuse. Later, in the Middle Ages, the word changed in a kind of respect for the industry of the bee.

weather That great object of conversation, the weather, is something we can depend on to change. The idea of weathering a storm is captured in the Old Norse roots of the word, meaning "to blow," though an Old Slavic word of similar origin referred to fair weather. "Under the weather" is an old phrase that could mean either "gone belowdecks or inside because I'm not well enough to take the weather" or "feeling like I've been left out in the weather"; both are unpleasant.

week Speaking of weather changing, for the English of over a thousand years ago any period of change was considered a "week," a time of turning. In other lands the notion of the seven-day week was thousands of years old. Of course, we all know the Bible story of the seven stages of creation, and the Hebrews based their lifestyle on that description, focusing mainly on the Sabbath, a time for rest. Even then there was a sense of living for the weekend. In Mesopotamia the seven-day cycle was based more on the influence of the sun, moon, and planets than on the labor involved in making those heavenly bodies. The Romans took that belief to heart and popularized it in their calendar. The *dies solis* was translated as the "sun's day" or *Sunday. Monday* was the moon's day, *dies lunae. Tiu* was a German god of war and the sky taken by the early English tribes as *Tiw,* so that when the Romans explained that the third day belonged to their god of war, Mars, these folk naturally named the same day after their war god: thus *Tuesday.* We can still hear what this day might have been called (had these ancestors not held to their deity) when we hear the French *Mardi Gras* (fat "Mars-day," or Tuesday). We also can see how the French took their name for the fourth day of the week, *mercredi,* from the Latin *dies Mercurii* (Mercury's day). To honor their own religious beliefs, the early Norse and English folk named that day for their chief god, Woden, thus giving us *Wednesday* ("Woden's day"). *Thursday* came from "Thor's day," just as the Romans felt that day went to their chief god and the mighty planet Jupiter, or Jove. When the northern tribes were told about the sixth day belonging to Venus (note the French *vendredi* as one of the carryovers), they decided to give it to Woden's wife, Frigg, the goddess of marriage and the home. Who knows whether compromise was made with the Romans or whether our Celtic ancestors were gone for the weekend, but "Saturn's day" stayed in our language fairly intact as *Saturday*. The pagan names continued in one form or another in their respective languages even after Emperor Constantine I made the Christian week, beginning on Sunday, official in 321 A.D.

weird   Man always seems to be caught between the idea that he has freedom of choice and the notion that his destiny is controlled by higher powers. Our many religious denominations will still argue the point, as will thousands of philosophy students. Sometimes what happens to you certainly seems to be more than chance and can make you scratch your head in wonder and say, "That was weird!" For the early tribes of England the "wyrds" were the Fates, who controlled man's future. The Norse called them "Norns" and believed that they ruled past, present, and future. The Romans took their three Fates from the Greeks: Clotho, the spinner, who created the thread of your life; Lachesis, who measured the length of that thread; and Atropos, who carried the shears to cut the thread, a kind of Greek Grim Reaper.

In all cases these spirits seemed to come in threes and all seemed to be female. Another side note: The word *weeds,* when applied to mourning clothes, has nothing to do with any reference to human life being as short as a weed's existence. This *weed* goes back to an old word for black woven linen and its root means "to weave," a reference to the spinning of the goddesses of fate.

west The name for this direction in which young men were once urged to go comes from the Greek word meaning "evening." When the sun sinks from the sky in that direction we certainly know night is not far away. The Latin root that was derived from the original Greek gives us the word for evening prayers or services, *vespers.* In today's political world the West represents a kind of people-oriented way of life, versus the East that seemed to subject people to the will of the state. These East-West delineations may be the stuff of history books before too long.

while Though now this just means a brief period of time, the original root meant "a time of quiet or rest." That initial meaning can still be heard in the phrase "whiling away the time." And although some people who believe that loafing is wicked may think this word was influenced by *wile* (in its earliest meaning: "to lure as by magic or trickery"), such relaxing can often be worth your while.

wife Well, I talked about the husband and now it's time for the wife. Our earliest Old English root for this title simply meant "woman," and so could be found in *midwife* ("woman with" or "woman assisting") or in "old wives' tale" (merely referring to an elderly female storyteller). The word probably goes back much farther to an older root dealing with wrapping, as in veiling or hiding. When early man and woman began to assume a kind of specific allegiance to one another, there was the notion that the role of the non-childbearer/rearer was to provide protection and security for the other. One way of doing that was to hide, cover, or lock away the woman. In northern climes and in the mixed hunting-agricultural societies, where survival meant everyone pulling together, a woman had plenty to do without the wrappings.

willow The beautiful weeping willow best represents the meaning of the parent word from the Dutch. "To twist, turn, or bend" was the description given to the tree. Baseball and cricket bats were once called willows, not because they twisted the ball into the field but because they were originally made of willow. Some homes may have willowware in their kitchens. This was a kind of inexpensive china designed in England in the late 1700s with patterns of willow trees next to rivers and pagodas, giving the feel of the Orient without the expense.

window Hundreds of years ago, in the chilly Norse winters, the home could be a place of eye-stinging smoke and the rank smell of damp fur. That was the reason for putting a "wind's eye" in the design of a house. That's the meaning of the earliest form of our word *window*. It was a place to let air in or out. These vents of the past are the stylish frames of today. With central heat and air condition-  ing they are more of a "light's eye" than a hole for the breeze.

winter To those same early Norse tribes or Gothic Germans, cold must have been a normal state of affairs, much as it is for some Minnesotans, who laugh about their miniature spring-summer-fall. For these tough outdoorsmen of the past, winter was "the wet season," which indicates what they seemed to notice most at that time of year, when cold storms blew in from the North Sea, the Baltic, and the Gulf of Bothnia.

wiseacre This term for people who think they know much more than they do came from a more "serious" root. The Old German word meant "prophet or seer." When the Dutch borrowed it, it kept its early meaning for a while, but time and the poor track record of some of those so-called prophets must have soured the people on those that claimed such wisdom about the future, because the word was gradually directed more toward foolish braggarts. Measurements of land have nothing to do with the second half of the word, which was merely altered in spelling from the Dutch "to say": *zegger*.

world   As you've read *Where in the Word?* you've seen how our world has changed, adding and deleting words, as each generation has its own experiences and passes them on. For the first people, that set of experiences was their world. In fact, the root for this word could be translated as "the age of man" or "the life of a man." Even today, each of us has our individual world with its beginning, middle, and end.

worry   "Worrying is like a rocking chair; it keeps you busy but doesn't get you anywhere," said Gordon Boggs. The origin of the Old English version of the word had a much more harmful sense, meaning "strangle or injure" and was related more to the way a dog will worry at a bone or some people will worry you to death with their pestering. The idea that mental distress and anxiety could bring you just as much pain and uneasiness came later in the word's life. These days it's mainly the troubling worries, those that choke the mind, that come to mind when we hear the word, and we scold ourselves for being *worrywarts* (so obsessed with insignificant things, like every little wart).

wrinkle   They're said to give a man character and a woman age, but in either case we've got to accept them as a natural consequence of life or run to the plastic surgeon to escape them. The Old English root means "to wind about" and was related to *wring,* meaning "to press or compress," which is what seems to happen to our faces after the weight of the world has been on them awhile. The idea of "a new wrinkle on an old idea" is related to our smile and worry lines, but is also kin to *wrench,* which meant both "to twist" and "to trick."

When the tool got the name, the sense of putting a new twist on something drifted away from that word.

Xmas   Many do not like what they consider to be an informal, sacrilegious name for Christmas: Xmas. But the word has its roots in sacred symbols. The early Greek Christians used the letter *X* to stand for Christ, just as the fish with the *X* in the tail also represented Jesus. The letter is transliterated into *Kh* as part of "Khristos," and the businessperson's seemingly less overt *Xmas* is even pronounced "Christmas" in some places. The "chi-rho," those first two Greek letters in Christ's name, is often seen on cloth vestments and looks like a *P* with an *X* crossing its base.

xylophone   Literally translated from its Greek roots, this word means "wood sound." Banging on wood for signaling, entertaining, or scaring away evil spirits is a pastime that is thousands of years old. The Africans refined the musical woodtapping by attaching little tubes under the wooden bars to make the notes fuller. From one of those languages we get *marimba.* We got the ultimate xylophone when the bars were made of metal and a keyboard was attached, making the *celesta,* which is French for "heavenly." And we even see this kind of percussion instrument in marching bands under the German name *glockenspiel,* meaning "playing bells."

yacht This word is now almost exclusively associated with the lifestyles of the wealthy and renowned, but the early Dutch version had a much more practical meaning. This was their term for a pursuit ship used to catch pirates. Yachts were fast, relatively small craft designed to chase or hunt down those buccaneers who preyed on shipping lanes. They were the PT boats of another  time. When piracy diminished, the ships were used for more frivolous pursuits, such as racing or pleasure cruises financed by the wealthy.

Yankee This word has certainly had its ups and downs during its several-hundred-year history. It was first a term of derision that English colonists used for Dutch settlers. The Dutch love for cheese was well-known and they sold it prolifically. This, when combined with a common Dutch first name, gave rise to the nickname "Jan (pronounced 'Yon') Cheese." Over time this ethnic slur got blurred into "Yankee." When the feisty revolutionaries were given the name by loyal Britishers, they wore it with pride, even adopting the song that was meant to make fun of foolish fops, "Yankee Doodle," as a proud tune for their cause. After the Revolutionary War the term "Yankee" was one of honor. This changed, however, with the War Between the States. Once again there was divided opinion as to whether it was good to be a Yankee. After the Civil War the word was applied to all those living north of the Mason-Dixon line and still carries some sting on the tongues of certain southerners. War again brought some pride back to the name, though, as the world wars saw American troops fighting overseas as part of the Allied forces. "The Yanks are coming" was a phrase of happy relief; ironically, to be a Yankee in England could be a very welcome thing. The wheel of victory can certainly change a word's connotation, though. When the wealthy United States began to get involved in developing countries and their governments, an American could be faced with an angry crowd shouting, "Yankee, go home!" Once more, *Yankee* became a word prompting mixed emotions. Still, we speak with pride about "Yankee ingenuity" and "the stubborn Yankee spirit." As a sidelight, the "doodle" in the song "Yankee Doodle" was probably originally "tootle" because it was written for the fife, a popular instrument of the day.

yard   Here's one last look at measurements. This word came from the old measurement using a rod, which is what its root meant. The first rod equaled the distance from the wrist to the backbone, and that was the length of the stick you used as a standard for measuring land. Later the rod got lengthened to the sixteen and a half feet it is today, while the yard stayed at about the three feet we use now. A foot in Old English days was the length of a foot. The words *inch* and *ounce* both come from the Latin for "twelfth." At first, ounces were twelfths of a pound, and they still are in troy weight (which takes its name from Troyes, France, where goods at medieval fairs were first weighed using this standard). Later the English divided pounds into sixteenths using *avoirdupois* weight (from French, meaning "the weight of the goods").

yarn The spinner of tales who tells yarns and the sockmaker who uses yarn both are creating something, either from the cloth of the imagination or from threads of wool. The root for the word is a bit different, however. It meant "gut or intestine." The word's birth gets all mixed up in the early use of gut for thread, the sooth-sayer who would read intestines and their contents to predict future events, and the cord of life I talked about with the Fates. So telling a yarn might have a more mystical beginning than darning with yarn.

year You already saw how time got organized in the words *calendar* and *week*. One other measurement of time, the year, also was more vague at first than it is today. For olden-day Germans the root meant "sum-mer." Early Bulgarians had a similar word meaning "spring." The English first took the root in its general sense, "that which passes," and the years certainly do that. In 46 B.C. the great Julius Caesar gave us our first standardized year, equal to 365 days and 6 hours. Somewhere his calculations were off, and our leap years were thrown in to compensate. By the 1500s Roman time-counts had pushed the first day of spring back from March 21st to March 11th. Well, Pope Gregory XIII thought this would never do: After a while, we'd have spring coming in January. He made the Roman Catholic world drop ten days off the calendar and use leap years for years ending in hundreds if they could be divided by 400. England refused to adopt this division of time until 1752, so Shakespeare's spring was earlier than the rest of Europe's. What's more, the Eastern Orthodox Church didn't accept this Gregorian calendar until this century . . . talk about behind the times!

yellow   The Germanic root that entered Old English and eventually became our word *yellow* was just a term to describe things that shine, like gold or the rays of the sun. You'd think, though, that we'd be ready to chuck the word onto the trashpile of slang for all the negative uses it's had. If you are considered a coward, you might be called "yellow" or "yellow-bellied." Did this come from a certain prejudice against the rather humble and shy Chinese immigrants who worked so diligently for the railroad? Such bigotry and aspersions concerning their courage were definitely present in the early West. Later, their threat to the world as we knew it was called the "yellow peril." If you wrote a sensational kind of article that came close to libel in its distortion of the truth, it might be called "yellow journalism." This expression was spawned in the late 1800s by one of the earliest tabloids, *The New York World,* which used yellow ink to attract readers to its pages, especially in a cartoon called "The Yellow Kid," which was vulgar and sensationalist and could make some of our modern grocery store mags blush. Even the name of the tropical disease yellow fever took advantage of the poor color in describing its jaundiced victims. But yellow can be mellow and even has some good uses in our modern phone books, where our digits do the strutting.

yen   Today we associate this word with Japanese money, so someone who says, "I have a yen for her" might be thought to mean his desire is materialistic. There is another "yen," however, from which we got the notion of a craving or wish for something. The Chinese root for this English word applied to opium and the addiction to the drug. That sense of the addict's yearning or longing remained the basis of the word after it entered English.

Yule   Here's another example of a heathen festival that got changed by Catholic priests into a Christian holiday. Northern celebrations of the winter solstice were widespread, since the shortest day of the year was a sign that winter was on its downhill run. A twelve-day feast was held, marked by burning a bit of a large scented log on each of the days and enjoying some of the stored harvest and a mug of mead. We know the priests' sales job won out, since we now have our twelve days of *Christmas,* with our yule log and Yuletide carols sung by its fire. *Yule* is Norse for "jolly."

Day Forecast for Latitude 40.39N and Longitude -105.75W (

Trail Ridge, CO

Enter Your "City, ST" or zip code

WS Denver-Boulder, CO
oint Forecast: Trail Ridge, CO
).39N -105.75W (Elev. 10529 ft)

Forecast Val

orecast at a Glance

Today	Tonight	Sunday	Sunday Night	Monday	Mc N
				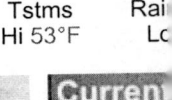	
Mostly Sunny	Mostly Clear	Breezy	Breezy	20% Slight Chc Tstms	Slig Rai
Hi 60°F	Lo 33°F	Hi 61°F	Lo 34°F	Hi 53°F	Lc

etailed 7-day Forecast

Curren

azardous weather condition(s):

Hazardous Weather Outlook

oday: Mostly sunny, with a high near 60. West wind between
 and 15 mph, with gusts as high as 24 mph.

Fa

zebra   It was the Portuguese who gave us this name for the striped African horse, though their term was originally used for a wild ass that is now extinct. When they found the unusually patterned zebra, they gave it the name of the disappeared donkey.

zest   Having a zest for life is a wonderful thing, lending a sense of enjoyment to every little experience. Zesty food, too, can be flavorful and a treat to the taste buds. Here is where the word got its start, from a French term for the peel of an orange or lemon used in cooking to add taste and pungency to a dish.

zigzag   The mad expressway driver we sometimes see weaving in and out of the lanes, passing all traffic with abandon, is carrying out a maneuver named after the German word for "tooth" or "prong." Something that goes up and down like a set of hound's teeth gets that doubled name. *Zinc* comes from a similar root because of the way zinc crystals form points in the smelting process.

zodiac   This word goes far back into ancient times and came from the Greek for "a circle of carved figures." As the belief in the influence of the stars on our lives was passed to early Rome, the *kuklos* part, meaning "circle" was dropped. After two thousand years the constellations are in different parts of the heavens than they were when the Assyrians spread the notion that all things are determined by the position of the stars and planets because of the way the earth rotates in an imperfect spin. The idea persists today and even our leaders are sometimes rumored to use these interpretations of celestial power. *Horoscope* had its beginnings as "one who observes the seasons or movement of time" and was the name given to an astrologer. The early Christian Church frowned on the practice and a pope condemned it in 1585, but these predictions still abound in your local newspaper.

INDEX

Note: Words marked with an asterisk are found within descriptions of other words.

About the Author

With a degree in English and a Masters in English Education, David Muschell taught for eight years in the public schools. He left to pursue a career as a playwright and worked in radio broadcasting during that time. On WGRG in Greensboro, Georgia, he began his "Word for the Day" series, which led to this book. He also has had seven plays published. David has returned to teaching English at Georgia College in Milledgeville.

About the Illustrator

Hatley Mason was born in Richmond, Virginia, and studied at Virginia Commonwealth University School of the Arts. Since 1983 he has worked at the Sacramento Bee. Mason's illustrations appear in the Sacramento Bee's feature sections and have been published and exhibited internationally. Recently a painting was acquired by President and Mrs. Bush for the White House.